AMERICAN INDIAN
WATER RIGHTS AND
THE LIMITS OF LAW

DEVELOPMENT OF WESTERN RESOURCES

The Development of Western Resources is an interdisciplinary series focusing on the use and misuse of resources in the American West. Written for a broad readership of humanists, social scientists, and resource specialists, the books in this series emphasize both historical and contemporary perspectives as they explore the interplay between resource exploitation and economic, social, and political experiences.

John G. Clark, University of Kansas, General Editor

AMERICAN INDIAN WATER RIGHTS AND THE LIMITS OF LAW

Lloyd Burton

 University Press of Kansas

Published by the University Press of Kansas (Lawrence, Kansas 66049), which was organized by the Kansas Board of Regents and is operated and funded by Emporia State University, Fort Hays State University, Kansas State University, Pittsburg State University, the University of Kansas, and Wichita State University

Library of Congress Cataloging-in-Publication Data

Burton, Lloyd.
    American Indian water rights and the limits of law / Lloyd Burton.
        p.   cm.
    Includes bibliographical references and index.
    ISBN 0-7006-0481-2 (cloth)   ISBN 0-7006-601-7 (pbk.)
    1. Indians of North America —Water rights. 2. Water—Law and legislation—United States. I. University Press of Kansas.
II. Title.
KF8210.N37B87   1991
346.7304'32—dc20   90-23088
[347.306432]

British Library Cataloguing in Publication Data is available.

Printed in the United States of America
10   9 8 7 6 5 4 3 2

The paper used in this publication meets the minimum requirements of the American National Standard for Permanence of Paper for Printed Library Materials Z39.48-1984.

This water policy study is affectionately dedicated to my wife, Abby, the Pisces Who Made It Possible; to my children, Robin and Ginger, who with their generation will inherit the water future we create; and to the memory of Charles F. Kettering, Jr., who knew that believing in positive social change involves believing in people.

CONTENTS

PREFACE

A few years ago I heard a talk by Navajo Tribal Chairman Peterson Zah, describing his tribe's efforts to ensure its water supply. "When I was a kid in geography class, I was taught that water always flows downhill," he said. "What I've learned since is that water flows to money and power, wherever they may be."

In addition to being a poignant comment on the politics of water in the American Southwest, Chairman Zah's remark also casts light on the fundamental interrelationship between environmental and social policy in the United States. The "life, liberty, and pursuit of happiness" of every social group in our country is inextricably linked with the question of how we should inhabit our environment and partake of the natural riches it provides.

Ever since the founding of the American conservation movement about a century ago, the political wisdom of focusing on this interrelationship has been debated. Many active and influential conservationists objected (and many still object) to the use of government authority to solve social problems. In order to build the coalitions necessary to make effective environmental advocacy possible, then, there has been a tendency to treat decision making in resource management and environmental protection as if these actions were somehow structurally separable from their social consequences.

But if developments in the environmental sciences in this century—especially ecology—have taught us anything, it is that we ignore these interrelationships at our peril. For example, a policy favoring the preservation of ancient forests and the life forms that inhabit them must also ameliorate its effects on those whose livelihoods depend on the availability of (usually low-paid and relatively hazardous) forest products jobs. To do otherwise robs public policy of moral force; it sets emerging concerns with environmental ethics squarely at odds with the welfare of people at the economic margin, who have few or no alternatives to employment in resource-extractive industries.

One of the most impressive challenges facing policymakers today is how to devise environmental policies that do not exacerbate socioeconomic inequities and economic policies which don't entail further environmental degradation. That admittedly ambitious challenge is taken up in this book, about half of which concerns the history of

American Indian water law and policy with the other half focusing on where we are now and the various paths we might follow from here. Inescapably, the intertwining themes of social justice and the ethics of environmental management arise often. The emphasis is mostly on the second half of the equation: the achievement of socially just resource distribution without additional environmental despoilation.

As indicated in the title, the role of law is also a prominent feature throughout. Generalizations in the area of American Indian law can be dangerous and to some extent inevitably misleading. But with this caveat in mind, it is nevertheless possible to characterize the last two centuries as a period during which state governments and some federal elected officials generally did what they could to divest indigenous peoples of their natural resource heritage, while (until quite recently) federal judges generally did what they could to preserve that heritage for the tribes' use and enjoyment. This is the story of a doctrine fashioned and enforced by the federal courts for the preservation of American Indian water resources, set against state water laws under which most of the waters of the West have already been allocated to non-Indian interests. One of the book's core findings is that while in the hands of federal judges the law (the reserved rights doctrine) has proved to be the salvation of the American Indian water resource heritage, we may be approaching the limits of what the law is able to do on the tribes' behalf in the pursuit of just and durable dispute resolution.

There is a vast literature bemoaning the immoral treatment of indigenous Americans, in part because there is no shortage of examples of such treatment. Less common is some consideration of how we might go about righting old wrongs (restoring tribal water supplies) without committing new ones (taking water from non-Indians who thought they had acquired good title to it under state law). That is another challenge this study confronts and deals with (Chapter 6). The decision to take on this task arose from the conviction that genuinely positive-sum solutions to such problems must be both socially and environmentally constructive. We may have inherited a tradition of one group damaging another for the sake of its own welfare, but that does not mean we are doomed to perpetuate it.

Near the end of the book are suggestions for a uniform negotiation process which addresses some of the serious fairness problems besetting the negotiations currently being encouraged and sponsored by the U.S. Department of the Interior. These suggestions, along with substantive solutions for resolving the American Indian water rights dilemma, would probably have to be legislatively authorized. However, some tribal advocates with whom I have spoken expressed concern about the sponsorship of any kind of uniform federal legislation at this point, fearing that western-state adversaries in Congress might be able to use the opportunity to statutorily destroy or diminish the reserved rights doctrine—the principal legal foundation for the Indian claims.

My first response to this concern has been that it is not my intent to recommend that any party to a legal conflict be coerced into using an alternative dispute resolution process not seen to be in its own best interest; that is the major problem I see with current negotiation efforts. The last two decades have witnessed a relentless boosterism for alternative dispute resolution techniques (negotiation, mediation, arbitration, neutral evaluation), followed by an equally virulent backlash against their use. The critics' central point seems to be that informality exacerbates inequity—that the less powerful party actually has a better chance of defending its rights in an open adjudicative forum like a court of law or administrative hearing than in a closed-door, informal proceeding.

Whether this will prove true in the American Indian water rights disputes remains to be seen; the cases reviewed in Chapters 4 and 5 provide some insights on both sides of this strategic argument. What experienced advocates know, however, is that *any* dispute resolution process—adjudicative, legislative, or conciliatory—has its attendant costs, benefits, and risks.

Knowing when and how to use each process, along with having a clear vision of one's immediate objectives and ultimate goals, is a lot of what effective advocacy is all about. The recommendations in Chapter 6 are predicated on the assumption that the greater the number of fair, reliable, effective dispute resolution alternatives available to the parties, the better are the chances of mutually achieving those goals and objectives in a positive-sum context. And at least as we have chosen to practice it in this country, the achievement of positive-sum solutions has all too often proved to be somewhat beyond the limits of law.

A great number of mentors, colleagues, friends, and associates helped this project along its path from a concept for a policy study almost a decade ago to the form which you hold today. They all deserve thanks for any contribution the book might make, although I must bear sole responsibility for any shortcomings it might contain. Acknowledged below in reverse chronological order (there certainly is no general order of importance) are some of these kind and helpful people.

The staff of the University Press of Kansas compassionately and professionally attended to all the routine birthing agonies of a first-book author. After an eight-year gestation period, I'm not sure why I assumed that the final labor and delivery of this book would be painless.

Bill Lord, former director of the University of Arizona's Water Resources Research Center, was one of the first to see the glimmerings of a book in a highly academic doctoral dissertation and gave freely of both his practical experience and analytic expertise in advising in its transformation.

Access to some of the literature as well as to some of the leading thinkers in the field was made possible by my capacity as cochair of the University of Colorado Conflict Resolution Consortium, which in turn was supported by a major grant from the William and Flora Hewlett Foundation. Robert Barrett, the Consortium's project officer at the foundation, took an interest in and encouraged my research in water rights dispute resolution long before either the Consortium or this book came into being.

Most of the legal research and analysis in this book—especially the historical materials—had an earlier incarnation as a Ph.D. dissertation in Jurisprudence and Social Policy at the School of Law (Boalt Hall), University of California, Berkeley. My committee members—law professors Martin Shapiro (chair) and Harry Scheiber and earth sciences professor Luna Leopold—provided the scholarly guidance and counsel necessary for nascent curiosity to develop into an extended program of research. My sincere thanks also to Rod Watanabe and the staff of the Jurisprudence and Social Policy program, who had to contend with the fluctuations between intellectual narcissism and self-doubt which sometimes characterize graduate student behavior.

Financial support for the dissertation took two forms. The first was a conservation fellowship from the National Wildlife Federation and the second was a grant from the University of California, Berkeley Chancellor's Patent Fund. My feelings about the intellectual property rights of university faculty members are and will continue to be strongly tempered by the fact that university-held patents—the fruits of my predecessors' labors—helped fund my own work.

While a student and (later) a teacher at the University of California, I had occasion to both consult for and learn a lot from the people at the American Indian Resources Institute in Oakland, California. My deep appreciation is therefore extended to AIRI director Richard Trudell and his ever-supportive staff.

Finally, as a college undergraduate I had the rare privilege of spending a semester as a legislative intern in the Washington, D.C., offices of Arizona Congressman Morris Udall. Such an opportunity provides the sort of critically important educational experience which the academic environment, in its necessary seclusion, never can. While Mr. Udall and his staff might look askance at some of what is suggested here, at least they know I was thoroughly apprised of the realities of western water politics before writing it.

My stay in Washington was made possible through the offices of the late Chuck Kettering, who died tragically several years ago. I only wish he were here to thank personally and to receive a copy of this book.

CHAPTER ONE

Reflections in a Glass Bead

Some stories of our nation's founding have such symbolic potency that, although rooted in fact, they have over time taken on the status of myth or legend. One such tale is that of the Dutch purchase of Manhattan Island from its native inhabitants. Correspondence from that era recounts the early seventeenth-century acquisition of title to the twenty-two-thousand-acre island from local tribes by the Dutch West India Company, which paid for the land with "some beads and trinkets,"[1] valued by nineteenth-century historians at about twenty-four dollars.[2] Some historians considered the amount "a trifle,"[3] even by the standards of 1626, and as the first documented demonstration of the European colonists' relentless intent to cheat indigenous Americans out of their land. Apologists for Dutch behavior, on the other hand, allege that the tribe involved in the transaction (the Canarsies) did not actually dwell on the island anyway, using it only for hunting, and further, that tribes in the area were fond of repeatedly selling the same parcel of land to fresh waves of European immigrants—in one instance deeding the same real estate to six different colonial purchasers.[4]

Whichever view of the event one wishes to take, its symbolic significance is undeniable. On that island on that spring day over a third of a millennium ago, a transaction occurred that had vastly different meanings for the parties involved. From what little is known of tribal norms in that place at that time, in all likelihood what the native peoples probably thought they were conveying was a limited-use right, just as they were accustomed to doing with neighboring tribes as an outcome either of trading with the friendly ones or warring with the others. But in the European mind, what had been acquired was exclusive and perpetual possession of the land itself and all that was on it: a "bundle of rights," including the unfettered power to develop and alter the land and its resources at will, to use it for any purpose, to divide it among individuals within the title-holding group, and to sell it to any buyer of the owner's choosing.

Members of two cultures with almost incomprehensibly different world views met to decide the fate of the land on which they stood. The legal traditions and institutions of Europe were set against the norms and customs of nonliterate, indigenous America. And as the next two-and-a-half centuries of history would reveal, the force of arms as well as the sheer force of numbers would determine which of those world views would come to dominate the American landscape.

This event is among the first recorded instances of the combined use of European legal instruments, symbolic wealth ("beads and trinkets"), and eventually military force (under the bloodthirsty New Amsterdam commissioner Kieft) to divest indigenous North American peoples of their natural resources.[5] From that day to this, American Indian tribes in the United States have been under continuous legal and economic pressure to relinquish claims to and control over those resources. For most of our nation's history the struggle was over land; the most severe and most protracted conflicts today concern water.

Litigation over American Indian water rights is—not coincidentally—now proliferating at the same rate as the urbanization and industrialization of the American West. Urban areas west of the hundredth meridian are growing at a breathtaking rate (quite literally, if measured by pollutant concentrations in the air over Denver, Albuquerque, Phoenix, and Los Angeles). Competition for water resources is increasing dramatically, along with the salaries of the battalions of lawyers who up to now have been the only clear winners in the latest round of western water wars. In the 1980s alone, over four dozen major Indian water-rights disputes were wending their way through state and federal courtrooms and administrative hearings throughout the United States. The great majority of these lawsuits and administrative actions are unresolved as of this writing and may well remain so into the twenty-first century.

At the heart of the legal controversy over Indian water rights is the fact that those rights were granted to the tribes in treaties and federal court decisions of the late nineteenth and early twentieth centuries— rights that the federal government (as trustee of all tribal resources) was to uphold and protect. Instead, the U.S. government more often acquiesced in the allocation of surface-water rights to non-Indian interests, using state water-rights doctrines. Most of the West's water has now been allocated to non-Indian people who believed they had acquired clear title to their water rights under state law, but the courts have begin to point out that the Indians' reserved water rights as a matter of federal treaty obligation are in most cases legally superior to non-Indian rights granted by the states.

The threat to non-Indian water rights posed by tribal claims of reserved rights has periodically resulted in the introduction of legislation in Congress that poses a direct threat to the future of the tribes. The proposal most frequently encountered would terminate Indian water rights without tribal consent by issuing a one-time cash payment to the tribes for waters taken (rather like condemning private land for highway construction). Although this policy seems to most members of Congress so unfair that it has yet to be adopted, each new Indian court victory brings renewed cries for a "final solution" to the Indians' asserted water-resource entitlements, and a policy of water-rights termination may still be enacted.

There is also growing interest in the possibility of settling these disputes through negotiation. Although several attempts have been made, only a small handful of cases have been resolved by means of comprehensive water-rights agreements ratified by Congress (ratification is necessary, for these agreements somewhat resemble "water-rights treaties"). In these few settlements, the tribes have agreed that under certain conditions they would accept money damages in lieu of water the federal government has promised to deliver—to forfeit water for symbolic wealth.

The Indian water-rights termination bills submitted to Congress would divest the tribes of their water forcibly, simply by taking the water and then paying the Indians for it; in the negotiated settlements, money damages would be paid only if Congress fails to honor its promise to deliver measured quantities of water to the tribes. In either situation, the result would be separation of the Indians from their water by tokens of wealth. The ultimate issue for the Indians in all contemporary controversies is how much water they will be able to retain, not how much money they will be able to get.

The dynamics of American Indian water-rights conflicts can also be illustrated by a metaphor drawn from Herman Hesse's 1943 novel, *Das Glasperlenspiel* (The Glass Bead Game). One evening, after returning from a conference of government officials, financiers, and construction-industry representatives involved in planning future western water projects, I read the following passage in Hesse's book:

> The atmosphere was like that in the corridors of a government ministry or aristocratic club, where the rulers and those who will take over their responsibilities in the near future meet and get to know one another. A muted polished tone prevailed in this group. Its members were ambitious without showing it, keen-eyed and critical to excess.[6]

He describes the gathering of an intellectual elite who have taken it upon themselves to transmit the essence of high culture down through the ages by means of an elaborately structured transaction, or game. What struck me at the time were the similarities between the gathering I had just attended and the one the novelist depicts. The main difference was that Hesse's characters are concerned with transmitting an intellectual essence and the goal of the group I had observed was to perpetuate the arrangements that we as a culture use to manipulate the environment—specifically, how we exercise power over water.

That the gathering I witnessed was an elite of sorts goes without saying. Even in a society as pluralistic and democratic as our own, decisions about water-resource management involving vast public wealth, massive environmental modification, and significant social dislocation are made by an astonishingly small group of people. For most of this century, a closely knit priesthood of key politicians, engineers, bureaucrats, lobbyists, and land developers has transformed the waterways of the West.[7] Sometimes with enthusiastic public support, sometimes amid complaints about costs, the work has gone on.

Beginning in the 1970s, however, the combined influences of recession, environmentalism, and competing water-rights claims began calling into serious question the judgments of the elite. Some critics contended that the reclamation goals our nation adopted at the beginning of this century have been substantially attained and are no longer relevant to emerging needs; others charged that the costs paid by all were benefiting a very privileged few. As a result, the game can no longer be played in quite the same way. Suddenly there are new players claiming seats at the table. And because of the legal strength of their claims, the most notable among these new entrants are the Indians.

The terms *American Indians* and *indigenous Americans* are interchangeably used in preference to *Native American* in this presentation. Some advocates of Indian rights self-identify with pride as American Indians; it is a term of choice among many indigenous peoples. The term also differentiates the tribes in the forty-eight contiguous states (whose rights are the subject of this study) from Eskimos, Aleuts, and Hawaiians, who are also indigenous to what is now American soil. Finally, in conducting this research I have found that the term ''Native American'' rubs salt in the old wounds of Indian/Anglo relations in many parts of the West. It is a pointed reminder of whose ancestors got here first and what happened to them when the next group arrived. Further, it reinforces the sense of transience and rootlessness which is already too much a part of the dominant culture. In the view of many, European-Americans desperately need to develop a more lasting sense of connectedness with the land before they will be capable of taking better care of it.

In the broader sense of the term, anyone born in the Americas is a native, including the light-skinned descendants of northern Europeans. The irony is that although ''American Indian'' communicates meaning more precisely, it is also a continuing reminder of the geographic ignorance of the early, land-hungry European immigrants and of their persisting ethonocentric need to regard this continent's dark-skinned original inhabitants as somehow foreign to American soil.

Since the central focus of this work is on the attainment of distributive and procedural justice in the settlement of water-rights disputes, the emphasis is primarily on the use of legal institutions. Euro-Americans originally used the law in combination with military might to strip indigenous peoples of most of their natural resources. Federal judges then used it primarily on the tribes' behalf to protect what was left and to restore some of what was lost. Now—in part because of changes in the federal judiciary—disputants are "bargaining in the shadow"[8] of conflicting water-rights doctrines in an effort to attain at the negotiating table what has eluded them after nearly a century in court: dispute resolution deemed just by both parties.

The force of public law—as fashioned in court and Congress—emerges from the historical portion of this study as a double-edged sword, defending the rights of some and decimating the rights of others, depending on who was grasping the hilt at a given time. The problem is that in distributive disputes over fully allocated resources (a situation characteristic of most Indian water-rights litigation), the court cannot defend without destroying, and for the most part Congress has not done much better. In some important ways, the tribes and non-Indian disputants in many of these water-rights conflicts have reached the limits of law. The Supreme Court has with the advent of Nixon and Reagan appointees largely abandoned its role of trust insofar as Indian water rights are concerned, and Congress is deadlocked over the consideration of comprehensive-settlement legislation. What remains to be seen is whether the disputants themselves, given a level playing field, may be able to achieve what legal institutions historically could not.

CHAPTER TWO

The Development of American Indian Water Rights

In the study of history there is a natural tendency to organize past events into periods, patterns, and themes; to punctuate the flow of time with a concept or event perceived as having measurably affected the course of human experience. In 1983, for instance, we observed the fiftieth anniversary of the birth of the New Deal, an occasion to compare the management of past crises with the handling of our own uncertain times.

January of 1983 also marked the seventy-fifth anniversary of a legal event, almost unnoticed at its occurrence, which was in retrospect just as significant for American Indian tribes as the New Deal was for the rest of American society. In January 1908 the U.S. Supreme Court issued its seminal decision in *Winters* v. *United States*,[1] the first case in which the federal courts explicitly affirmed the water rights of Indian reservations. The *Winters* decision would arouse little more interest now than it did three quarters of a century ago but for its impact on contemporary resource management. Armed with the reserved water rights (or "*Winters* doctrine") first articulated in this decision, over forty tribes are now locked in combat with non-Indian interests in administrative hearings and courtrooms throughout the western states, claiming their share of the water resources on which the entire economic future of the West depends.[2] The quantities of water in controversy are huge, as are the economic benefits accruing to whichever parties eventually win.[3]

The news media have come to recognize the magnitude and importance of Indian water-rights claims,[4] giving the impression that the structure of current Indian-related controversies over water rights is a contemporary phenomenon. In fact, just the opposite is true: the roots of these conflicts extend at least to colonial times and the patterns of conflict emerging over the last two-hundred-fifty years may have a determinative effect on the outcome of present disputes.

Historical developments in the law of American Indian water resources have been characterized by three recurrent themes or trends. First, in entitlement disputes over natural resources, the federal judiciary has generally tended to treat North American Indian tribes as individual, nationlike entities, in accordance with the status implicitly

6

assigned them by original provisions of the U.S. Constitution.[5] Second, however, in keeping with the realpolitik of westward expansion, congressional and executive branch policy makers—unlike the judiciary—have come to regard the tribes not as separate, semiautonomous nation-states with ancient rights to natural resources but collectively, as just one more ethnic minority group struggling for parity in the distribution of national wealth. This historic divergence in perspective between the courts and the more politically sensitive branches (a divergence that in modern times may be waning) has left the federal government beset by a fundamental ambivalence regarding the status, rights, and entitlements of American Indian tribes.

A useful image is that of a ship with three rudders, each controlled by a different helmsman. When in disagreement, the courses the three helmsmen set tend to cancel each other out. When in accord, they have sent American Indian policy veering off in wildly different directions at various times in our history. The tribes have usually fared worst in retaining control of their natural resources (land, water, minerals, wildlife) during periods when national governmental institutions were paying maximum deference to the rights of states since the states compete most directly with the tribes for economic benefits arising from control of resource development.

Third, a stark parallel may be drawn between the process which created the Indian reservations in the nineteenth century, when the tribes relinquished theoretical sovereignty over vast areas in return for federally protected control over much smaller amounts of land, and the process of current western water-rights negotiations, in which the federal executive branch, the states, and assorted business interests are urging the tribes to abandon theoretical water-rights claims in return for federal delivery of much smaller amounts of water.[6]

Only those aspects of U.S./Indian relations specifically related to control of natural resources are reviewed here, along with elements of early history, supplied for context. Greater detail is provided in describing the chain of events that began with the *Winters* decision at the outset of this century.

INDIGENOUS NORTH AMERICANS AND
EARLY EUROPEAN CONTACT

As with nearly every other aspect of the study of North America's indigenous peoples, considerable controversy surrounds the issues of when they first appeared on the continent and when contact with European cultures first occurred.[7] Addressing the former question, a minority of archeologists claims evidence of human habitation in North America as far back as one-hundred-thousand years ago;[8] a more broadly accepted theory is that humans entered the Americas via the Bering land bridge from about twenty-eight to twenty-five-thousand years ago.[9] The most conservative estimates of continuous habitation, based on the radiocarbon dating of indisputably man-made artifacts, confirm the existence of human settlement in several areas of western North America by about 12,000 B.C.[10]

There is more agreement on the development of aboriginal life-styles after that period. The first human inhabitants were nomadic hunters, subsisting on the herds of large mammals which roamed the nonforested areas of the continent. However, by about 7,000 B.C. a combination of climatic change and wasteful hunting practices had drastically reduced the big game population (especially the prehistoric bison); the hunters were then forced to rely on a wide variety of smaller game and on the gathering of edible plants. As a result of becoming more dependent on plant distribution they also developed a more sedentary life-style[11] keyed to a limited seasonal migration along fixed routes with semipermanent campsites and eventually a rudimentary agriculture.

Although it is difficult to pinpoint the time when some Paleo-americans shifted to cultivated plants as a principal food source, there is ample evidence that by the time of Christ's birth peoples residing in what are now the southeastern and southwestern United States were successfully growing and preserving several crops, using methods perfected by the great agricultural civilizations already flourishing in Central and South America. Among these first North American farmers, the culture groups of the greater Colorado River basin devised the most elaborate and sophisticated techniques for coaxing large crop yields from short supplies of both arable soil and water.

Three clearly distinguishable groups inhabited the greater Colorado basin by about 300 B.C. On the desert floor of what is today south-central Arizona there arose the *Hohokam* culture (a Pima Indian word meaning "those who have gone before"). The Hohokam populated the Salt, Verde, and Gila river valleys, developing after 800 A.D. the most advanced irrigation system to be found in that region until the late eighteenth century. A vast series of main and lateral canals carried water from the rivers to carefully terraced fields of maize and beans; the runoff from each field drained to the terrace below, so that one lateral canal could serve several acres.[12]

The extent and complexity of these systems suggest a highly organized and well-coordinated social structure.[13] There were over two-hundred miles of canals in the Hohokam irrigation works—some excavations were as much as eighteen feet wide and fifteen feet deep, possibly lined with clay to impede water loss.[14] Although a succession of alternating droughts and floods and increasing soil salinity forced the dispersal of this group by about 1400, most experts consider the Tohono O'Odham and Pima tribes, who were irrigating the same lands on a reduced scale at the time of first contact with the Spanish, to be direct descendants of the Hohokam.[15] The size of these descendant populations at the time of first contact with the Spaniards in the mid-1500s has been estimated at about thirty-thousand.[16]

To the east and north of the Hohokam, in the mountainous region along the present Arizona-New Mexico border, the *Mogollon* group had also evolved an independent cultural tradition by about 300 B.C. Unlike the Hohokam, who relied predominantly on irrigated agriculture for subsistence, the hill-dwelling Mogollon developed a more diverse resource base, combining agriculture with hunting and the gathering of wild plants. The Zuni and some Pueblo tribes are considered to be their historic descendants.[17]

Further north, on the Colorado plateau in the region where the borders of Arizona, Colorado, New Mexico, and Utah meet, another culture group—the *Anasazi*—had also established itself by the beginning of the Christian Era. The Anasazi are best remembered for their architectural and engineering prowess; this group constructed the massive, multistorey dwellings in the cliffs and canyons of the Four Corners region, structures which are still the most impressive examples of Paleoamerican architecture ever found north of Mexico.[18]

Evidence also indicates that the Anasazi were adept at irrigated agriculture. By the twelfth century, in a twenty-mile segment of Chaco Canyon in northwestern New Mexico, their crop yields supported an essentially urban population of nearly ten-thousand people who lived in towns comprised of multilevel buildings capable of housing as many as twelve hundred persons each. The structures were linked by a system of paved roads.[19]

Recent studies suggest that this dense population had exceeded its environmental carrying capacity by the end of the thirteenth century. Forests were stripped of all mature trees for roof supports and fuel,[20] and the resulting erosion, along with increasing soil salinity and abrupt climatic changes, ensured successive crop failures. Most of the Anasazi from this and similarly over-used settlements eventually migrated east to the upper Rio Grande and established smaller, less centralized communities; there the Spaniards found them in the 1500s and assigned them their present-day name: the Pueblos ("town-dwellers"). Some peripheral Anasazi groups whose communities never achieved the scale of the ill-fated Chaco Canyon settlement were able to adapt their agricultural practices to changing climatic conditions, thereby avoiding forced relocation. The Hopi, in northeastern Arizona, are the present descendants of one such group.[21]

The popular portrayal of early European/Indian contact is usually that of a technologically sophisticated agrarian culture (the West Europeans) encountering crude, nomadic bands of hunters and scavengers (the Indians); the hapless Stone Age wanderers inevitably fall before the advancing agricultural millennium. This scenario may be marginally related to what actually transpired in the plains and forests. But at the outset of continuous European presence in the New World in the early sixteenth century, significant portions of the Mississippi valley and Colorado basin had been under continuous intensive cultivation for more than fifteen hundred years. When Giovanni da Verrazano anchored off Cape Hatteras in 1524, he unknowingly beheld a continent inhabited by at least a million persons of roughly five-hundred distinct language groups.[22] A substantial number of these people were skilled, experienced farmers, already permanently settled on and using that resource which subsequent waves of European immigrants would most ardently desire: arable land.

More than two-hundred years elapsed between Coronado's and De Soto's advances into the southeast and southwest regions of North America in 1540 and England's success in establishing itself as the dominant military presence on the continent.[23] During these two centuries the Dutch, English, French, Spanish, and Swedish governments all vied for control of the North American land mass and for trade with its native inhabitants. The Dutch and Swedes were eliminated rather early in the game, but French/English competition in the northeast resulted in full-scale war during the latter half of the eighteenth century. At this time, there were roughly three-hundred-thousand Indians residing east of the Mississippi River (many of them well organized and somewhat warlike) and fewer than two-hundred-thousand European colonists;[24] both of the European powers understandably perceived Indian support for their cause as necessary to victory.

By most accounts, the French were considerably more humane in their economic and social relations with the eastern tribes than were the English, which enabled the French to command the loyalty of more tribes during the French and Indian War.[25] England avoided defeat partly by exploiting intertribal hostilities, enlisting the aid of the Iroquois Confederacy in combat with their enemy tribes to the west.[26] Like the Iroquois, the twenty-thousand-member Creek Confederacy in the Southeast was considered by the British as the most powerful Indian confederation known and was thought to hold the balance of power in the Alabama-Georgia area during the Europeans' fight for control of the continent. British diplomats labored fervently to keep the Creeks and Choctaws neutral during this period—an effort impeded by the encroaching settlements of Georgia colonists.[27]

Among the reasons for England's troubled relations with the tribes was that each of its colonies was originally allowed to establish its own Indian policy. Particularly along the western frontier this brought about intercolony competition for Indian trade, the involvement of individual colonies in intertribal wars, aggressive land seizures by whites, and retaliatory attacks by the affected tribes. By the end of the French and Indian War in 1763, the British were aware that their fragmented, uncoordinated Indian policy had been a serious military liability. In his Proclamation of 1763, therefore, King George III stripped the individual colonies of all treaty-making powers with the tribes, drew boundaries to separate Indian from non-Indian lands, and appointed his own commissioners to control relations between the colonies and the Indians; colonial officials were ordered to prohibit white incursion into the newly created "Indian Country."[28] Thus began the acrimonious debate over centralized versus local government control of Indian relations which has continued to the present day.

The Proclamation of 1763 proved to be just one more log on the revolutionary fire; colonists were incensed at being denied access to Indian Country lands and free trade with the tribes. During the American Revolution, the Continental Congress tried to stay on peaceful terms with the tribes by means of treaties forbidding white settlement on Indian lands and by reserving to Congress all authority for Indian affairs. However, compliance with the policy was voluntary and it was utterly ignored by settlers and land speculators after the war. Several tribes had supported the Crown during the Revolution in an effort to stem colonial encroachment, and there was strong sentiment among the victorious colonists for appropriating Indian lands in retribution.[29]

By the time of the Constitutional Convention of 1787, relations with some tribes were nearly as bad as they had been prior to the French and Indian War some thirty years earlier. On returning from a tour of the western territories in 1784, George Washington observed, "In defiance of the proclamation of Congress they [white settlers] roam over the country on the Indian side of the Ohio, mark out Lands, Survey, and even settle them. This gives great discontent to the Indians, and will unless measures are taken in time to prevent it, inevitably produce a war with the western tribes."[30] His warning was prophetic. Unauthorized settling northwest of the Ohio River did indeed goad the Indians into combat in the late 1780s, which in turn brought about a punitive U.S. Army expedition into Indian Country in 1791. There the Shawnees soundly defeated General St. Clair's army, killing more than six-hundred soldiers. The federal government was not able to gain military superiority in western Ohio until Gen. Anthony Wayne's victory at Fallen Timbers in 1794.[31]

Participants in the Constitutional Convention were acutely aware of the problem Washington had pointed out; they also perceived the total inability of the weak central government established by the Articles of Confederation to do anything about it. If they wanted to avert a fresh round of Indian wars (something the new American nation was ill-prepared to undertake), the framers of the Constitution would have to find more effective means of making and maintaining peace with the Indians.

Congress had acknowledged the sovereignty of the Indian tribes and had claimed exclusive authority to coordinate U.S./Indian relations, both in Article 9 of the Articles of Confederation and in the treaties it had been making with the tribes since 1778. These treaties provided that Indian lands were to remain inviolable, to be acquired by the United States only by purchase and not by right of conquest.[32] Thus as the framers set about structuring a more powerful central government, an established Indian policy was built into the Constitution in three different ways. First, existing and future treaties with the Indians (and with foreign nations) were elevated to the status of supreme law of the land, preempting state law whenever the two conflicted.[33] Second, the president was directed to negotiate such treaties in the future, subject to Senate ratification.[34] And third, Congress was assigned responsibility for the general regulation of "commerce with foreign nations, and among the several states, and with Indian tribes."[35]

U.S./INDIAN RELATIONS IN THE NINETEENTH CENTURY

Although the Constitution alluded to a tribal status vaguely akin to that of a sovereign foreign nation, the steadily deteriorating relationship between Indian tribes and neighboring state governments was a phenomenon the new Constitution was powerless to reverse. In addition to the bloody skirmishes and pitched battles in the Ohio valley in the early 1790s, events in the South were also moving the tribes and settlers into protracted conflict. Especially in the Carolinas, Georgia, and what would become Alabama and Mississippi, there was intense and unrelenting competition for agricultural land. The Indians of the Northeast had been primarily hunters and gatherers and had been persuaded by one means or another simply to migrate to more westerly forests as the East was settled, but most of the southern tribes were agriculturally oriented and permanently established on their lands. Four of these "civilized tribes"—the Cherokees, Chickasaws, Choctaws, and Creeks—collectively numbered more than sixty-thousand members and inhabited rich farmland ranging from the southern Appalachians to the Mississippi marshes.[36]

White settlers in Georgia saw the Cherokees as a direct impediment to land development and wanted them removed. During negotiations over ratification of the U.S. Constitution, Georgia representatives demanded a federal agreement to move all Indians out of the state in return for Georgia's willingness to cede its western territories and ratify the Constitution. The agreement was made, and Georgia ceded its western holdings in 1802[37] with the understanding that the United States would "at their own expense extinguish for the use of Georgia as early as can be peaceably obtained on reasonable terms" title to all Indian lands within state boundaries.[38] However, the Indians were not in a mood to sell out and move west, and the federal government was unwilling to force them.

While this situation festered in the South, similar tensions erupted into open warfare further north. The Shawnee leader Tecumseh had been advocating unified tribal resistance to land cessions to white settlers throughout the first decade of the nineteenth century. While he was trying to bring southern tribes into his pan-Indian coalition, Americans in Ohio attacked and destroyed "Prophet's Town," his home base.[39] In retaliation, he persuaded certain tribes to launch a full-scale war against the Americans along the western frontier in the spring of 1812. When the United States and Great Britain went to war later that same year, he allied his forces with the British. Tecumseh was slain in battle a year later.[40] Although the majority of tribes had not joined Tecumseh's coalition, all Indians suffered for it. White settlers regarded most Indians as traitorous after the War of 1812 and renewed their demands that the tribes be relocated west of the Mississippi. By 1820 the settlers had acquired nearly 200 million acres of land formerly held by the Indians, at treaty-negotiated prices ranging from one cent to one dollar per acre.[41]

The southern "civilized tribes" had for the most part remained neutral during the war and still would not relinquish their lands. This reluctance to move presented southern political leaders with what one historian has called "a practical and moral dilemma. For if they [white southern statesmen] were avaricious, they were also 'honorable men.' They recognized . . . that the Indians had some claim on the land they occupied. . . . Yet the lands must be obtained. It is not easy to reconcile avarice with honor or force with voluntarism, but the Jacksonians tried it."[42]

President Jackson and his followers finally succeeded in establishing Indian removal as official federal policy through passage of the Removal Act of 1830, which mandated negotiation with all the remaining eastern tribes for the cession of their lands in return for holdings in Indian Country west of the Mississippi River.[43] Debate over this measure was prolonged and heated, as religious groups in the Northeast railed against the immorality of evicting the tribes from their native lands. Southerners pointed out in response that New Englanders were in a position to flaunt their moral superiority only because their forefathers had already rid the Northeast of most of its indigenous population.[44] It was a classically regional dispute with strong economic overtones (the South needed land to expand agricultural production), anticipating some of the arguments which would later lead to the Civil War.[45] Opponents of the Removal Act were able to gain one concession: the stipulation that all removals would be "voluntary," a result of treaties with the tribes rather than forced relocation. This requirement of tribal voluntarism naturally caused problems of implementation. Some removal treaties negotiated before the act's passage had been obtained by bribing the tribal officials who had signed them. The "civilized tribes" moved to prevent this practice by establishing a compact among themselves, vowing to cede no land to federal or state governments; one chief who violated the compact was assassinated.[46]

Georgia legislators finally lost all patience with the obstinacy of the "civilized tribes" and the federal government's failure to evict them. In 1827 the legislature passed the first of a series of acts annulling all tribal laws and extending state jurisdiction over all Indian-occupied lands.[47] In so doing, they were aware of actually trying to assert state authority over federal land; in 1823 in *Johnson* v. *McIntosh*[48] the U.S. Supreme Court had ruled that although the rights of the Indians to their lands were good against all third parties, those rights were maintained only at the behest of the federal government, which held ultimate title and "exclusive power to extinguish the Indian right."[49] The tribes retained a "right of occupancy."

The Cherokees sought to enjoin the state legislation in an original action before the Supreme Court on the theory that the tribe was a sovereign nation and therefore not subject to state regulation. But in *Cherokee Nation* v. *Georgia*,[50] Justice Marshall rejected this argument, holding instead that the Indian tribes were "domestic dependent nations" and that their relationship to the United States "resembles that of a ward to his guardian."[51] As in *McIntosh*, the Marshall Court again unequivocally subjugated Indian rights to the federal will. History suggests the Court did so in part to avoid having to assert jurisdiction over the case; Georgia had refused to acknowledge federal authority to hear the dispute by failing to file a written response to the suit or to appear for oral arguments before the Court.[52] If the Indians were not foreign nations, there was no Article 3 jurisdiction.[53]

In the following term, however, a related issue came before the Court, and this time the result was different. The law in question was a new Georgia statute requiring all white persons living on Indian lands to obtain state permission to do so. Two missionaries violated the law, were imprisoned by the state, and appealed their convictions on the grounds that Georgia had no jurisdiction over Indian lands.[54] Having earlier fully subjugated tribal rights to federal authority, the Marshall Court now proceeded with equal vigor to bar the states from any control over lands occupied by the Indians. In *Worcester* v. *Georgia*[55] Justice Marshall held that the Cherokee Nation was a federal protectorate in which the laws of Georgia could "have no force, and which citizens of Georgia have no right to enter" absent Cherokee assent or an act of Congress.

President Jackson and his followers were infuriated by the Marshall Court's decision, and the chief executive essentially refused to enforce it. Removal of the tribes to lands west of the Mississippi proceeded at a brisk pace, with relatively vast territories assigned to them in what would later become the central plains states. Some tribes were so disrupted by the relocation in an alien environment that they failed to survive as cultural and economic units, though other tribes apparently prospered.[56]

Thus in the space of ten years, the Court demoted the Indian tribes from the sovereign status alluded to in the Constitution to "domestic dependent nations"—wards of the federal government—without title to their lands, which the Marshall Court claimed the United States would thenceforth hold in trust for the tribes. Yet in *Worcester* Justice Marshall also repelled state efforts to assert any jurisdiction over the Indian trust holdings.

In carving out this enigmatic legal niche for the Indians (subordinate to the United States but not to individual states), the Marshall Court was acknowledging from the bench what the U.S. Army had already asserted on the battlefield: ambiguous and ill-defined dominion over the continent's indigenous population. Original articles of the Constitution may have alluded to the tribes as sovereign and independent nations, but the political and military realities of the early 1800s no longer reflected that perspective. As demonstrated in *Worcester*, after presiding over this legal diminution the federal judges took very seriously their new role as guardians of the wards they had created.

Subsequently, the federal courts would sometimes deflect federal legislative and executive actions—as well as those of the states—which
seemed too blatantly inimical to Indian interests.

In the long view, the removal policy proved to be only a temporary
solution to Anglo/Indian tensions over land control. Following the
discovery of precious metals in the west and after the Civil War, a flood
of settlers streamed westward seeking land. What they found was
Indian Country—the vast prairies where the federal government had
relocated the tribes displaced by the removal policy and where plains
Indians had by treaty been guaranteed the freedom to continue traditional patterns of life through subsistence on the buffalo herds. But the
buffalo required expansive range that incoming settlers were eager to
fence off and farm.[57] In response to this cry for more land, the federal
government fully embraced a policy it had been experimenting with
since the early 1850s: the establishment of Indian reservations.

The tribes originally removed from the eastern states to Indian
Country in the plains west of the Mississippi were assigned huge
contiguous territories in which no whites were settled. But in the
Southwest, many of the tribes inhabiting areas the United States had
acquired after the Mexican War in 1848 (the present-day states of
Arizona, California, Colorado, Nevada, New Mexico, and Utah) were
living on islands of reserved lands surrounded by Spanish (and later,
Mexican) settlements. Seeing that this pattern of concentrated distribution freed much more land for development, the federal government
quickly negotiated treaties with Indians in the thinly populated western
territories. The tribes relinquished dominion over most of their land
(which they hadn't the martial force to control anyway) in return for a
much smaller reserved area, which the United States promised to keep
free of white incursion and where Indian rule would be exclusive. From
1853 to 1856, fifty-two such treaties were negotiated, involving federal
acquisition of about 174 million acres of land from the western tribes.[58]

But for those tribes which did not acquiesce in the new reservation
policy after the Civil War, a tragically familiar sequence of events
occurred. The completion of the first transcontinental railroad in 1869
stimulated some unauthorized white settling and ranching on tribal
territories. This provoked retaliatory Indian attacks, usually countered
by the U.S. Cavalry. A peace treaty would ensue; and the tribes would
give up most of their lands in return for a smaller reserved area, rations
and other supplies as needed, and implements for conversion to
farming, animal husbandry, and other "arts of civilization."[59] The
fighting was particularly vicious in the Southwest. While the sedentary
agrarian tribes (e.g., the Hopi, Papago, Pima, and Pueblo) had been
more or less peacefully coexisting with the Spanish and Mexicans for

two centuries by the time of the Civil War, the more warlike hunting and gathering tribes had not. In much of Arizona and New Mexico, the Apache and the Navajo constituted the dominant military presence until the latter half of the nineteenth century. Early efforts by the U.S. government to treat with the Apache and the Navajo[60] failed, and continuous guerilla warfare persisted for nearly a decade. In the late 1860s and early 1870s hostilities escalated into reciprocal massacres, with entire villages of friendly Indians or white farming and ranching communities destroyed and all inhabitants slain or enslaved.[61]

It was in this climate of extreme hostility that Congress began to adopt openly retributive Indian policies, which also had the effect of freeing more land for non-Indian resource development. First and foremost, in 1871 it took the constitutionally questionable action of declaring that thereafter no Indian tribe would be recognized by Congress as a nation capable of making treaties. Existing treaties were unaffected.[62] Since the Constitution empowered the president to treat with the tribes subject to Senate ratification and established such treaties as the supreme law of the land (see notes 33–35), the net effect of this remarkable legislation was to serve notice to the president that no more treaties would be ratified and that Congress intended in future to assert its own reservation-making powers. (The federal courts dealt with this modification of constitutional intent not by overturning the act but by according subsequent "agreements" between Congress and the Indians the same status that they earlier had given to treaties—much to the consternation of western water users and other advocates of states' rights.)

Other Congressional actions during this era would have a less direct but equally detrimental effect on Indian resource rights. In post-Civil War debates over resource-development practices on federal lands, western proponents of states' rights vigorously sought and eventually obtained a policy which encouraged the outright sale of resource-rich federal lands to private parties for nominal fees (thus expanding the western states' tax base)[63] and allowing state systems of water-rights allocation to prevail in watersheds where the federal government owned property.[64] Since the federal government had asserted ultimate title to all Indian lands a half-century earlier in *Johnson* v. *McIntosh*, states' advocates would later conclude (and still hold) that in these acts—as well as in section 8 of the 1902 Reclamation Act—Congress gave over to the states authority to determine the water rights of Indian tribes.[65]

In the century immediately following constitutional ratification, the United States government unilaterally adjusted the legal status of the Indian tribes down from the sovereign nations (of Revolutionary days) to "domestic dependent nations" in 1823 (in *McIntosh*) to nonnational entities in 1871. Concomitant with the loss in status had been the loss of land, first through the Jacksonian removal policy and later through reservation-creating treaty negotiations and guerilla warfare. Congressional policy makers now took what they assumed to be the final step in assimilating the Indians into white society and freeing their remaining lands for maximal resource development: passage of the General Allotment Act (also known as the "Dawes Act") of 1887.[66] The purpose of the act was to facilitate the dissolution of Indian tribes by authorizing the president to allot communally held tribal lands in 160-acre parcels to individual tribal members. After all members had received individual allotments, the secretary of the Interior was to negotiate with the tribes for the sale of the remaining lands to non-Indians.[67]

The act proved to be a disastrous failure for the Indians. It fell even further short of its stated goals than the Homestead Act (on which it was nominally patterned) and for similar reasons: non-Indian interests managed by various means quickly to accumulate title from the individual allottees, who were naive about legal matters. Of the 155.6 million acres held by Indian tribes in 1881, title to roughly 90 million acres (more than half of preallotment holdings) had fallen into non-Indian hands by the time the allotment policy was repudiated fifty years later.[68] Further, about 20 million acres of the reservation lands not allotted were unirrigated desert, considered essentially valueless by most whites.[69] Whether intended or not, the allotment policy's most effective means of encouraging the tribes to meld into white society was simply to relieve them of much of their well-watered, arable land. Throughout the periods of removal, reservation, and allotment, the size of the Indian population in the United States steadily declined. From an estimated one million indigenous people at the outset of continuous European presence, by 1900 the total Indian population had fallen to 237,196—a decline of more than seventy-five percent, according to Edward Spicer in *The American Indians* (see n. 22).

WATER RIGHTS AND INDIAN POLICY IN THE TWENTIETH CENTURY

Justice, Politics, and Planning in the Western United States before the New Deal

The Great Blackfeet Reservation of 17.5 million acres was set aside for several northern plains tribes in 1855, but in keeping with the established pattern it was greatly reduced in size later in the nineteenth century. Under extreme pressure from post-Civil War settlers and other development interests, the Gros Ventre and Assiniboine tribes finally abandoned claim to all but 600,000 acres of their land in Montana in 1888 in return for a federal promise of shelter, livestock, medical care, and farming implements.[70] Since Congress had unilaterally abolished treaty making in 1871, the federal agreement to provide these goods and to establish the smaller reservation at Fort Belknap, Montana, took the form of a congressional enactment.[71]

Two years later railroad lines penetrated the former 17-million-acre reservation area, and the land was soon acquired by non-Indian development interests. The Fort Belknap Reservation experienced its first water shortage in 1905, after newly arrived ranchers and farmers built diversions in the Milk River upstream from the reservation. Convinced that the tribes at Fort Belknap would starve if unable to water their crops that summer, the reservation superintendent solicited the aid of the U.S. attorney general's office. This was the first year of Theodore Roosevelt's second presidential term, and his administration was strongly urging the reservation and conservation of natural resources on federal lands. Perhaps in part for this reason, the Justice Department responded immediately to the Fort Belknap superintendent's request.[72] The U.S. attorney used a variety of theories in defense of Indian water rights. In petitioning the federal courts for an injunction against further non-Indian diversions from the Milk River, he in fact relied on elements of two opposing water-rights doctrines.

The humid eastern states had early on inherited the English common law of riparian water rights, a doctrine that included the following features: (1) title to land abutting a stream carries the right to withdraw for "reasonable use" waters from the stream; (2) the rights of all riparians on a watercourse are correlative, in that no user may alter water flow or quality to the degree that a neighboring riparian's use is harmed or precluded; (3) the amount of water withdrawn is not quantified, "reasonable use" and harm to neighboring riparians being the only limitations on withdrawal; and (4) a riparian right is not lost through nonuse, since the right inheres in title to riparian land.[73] Based on this doctrine, the U.S. attorney alleged Indian rights to the Milk River because it abutted the Fort Belknap Reservation.

However, Montana and other relatively dry western states had rejected riparian doctrine, primarily because the equal sharing of waters from sparse streams with wide seasonal fluctuations in flow would not assure any one user a water supply sufficient for most agricultural or industrial uses. What therefore evolved was the doctrine of prior appropriation, in which (1) a strict hierarchy of rights is based on the chronological order in which users first began to appropriate waters from a given source (ownership of riparian land not being a prerequisite to such withdrawals); (2) the right is limited to a specific amount of water dedicated to an approved "beneficial use"; (3) nonuse of an appropriative right can result in its forfeiture to other appropriators; and (4) in times of shortage the rights of users are honored in the order of their original appropriation of the waters, with the result that senior appropriators can receive their full share while junior appropriators may get little or nothing.[74] Citing this doctrine, the U.S. attorney claimed an Indian right based on the date when the reservation first diverted Milk River waters for agricultural purposes. He also alluded to "other rights" necessary to accomplish the ends for which the reservation was founded.[75]

But in granting its permanent injunction, the court relied far less on conflicting state water-rights doctrines than it did on its interpretation of the federal government's responsibility to the Indians as expressed in the Fort Belknap agreement. Although Congress had arguably abolished treaty making seventeen years prior to enactment of the Fort Belknap Reservation agreement, when in 1906 the federal trial judge issued an injunction against the white settlers, he held that "when the Indians made the treaty granting rights to the United States, they reserved the right to the use of the waters of the Milk River, at least to an extent reasonably necessary to irrigate their lands."[76]

On appeal, the 9th Circuit Court of Appeals unanimously concurred in what it found to be the lower court's "true interpretation of the treaty of May 1, 1888."[77] Citing treaty obligations of the U.S. government to the Indians as supreme law, the courts unambiguously upheld the Indian right. The appellate court also determined that for the purposes of state water-rights administration, the Indians were to be assigned as an appropriation date the day Congress enacted the Fort Belknap reservation legislation.[78] The circuit court also determined that its finding in *Winters* was not unduly violative of state water-rights law, in that two years earlier the Montana Supreme Court had acknowledged that it was unnecessary for the federal government formally to appropriate unclaimed water on its reservations, as that government "owned it already. All it had to do was take it and use it."[79]

On appeal, the U.S. Supreme Court voted eight to one to solidly uphold both the reasoning and the findings of the lower courts.[80] Although it refrained from referring to the 1888 agreement as a treaty, it nonetheless fully supported the intent of the federal government in creating a reservation as a concomitant intent to set aside that amount of water necessary to fulfill the purposes for which the reservation was established. The decision was not altogether clear in stating whether it was the Indians themselves who had reserved the waters or the federal government acting on their behalf (an important distinction),[81] but it explicitly affirmed the principle that creation of an Indian reservation automatically if impliedly creates a federally sanctioned water right for that reservation.

In upholding the circuit court decision, the Supreme Court agreed (1) that in keeping with the policies of western states' water rights, the date a reservation was established was to be considered as the date the waters were reserved (thus making Indians the senior appropriators on many western streams since most reservations were founded from the 1850s through the 1880s); but (2) that unlike state prior-appropriation doctrine, the reserved right was not liable to extinction through nonuse; and (3) that the right need not be quantified if the appropriated waters are used to fulfill the reservation's purpose.[82]

This principle—that rights of natural-resource development were impliedly retained by the Indians in treaties and agreements which set aside land for reservations—was not an entirely novel concept before the Court. As early as 1832 in a concurring opinion in *Worcester* v. *Georgia*, Justice M'Lean had set forth as a federal rule of treaty interpretation the principle that owing to the inferior bargaining position of the tribes, ambiguities in treaties were generally to be decided in the Indians' favor; that "the language used in treaties with the Indians should never be construed to their prejudice. . . . How the words of the treaty were understood by this unlettered people, rather than their critical meaning, should form the rule of construction."[83] This principle was honored with some consistency by the Court throughout the nineteenth century; and prior to *Winters* it had been most recently affirmed in *U.S.* v. *Winans*,[84] a 1905 case in which Justice McKenna (who also wrote the majority opinion in *Winters*) found that all resource-development rights not specifically surrendered by the tribe in treaties or agreements were to be considered as having been retained by the Indians. The *Winters* ruling simply applied the general treaty-interpretation doctrine set forth in *Worcester* and clarified vis-à-vis natural resources in *Winans* to the protection of Indian water rights.

Given the clarity with which the Court manifested its intent to protect the Indian right, it would later prove unfortunate for all western water-rights holders that the federal executive and legislative authorities responsible for development of western water resources did not heed these judicial signals, for they assuredly did not. More water for the Indians would have meant less water for far more politically powerful non-Indian interests. Honoring the Indian right played a minimal role in early federal-reclamation project planning and interstate stream apportionment, and all parties concerned are now paying the price for that inattention.

By the end of the nineteenth century, western water users were painfully aware of the disparity between a legal right to divert surface waters for a beneficial use and the financial and technical ability to develop that right profitably. As many of the small private irrigation companies that had been formed to deliver water to agricultural lands in the western states went bankrupt in the depression of 1894, it became ever more apparent that only the federal government possessed both the technical expertise and financial resources necessary to exploit fully the surface waters of the arid states.[85]

The Reclamation Act of 1902[86] acknowledged this fact in establishing within the Interior Department an authority to locate, design, and construct large irrigation projects in sixteen designated western states, using federal funds. Although the Reclamation Fund established by the act was intended to become self-perpetuating through the sale of newly irrigated federal lands adjacent to the projects, neither those land sales nor contracts for the sale of waters impounded ever fully recouped reclamation project costs. Since the program's initiation, irrigators have in actuality had the real cost of their water subsidized by municipal users (who pay higher rates), the sale of hydroelectric power, repeated extensions of payback periods, or straight-out donations to the fund by Congress from the federal treasury.[87] In creating what would later become the U.S. Bureau of Reclamation, the act vested great discretionary authority in the Interior secretary to determine the nature, size, location, and timing of projects to be built. Congress soon gained substantial control over these decisions through the appropriations process, and planning reclamation projects became as much a function of political bargaining as of rational analysis.

Since in the early 1900s Congress was still pursuing a policy of allotting Indian lands to individual tribal members, selling the remainder to non-Indians, and otherwise trying to assimilate the Indians into white society, it is hardly surprising that neither the Interior secretary nor congressional appropriations committees hastened to perfect any tribes' reserved water rights through construction of Indian reclamation projects. In fact, one of the first projects actually constructed under reclamation program auspices—the Roosevelt Dam, built to serve irrigators and (later) municipal users in the Phoenix, Arizona, region of the Gila River basin—would later become the subject of rancorous and protracted litigation seeking to restore the water rights of the Pima Indians.[88]

Another significant feature of the Reclamation Act was its provision for federal compliance with state water-rights law in administration of the reclamation program.[89] The effect of this statutory section was to encourage state residents further in their belief that as they appropriated waters from surface streams according to state prior-appropriation doctrine, they held that right free from any superior claim of the federal government and that the Interior Department would file for water use before state agencies and courts, just like any other property owner.

An enduring, intractable, and—from the standpoint of legal ethics— morally indefensible conflict of interest pervaded this situation and continues to do so to this day. The Interior Department, which through its Bureau of Reclamation (BuRec) was encouraging the rapid appropriation and development of water resources by non-Indian users under state law, was also responsible through its Bureau of Indian Affairs (BIA) for protection of the Indians' reserved water rights in the federal courts. Sadly but predictably, Interior was far more active and successful in discharging its former responsibility than its latter one.

Indian federal reserved water rights were understood and honored by the federal courts and had their infrequent defenders in the Justice Department and BIA, but they had little support in BuRec and even less in Congress. Without the political power necessary to get budgetary appropriations for Indian reclamation projects, the tribes were incapable of converting the *Winters* rights guaranteed them by the Supreme Court into actual beneficial use of their waters. Meanwhile, the remaining water resources were being rapidly appropriated by non-Indians, with BuRec acquiescence and support, under state law.[90] Periodically, however, the federal executive would rise in defense of the Indian right, and the judiciary would reaffirm it. In 1921, in *Skeem* v. *United States*,[91] the 9th Circuit held that the *Winters* right was not limited to use on those lands under present cultivation on an Indian reservation but could be expanded to include the entire land holding of a tribe. This decision also supported the ability of a tribe to lease its *Winters* rights in conjunction with the lease of tribal lands.

Meanwhile, the quickening pace of water-project construction in the western states was also leading to an increase in the scope of interstate water-rights litigation. The situation was particularly acute among the states in the Colorado River basin, since it was feared that if the Supreme Court steadfastly applied the prior-appropriation doctrine to interstate disputes, California—as the wealthiest, largest, and fastest-growing basin state—could and would establish prior claims to the lion's share of the flow of the Colorado.[92]

In order to avoid costly and protracted litigation which would cloud all state rights for an indeterminate period, in 1922 the seven Colorado River basin states[93] negotiated a compact for allocation of the river's waters among themselves. Commerce Secretary Herbert Hoover chaired the negotiations as a principal representative of the federal government. Conspicuously absent (because they had not been invited) were representatives of any of the scores of tribes inhabiting the basin, whose rights if enforced would constitute the largest claim on the river. Nor were Indian interests represented in compact negotiations by the Bureau of Indian Affairs. In historian Norris Hundley's characterization of this and parallel events, "Indians were a forgotten people in the Colorado Basin, as well as in the country at large; and their water needs, when not ignored, were considered negligible."[94]

Consensus on a precise formula for allocation of the waters proved impossible to achieve, so the resulting agreement was long on general principles and short on technical detail. The total drainage area of the Colorado was divided into upper and lower basins at a point on the river just above the Grand Canyon; half of the annual flow was to be allocated to the upper basin states and half to the lower ones (i.e., Arizona, California, and Nevada). Apportionment was quantified in absolute terms (7.5 million acre-feet* each to the upper and lower basins) rather than on a percentage basis, much to the consternation of current upper basin-state government leaders, since it now appears that the negotiators in 1922 based their agreement on erroneously optimistic data on the annual flow of the Colorado.[95]

The Arizona legislature refused to approve the compact as drafted,[96] but the agreement nevertheless received its constitutionally required congressional ratification in 1928.[97] The Supreme Court had warned western water users of the Indians' prior and superior rights in *Winans* and *Winters,* and the 9th Circuit (whose decisions are controlling in the lower basin states) had clarified and reinforced the *Winters* right in *Conrad*[98] in 1908 and in *Skeem* (see n. 91) just one year prior to the drafting of the Colorado River Compact. But those rights hardly figured in the final agreement: a one-sentence article stating that nothing in the compact was to be "construed as affecting the obligations of the United States of America to the Indian tribes"[99] was its only allusion to tribal water rights.[100] The federal courts may have had a clear vision of what the U.S. obligation to the tribes was, but the courts were not planning and funding reclamation projects. Certainly congressional and executive interpretations of the federal obligation bore little resemblance to the view from the bench.

Acre-foot is the unit of water measurement used throughout this study. Developed for use in reclamation-project planning and in calculating the quantity of water essential for irrigating various crops, it is that amount of water necessary to cover one acre of land to a depth of one foot. This equals 43,560 cubic feet, or 325,851 gallons—about the amount of water used in a conservative four-member household in a year's time. Quantities are usually expressed in acre-feet per year.

Federalism and Indian Sovereignty: The New Deal,
the Eisenhower Years, and the Civil Rights Era

The willingness of Franklin D. Roosevelt and his congressional supporters to alter existing policies significantly in the interest of economic
stabilization and the public welfare had just as substantial an impact on
Indian policy as on any other realm of federal endeavor. In 1928 a
prestigious privately funded study had revealed the disastrous social
and economic effects the allotment policy was wreaking on the Indian
tribes;[101] six years later, Washington was ready to follow the report's
recommendations and offer the Indians their own new deal.

The offer took the form of the Indian Reorganization Act of 1934.[102]
Most important, the act halted the practice of allotting tribal lands to
individual Indians and their subsequent sale to non-Indian interests.
The sale of remaining unallotted tribal lands to non-Indians was also
prohibited, as was the subjection of allotted trust lands to state intestacy
laws.[103] Although all matters regarding the use or disposition of natural
resources by reservation Indians remained subject to the Interior secretary's approval, the act did empower the tribes to retain their own legal
counsel (again, subject to Interior approval). Previously, the federal
government had been the only entity with authority to represent tribal
property interests in court. New Deal legislators did enact a series of
measures to foster state-federal cooperation in the provision of services
to Indian tribes,[104] but the net effect of the Reorganization Act's
repudiation of the allotment policy was to reduce greatly state influence
over Indian resources. Local governments could no longer gain control
of tribal lands through state tax and inheritance laws,[105] and lands could
no longer be given to individual tribal members and subsequently sold
to non-Indians (thereby increasing the state tax base).

The federal case law on American Indian water rights during this
period was mixed. In *United States* v. *Walker River Irrigation District*[106] the
9th Circuit held that reserved water rights accompany Indian reservations created by executive order as well as by treaty or agreement with
Congress, thus putting most tribes on equal footing regarding the
validity of their water-rights claims. But in *United States* v. *Powers*,[107] the
U.S. Supreme Court held that when a non-Indian takes title to allotted
lands from an individual tribal member, some measure of the reserved
water right is also transferred. Since the federal government's suit on
behalf of the Indians was dismissed on a procedural technicality,
however, the Court specifically declined to rule on what quantum of
water is transferred to non-Indians who purchase allotted reservation
lands.[108]

To understand fully why the western tribes had so little success in securing access to water up through the 1950s first requires an understanding of the unprecedented competition for water resources that accompanied post-World War II development of the American West. Denver, Albuquerque, Phoenix, Tucson, and Los Angeles all experienced explosive growth during the United States' postwar economic boom. An exemplary case in point is the city of Tucson, whose population grew nearly four hundred percent from 1950 to 1960 alone and another twenty-five percent the following decade; a similar if slightly less dramatic pattern was repeated throughout the West.

With this population growth came a parallel expansion in national political influence. In the U.S. House of Representatives, where all taxing and spending bills originate, the size of a state's congressional delegation is based on the size of its population. As the westward tilt in American population distribution began with wartime West Coast industrialization and continued throughout the latter half of this century, western states gained more and more influence over both the creation and distribution of national wealth. And what the western cities wanted was water delivered to their doorsteps. Mining, light and heavy industry, residential and commercial construction, transportation facilities, recreation, and huge population increases all demanded unprecedented quantities of water. Moreover, technological, biochemical, and genetic breakthroughs in American agriculture enabled the development of ever larger farms, ranches, and feedlots. Even subsequent to the urbanization and industrialization of the American West in the latter half of the twentieth century, agriculture and livestock still consume more than eighty percent of the water in every arid state.

For a variety of reasons, indigenous peoples of the region did not share measurably in the generation of wealth occasioned by western resource development in these middle years. First, they were not wealthy and powerful to begin with and were thus poorly positioned to convince private and public sector decision makers to underwrite tribal economic development. In contrast, banks, land developers, construction companies, railroads, agribusiness, and mining interests made hundreds of millions of dollars during the course of midcentury western-resource development, in no small part because of their ability to convince political leaders to lend government support to their development plans.

Second, the lands to which western tribes were confined during the reservation era of the latter nineteenth century could hardly be described as having the same potential for generating wealth as other areas of the West. Relative to areas inhabited by the Euro-American population, these regions were and are some of the poorest lands in the western United States.

And third, the attitudes of many Euro-American western politicians toward their indigenous American neighbors with a few notable exceptions tended to range from indifference and neglect to overt racist hostility. A telling example of this latter attitude is the remark of U.S. Senator Arthur Watkins of Utah. When one of his colleagues pointed out that legislation he was advocating (for the termination of Indian reservations) would have the effect of abrogating several important treaties with the tribes, he responded, "It is like treaties with Europe. They can be renounced at any time. . . . So that that question of treaties, I think, is going to largely disappear."[109]

Just as the New Deal's Reorganization Act abruptly halted the loss of Indian lands through allotment, a practice similar to allotment was just as abruptly resumed by the Congress which came to power with Dwight Eisenhower. With Republican champions of states' rights creating a majority in both houses, the Eighty-third Congress undertook a legislative program which transferred billions of dollars worth of federally controlled natural resources to state and private ownership and dealt a heavy blow to the concept of Indian sovereignty as well.

Even before President Eisenhower's election, Congress had been provoked by positions taken by the federal executive in natural-resource disputes with the states. For example, in state-federal water-rights litigation the Justice Department had regularly used the sovereign immunity defense to preclude quantification of federal water rights in (assumedly unsympathetic) state courts. The Eighty-second Congress put a stop to this practice in 1952, in the last year of the Truman administration, through passage of the McCarran Amendment[110] to the Reclamation Act. In this action, Congress waived federal sovereign immunity in certain types of water-rights cases, permitting the U.S. government to be joined in general stream-adjudication proceedings in state tribunals.[111] This was to have profound implications for the defense of Indian water rights.

The federal government and several coastal states had also been wrangling for years over title to submerged lands along the nation's shores. In 1950 the federal claims prevailed in the U.S. Supreme Court,[112] and just before leaving office President Truman declared the entire continental shelf to be a naval petroleum reserve.[113] In response, an early action of the Eighty-third Congress in 1953 was legislation cancelling President Truman's order and giving all submerged lands from the coastline three miles seaward to the respective coastal states.[114] Also enacted in that year was most of the current statutory arrangement for leasing federal submerged lands seaward of the three-mile limit to private mineral developers.[115]

The postwar, prodevelopment vigor of the American economy combined with states'-rights majorities in both houses of Congress set the stage for another assault on tribal resource rights. Having freed offshore petroleum and natural gas reserves for private development, the Eighty-third Congress now turned its attention to Indian lands. Two major pieces of legislation, both enacted fairly early in the first session, formed the core of a new Indian policy.

The first was a resolution[116] establishing procedures for the future legislative "termination" of Indian reservations: that is, the cessation of all federal trust responsibility for and supervision of reservation lands. Under this new program, the tribes in terminated reservations (1) became subject to state criminal and civil jurisdiction and to state property taxes; (2) were cut off from all federal health, education, welfare, and employment assistance; and (3) in cases where all their lands were sold to non-Indians, experienced a total loss of sovereignty as a governmental entity.[117] Some of the termination acts passed under the Resolution 108 guidelines arranged for entire reservations to be appraised and sold to the highest bidder, with the proceeds distributed to the tribe. A total of 109 bands and tribes were "terminated" during the life of this program, involving a loss of about 1.4 million acres of tribal land.[118]

A companion act to the termination program in the Eighty-third Congress was Public Law 280,[119] which extended state criminal and civil jurisdiction to all Indian lands in five states (California, Minnesota, Nebraska, Oregon, and Wisconsin) whether or not the reservations were being terminated and which also made provision for such extensions in any other reservation-bearing state requesting such authority. Tribal consent was not required. Thus, one-hundred-thirty years after Justice Marshall's finding that an Indian reservation was a land in which state law "can have no force" (*Worcester* v. *Georgia*, 1832), Congress finally came to the point of openly repudiating his decision. With a states'-rights oriented Congress and president in power, the 1950s witnessed a radical change in course for American Indian policy that once again suggests the analogy of the three-ruddered ship.

The major Indian water-rights case decided during the Eisenhower administration was *United States* v. *Ahtanum Irrigation District*,[120] in which the 9th Circuit restated and enlarged upon its finding thirty-five years earlier in *Skeem*, pointing out once more that the Indians' federally reserved water right need not be fixed in quantity but may expand with the needs of the tribe. The U.S. Supreme Court denied an immediate appeal from the 9th Circuit's decision.[121] In a now-familiar pattern, the federal courts continued to honor the historic U.S. obligations to the tribes as semisovereign peoples by upholding the water rights on which the continued existence and development of the reservations depended while the Congress was simultaneously working to dissolve the tribes and sell off their lands. Meanwhile, the executive branch continued to play its somewhat schizophrenic role of actively facilitating non-Indian western water-resources appropriations under state laws (via reclamation projects) on the one hand and occasionally defending the Indian reserved water right in federal court on the other.

Several commentators[122] have observed that the 1922 Colorado River Compact was so general because its signatories could agree on so little. A principal area of disagreement among the lower basin states was over the formula for apportioning the river's annual flow. Failing to come to terms over this issue, Arizona sued California in 1931 to have the compact overturned. Unsuccessful in this effort, in 1934 Arizona called out its National Guard to prohibit by military force the construction of projects to divert California's share of the Colorado. Arizona finally signed the compact in 1944 and contracted with BuRec for the delivery of its share of the river but initiated another suit in 1951 to establish a final apportionment of the Colorado in order to facilitate congressional authorization of the Central Arizona Project.[123]

When the Supreme Court rendered its decision in this case[124] in 1963 (more than thirty years after Arizona had filed its first action), it became apparent that compact negotiators had ignored the Indian rights at their peril. The U.S. government had defended the rights of five lower-basin tribes living along the main stem of the Colorado between Hoover Dam and the Mexican border. In response, Justice Black's majority opinion awarded the tribes (which collectively numbered fewer than thirty-five hundred persons)[125] more than ten percent of the entire annual lower-basin share of the Colorado River (about three times the amount granted to Nevada). Further, the Indians' portion of the annual flow was to be subtracted from the allotments to the states in which the various reservations were located. The Court also chose to quantify the *Winters* rights in this case, reserving enough water to service all "practicably irrigable acreage" on the reservations.[126] In a resounding reaffirmation of the doctrine it had articulated half a century earlier, the Supreme Court again let it be known that the creation of Indian reservations also created substantial and (in most cases) superior Indian rights to appurtenant water resources.

As it turned out, this supportive stance of the Warren Court presaged another change of heart in Congress over Indian policy. Just as

Congress had begun to follow the Court's lead in the early 1960s on matters affecting the status of other traditionally disenfranchised groups, it once again overhauled federal relations with the tribes. Its first actions in changing Indian policy were actually inactions, by failing to pass any reservation termination bills after 1962 (see n. 118). Yet the most striking restatement of policy came in 1968, when the Ninety-first Congress produced the Indian Civil Rights Act.[127] Although this legislation may be seen in one light as a continued limitation on Indian sovereignty (since it imposed Fourteenth Amendment restraints on tribal governments), it also effectively halted broader implementation of Public Law 280, by denying states not already having done so the authority to extend their civil and criminal jurisdiction over Indian lands without tribal consent. By the late 1960s, then, the accretion of state control over Indian lands had ended, and the flow of power was once again toward Washington. By the early 1970s, some tribes had actually convinced Congress to repeal the statutes terminating their reservations and to resume federal trust responsibility for their remaining lands.[128]

The Navajo Indian Irrigation Project

The federal government's advocacy of Indian water rights before the Special Master in *Arizona v. California* (and the findings in his report) made it apparent that the *Winters* doctrine had become a force to be reckoned with in all future western water-resources planning. Those proceedings had an immediate impact on negotiations in progress over a proposal to construct an irrigation project on the Navajo Indian Reservation.

The project under consideration would divert water from the San Juan River (a tributary of the Colorado) for the irrigation of Navajo lands near Shiprock, New Mexico. The proposal had been considered by federal agencies in one form or another since the late 1940s, when the upper basin states negotiated their own compact for apportionment of the upstream share of the Colorado River.[129] Federal representatives at the upper-basin compact negotiations had suggested that the Navajo could reasonably lay claim to an annual flow of about 787,000 acre-feet of water from the San Juan for irrigation purposes.[130] A reclamation plan prepared soon after at the Navajo Tribe's request by the BIA and BuRec called for project development of this approximate scope, but the upper basin states refused to support congressional authorization because of concerns that their own claims to the San Juan might be impaired.[131]

It was evident that the upper basin states' approval of the Navajo Indian Irrigation Project would be forthcoming only if the tribe agreed to limit and define its rights to the San Juan River. Finally, at about the same time as the Special Master's report in *Arizona* v. *California,* a bargain was struck. First, New Mexico agreed to support the Navajo proposal if its authorizing legislation provided for the construction of a companion project to divert water out of the San Juan and into the greater Rio Grande watershed for non-Indian use within New Mexico. Second, the Navajo Tribal Council agreed to the guaranteed delivery of 508,000 acre-feet of water annually through its proposed project in return for sharing water shortages during dry years with other San Juan water users. They also agreed that during drought years they would not assert senior rights based on the 1868 founding date of the Navajo Reservation.[132] Congress enacted authorizing legislation embodying this agreement in 1962.[133]

Congressional authorization is only the first step toward project realization, however. Next must come appropriations—the annual process by which Congress actually diverts funds from the federal treasury into project construction. Although the Navajo Indian Irrigation Project (NIIP) and New Mexico's San Juan-Chama Project were authorized by the same act, funds for the two were appropriated at vastly different rates. Eight years after authorization, NIIP was only seventeen percent completed; New Mexico's San Juan-Chama Project was about two-thirds built.[134] During this interim period NIPP's project design and technology were reassessed, with the discovery that use of a sprinkler-irrigation system rather than a gravity-flow system would irrigate the same amount of Navajo land with 370,000 acre-feet of water instead of the 508,000 acre-feet written into the legislation authorizing the project (see n. 132). This in turn stimulated a legal opinion within the Interior Department[135] to the effect that the Navajo were entitled only to enough water to irrigate the amount of land mentioned in the NIIP legislation and not to the specific amount of water cited. In effect, Interior was saying that it was obligated to deliver only 370,000 acre-feet of water annually through the project. Then in 1975, in response to an unquantified *Winters*-doctrine claim on the San Juan River by the Jicarilla Apaches, New Mexico filed for an adjudication of all rights (Indian and non-Indian alike) to the New Mexico segment of the San Juan in its own state courts.[136] Efforts to remove the case to federal court were ultimately unsuccessful.[137] As of this writing, the largest Indian reservation in the United States has still not had access to more than a small fraction of its theoretical water rights entitlement.

This and other examples of negotiated settlements of *Winters*-doctrine rights bear a striking resemblance to nineteenth-century negotiations over the establishment of reservations in the western territories, when tribes such as the Assiniboine and Blackfeet forfeited rights to millions of acres of land in return for federal assistance in the economic development of much smaller protected areas. Similarly, the Navajo waived their reserved rights to the San Juan—which the federal government itself estimated in 1948 to be at least 787,000 acre-feet—in return for the guaranteed delivery of 508,000 acre-feet (as authorized in the NIIP legislation), only to see this amount unilaterally adjusted to 370,000 acre-feet by the Interior Department in 1974. As a final irony, the Navajo were then called upon to defend their remaining rights in New Mexico's own courts. The strength of this historical comparison (i.e., the pitfalls involved in negotiating resource entitlements) has not been lost on Indian leaders, some of whom now have vowed "never again to discuss water rights outside the courthouse"—preferably the federal one.[138]

It is clear that Indian policy has not been made in a vacuum; it has in many instances been a by-product of government efforts to achieve other purposes altogether. To continue with the analogy of the ship with three rudders, although the name on the vessel may have been "Indian policy," it was often hauling different freight altogether. Consider the first three landmark decisions of the Supreme Court, as it began to shape and define Indian rights. *Johnson* v. *McIntosh* in 1823 stripped the tribes of fee simple ownership of their lands (vesting title instead in the federal goverment), and *Cherokee Nation* v. *Georgia* in 1831 reduced tribal status to that of "domestic dependent nations"—a sort of perpetual legal childhood in which the tribes have dwelt ever since. But in the very next term, the Court's 1832 decision in *Worcester* v. *Georgia* totally barred state governments from exercising any jurisdiction over Indian lands unless they had explicit congressional permission to do so.

How can the first two of these cases—which significantly diminished the status implicitly accorded the tribes in the Constitution—be reconciled with the third, which extended to the tribes an important shield against local avarice? In analyzing these cases, sometimes referred to as the "Marshall trilogy,"[139] it is instructive to remember that they were all authored by Chief Justice John Marshall, the most articulate, ardent, and forceful advocate of federalism on the court in the first half of the nineteenth century. His overarching goal was the assertion of federal control—over the tribes and their lands when they sought sovereign nation status independent of the United States and over the states when they sought control over Indian Country. American Indian policy in the Marshall Court was a highly suitable vehicle for the furtherance of federalism.

Likewise, the Removal Act of the 1830s, the reservation policy of the mid-nineteenth century, and the Allotment Act in the 1880s were all perfectly attuned to Congress's avowed goals during that period of acquiring as much of the North American continent as possible by whatever means from whomever possessed it and then just as quickly converting it to private ownership and development by U.S. citizens and corporations.[140] Indians were ejected from the most desirable lands right along with the French, Spanish, Mexicans, and Russians.

And further, mere coincidence does not explain the U.S. attorney's politically unpopular but highly successful advocacy of tribal reserved water rights in the *Winters* case in the early days of this century at the very same time President Theodore Roosevelt was using every means at his command to shield federally owned resources from private local exploitation. (Roosevelt also later tried to withdraw tribal lands from tribal use but did not prevail.)[141] Finally, repudiation of the allotment policy and reestablishment of tribal governmental authority over reservation lands in the 1930s came at a time when a New Deal president and Congress were discouraging resource development in order to stabilize prices and markets,[142] just as the termination policy of the 1950s coincided with a renewed postwar congressional zeal for the rapid, minimally regulated private development of federal resources.

Even in light of the argument that "Indian policy" has often been a convenient rubric for attaining other governmental ends, three generalizations about the legal history of American Indian water resources still hold true. First, from the 1908 *Winters* decision up through the 1960s, the federal courts for the most part[143] have tended steadfastly to uphold Indian water rights as preemptive federal obligations, while Congress and the executive—because of the Indians' relative lack of political clout—have tended either to ignore the Indian right or to subvert it indirectly (by facilitating non-Indian water appropriation under state laws). Infrequently, the executive branch has defended their right, in keeping with its court-assigned role as trustee of Indian resources and also when it coincided with other policy objectives. Second, at times when Congress has been most deferential to the states and private developers regarding access to federally protected natural resources, diminution of the Indian resource base has been the greatest (as in the Removal Act, the Allotment Act, the termination acts, and Public Law 280). And third, a strong parallel exists between negotiations over the creation of Indian reservations in the nineteenth century and current negotiations over the development of Indian water resources. In both instances, the tribes have been urged to relinquish resource rights, for which the federal judiciary had afforded strong constitutional protections, in return for congressional and executive promises of assistance in the economic development of a much smaller resource base, which grew even smaller once the original right had been bargained away.

As the governmental institution ostensibly least susceptible to shifting political currents and most sensitive to the honoring of governmental obligations, the federal judiciary has emerged over the course of this century as the primary definer and defender of the Indian water right. Congress has been called upon repeatedly to declare a general policy on these rights, but it has resolutely avoided action on any of the dozens of proposals it has considered;[144] federal executives market water to non-Indians under state law on Monday, defend the Indian right in court on Tuesday, and spend the rest of the week hoping the problem will just go away. Since the federal courts stand at the vortex in this swirl of ambivalence and uncertainty, any perceptible shift in their support for the Indian right will affect the future of that entitlement profoundly. Thus the courts' views on federal-state relations and on the nature and extent of the U.S. obligation to the tribes are of special relevance.

The following chapter argues that in the U.S. Supreme Court just such a shift has occurred, as the Court has become increasingly accommodative of states' rights in the area of water resource management. And the examination of dispute handling methods in contemporary cases reveals that changing court attitudes are continuing to have a major ripple effect on efforts to negotiate the settlement of Indian water-rights disputes. We will explore the nature of that effect in detail, as well as the tenuous bargaining position in which many of the western tribes therefore now find themselves.

Legal Issues and Dispute-Managing Methods in Contemporary Water-Rights Conflicts

Of the myriad issues raised in contemporary Indian water-rights disputes, judicial answers to about half a dozen principal questions will continue to form the core of the Indian right, unless Congress chooses to intervene: (1) Which court system (state or federal) should have primary jurisdiction over Indian water-rights cases? (2) How much water is reserved for tribal use? (3) To what uses may these waters be devoted? (4) What interests in water rights may be conveyed to non-Indians? (5) What is the extent of tribal authority and responsibility over management of water resources and water quality? And (6) Who is authorized to represent Indian interests in water rights?

These issues have more than simply legal and academic significance, for it is in their resolution—whether through litigation, negotiation, or legislative policy—that the economic and social future of many western tribes will be largely determined. Almost uniformly throughout the western states, the two most significant limiting factors on economic development are capital and water. Further, the resolution of these questions will do much more than determine whether the western tribes will be able to move toward economic parity with their non-Indian neighbors. An equally important principle at stake in these disputes is the sovereignty of the tribes. Will they be able to govern their own affairs and exercise the same degree of functional control over those necessary resources as do the state, regional, and local governments with whom the tribes coexist in the West?

Although as a matter of federal policy tribal sovereignty seems to be increasing in areas such as criminal jurisdiction, child welfare, and even the regulation of energy-resource development,[1] most western tribes have far less legal and functional control over reservation water resources than do neighboring governmental jurisdictions. As a matter not only of economic sustenance but also of tribal independence and self-determination, the resolution of these issues is inextricably intertwined with the future governmental status of Indian tribes.

Dispute management is used frequently in the latter part of the study in preference to "dispute settlement" and "conflict resolution," which appear more commonly in the social science literature. This choice of terms reflects the fact that for one or more parties in a dispute, settlement may not be a primary goal. Indeed, keeping the dispute unsettled, active, off balance, and costly to all concerned may in some situations be the preferred strategy. Also, in the disputing process each party plans and executes strategy to get the dispute into the friendliest forum under the most favorable conditions possible at the lowest cost to themselves and the greatest cost to their opponents. In short, each party tries to manage the dispute (regarding forum, transaction costs, movement toward or away from settlement, and so on) to its own advantage.

Jurisdiction to Adjudicate Indian Water Rights

Although Congress agreed to permit the quantification of federal water rights in general-stream adjudications in state tribunals in the 1952 McCarran Amendment,[2] it was not until 1976 that the U.S. Supreme Court was called upon to determine whether this provision also included the water rights of Indian tribes. Before then, the proposition that disputes over Indian water rights would be heard in federal courts had been so accepted that the question of jurisdiction over Indian water resources had not even appeared in treatises summarizing Indian rights.[3] But in a 1976 case, *Colorado River Water Conservation District* v. *United States*,[4] the Supreme Court declared that certain states did have jurisdiction to quantify the Indian entitlement rights. It held that a "general stream adjudication" such as that being conducted under Colorado law was just the sort of unified proceeding in which the McCarran Amendment directed the federal government to participate and that since the federal government was acting as trustee of the Indian interests, Indian rights were subject to quantification in state proceedings. The Supreme Court did reserve concurrent federal-court jurisdiction in future cases, however, and left open the question of a tribe's ability to perfect its rights in an original federal court action in the absence of a state proceeding.

This was a substantial setback for Indian rights. Judges in several of the western states are elected by popular vote (some with party affiliation) and periodically stand for reelection. Also, in some states members of the state boards who make initial findings of fact in stream adjudications are usually appointed by the governor, subject to legislative consent. With this degree of local political influence over water-rights adjudication, Indian concerns about fairness and objectivity are understandable.[5] The issue was further clouded by subsequent conflicting decisions in the circuit courts. These cases all interpreted language in the congressional enactments which admitted several of the western states to the Union or in the provisions in the constitutions originally drafted by these states. Provisions in these acts and constitutions waive any and all state claims to the ownership of or regulatory jurisdiction over Indian lands within those states.[6]

In 1979, in *Jicarilla Apache Tribe* v. *United States*,[7] the tribe sought to avoid state water-rights adjudications on the basis of such provisions. The 10th Circuit rejected the tribe's argument, finding that the McCarran Amendment and the Supreme Court's interpretation of it in its 1976 decision (see n. 3) authorized state adjudication of the Indian right. The Supreme Court declined to hear an appeal from this decision. But the 9th Circuit then heard three cases raising precisely the same issue, and in all of them it reached conclusions diametrically opposed to the 10th Circuit finding. In *Northern Cheyenne Tribe* v. *Adsit*,[8] the 9th Circuit explicitly rejected the reasoning in *Jicarilla* and found instead that states constitutionally disclaiming jurisdiction over Indian lands were barred from adjudicating Indian water rights. Likewise, in both *San Carlos Apache Tribe* v. *Arizona*[9] and *Navajo Nation* v. *United States*[10] the immunity of Indian reservations from water-rights adjudication in states with disclaimer provisions was upheld.

The U.S. Supreme Court heard all these cases on consolidated appeal and in July 1983 rendered a decision substantially reiterating the position it took in the Colorado River Conservation District case in 1976: Indians named in state general-stream adjudications would be compelled to participate in those proceedings for the purpose of quantifying their entitlements. The federal courts would retain concurrent jurisdiction to review state adjudicatory outcomes.[11] Moving beyond its 1976 holding, the Court also found that it made no difference whether the tribes were representing themselves or if the Justice Department was adjudicating on their behalf; the Indians would be compelled to defend their rights in state court.

Just how damaging a decision this was to the Indian cause is amply demonstrated by more recent state-court actions and the Supreme Court's response. In 1988 the Shoshone and Arapahoe tribes and the U.S. government suffered what some see as at least a partial defeat before the Wyoming Supreme Court: It ruled that (1) "practicably irrigable acreage" was the sole measure of the tribal water right; (2) tribal water could be reserved only for agricultural and domestic/municipal use, thus disallowing the reservation of waters for fisheries maintenance, minerals development, or wildlife protection; (3) the tribes were prohibited from selling their water to non-Indians outside the reservation; and (4) groundwater underlying the reservation belonged to the state—not to the Indians—and was therefore subject to exclusive state regulation.[12] Making this last point required a tortured reading of federal case law by the Wyoming court, for in 1976 the U.S. Supreme Court had ruled in *Cappaert* v. *U.S.*[13] that the reserved-rights doctrine extended not only to groundwater underlying a federal reservation whenever a ''hydrologic connection'' between ground and surface water could be demonstrated but also to a federal reservation's power to enjoin groundwater pumping by adjoining private citizens on their own land if such withdrawals were negatively affecting the water table underlying federal lands.

Since the Wyoming Supreme Court's holding basically stripped the tribe of its reserved rights to groundwater and in the process rendered impotent the U.S. Supreme Court's 1976 groundwater decision in *Cappaert* (at least insofar as tribes in Wyoming were concerned), the state action generated intense interest in what the U.S. Supreme Court would do in response to such an open challenge to its own authority and to such a substantial derogation of Indian rights regarding groundwater jurisdiction, off-reservation sale of water, and purposes for which water could be reserved.

In essence, the U.S. Supreme Court did nothing. First, it refused to hear an appeal from those portions of the Wyoming decision to which the tribe objected.[14] After agreeing to hear an appeal from those aspects of the decision to which the state objected (on the quantification issue), the Court became deadlocked over the question of whether to reverse Wyoming's action (Justice O'Connor did not participate in the vote) and thus let stand as binding the Wyoming Supreme Court decision.[15]

As a result, observers of Indian water-rights conflicts learned two lessons from these developments: State courts are indeed ready and willing to adopt somewhat restrictive views of Indian reserved rights—at least insofar as tribal jurisdiction and marketing power are concerned— and the U.S. Supreme Court does not seem prepared to stop them. At the same time, it should be pointed out that some observers are considerably more sanguine in their evaluation of how the tribes fared in the Big Horn River litigation, in that the state court did find that the tribes had prior and senior rights to a considerable amount of water (based on a priority date of 1868, when the treaty establishing the reservation was signed). The determination of ''practicably irrigable acreage'' was relatively generous, and there is no language in the Wyoming decision explicitly limiting the uses to which the Indians may put their waters, although agricultural and municipal/domestic were the only uses for which they could be reserved.[16]

It is currently unclear just how far the lower federal courts will be willing to follow the U.S. Supreme Court in its apparent abandonment of its trust responsibility for tribal water rights. In its 1983 ruling in *San*

Carlos Apache, the High Court listed three narrow exceptions to its finding that Indian water-rights cases must be adjudicated in state courts. It held that a federal court action could be maintained (1) if a state government voluntarily stays assertion of jurisdiction, (2) if the arguments for and against dismissal of the federal case are "closely matched," and (3) if the federal action is already so far advanced that removal to a state tribunal would be duplicative and wasteful of judicial resources.[17] Citing all three of these exceptions, in 1983 the 9th Circuit denied an appeal by the state of Oregon from a lower court decision barring the state from adjudicating the water rights of the Klamath Indians.[18] Since then the 9th Circuit has again marginally trimmed the states' jurisdictional victory in the *San Carlos* decision by holding that the federal courts maintain current control over implementation of historic-consent decrees involving Indian rights—decrees entered before passage of the McCarran Amendment in 1952.[19] The U.S. Supreme Court refused to hear an appeal from this decision and also from a later 9th Circuit decision removing an Indian water-rights case from state to federal court in the interests of "timely resolution" of the dispute.[20]

These circuit decisions are significant for two reasons. First, there are more Indian reservations involved in water-related legal conflicts within the jurisdiction of the 9th Circuit than within any other federal appellate circuit in the United States. The 9th Circuit is thus the second most influential court in the nation (after the Supreme Court) in terms of the geographic scope of its Indian water-rights decisions. Second, the Supreme Court declined to hear an appeal from any of these 9th Circuit rulings, thus letting stand a string of decisions favoring federal over state-court jurisdiction. This is in contrast to actual rulings of the Supreme Court in the 1976 *Colorado River Conservation District* case, its 1983 *San Carlos Apache* decision, and its affirmation of the jurisdictionally restrictive *Wyoming* v. *U.S.* in 1989.[21]

At the Supreme Court level, how can these rulings be reconciled with the observation that one of the federal court system's traditional trust functions has been to shield the tribes from state jurisdictional intrusions, absent explicit congressional instructions to the contrary? The answer lies mostly in the changing composition and orientation of the Supreme Court. It appears that the more deferential an individual justice tends to be toward the traditional powers of state government, the more likely he or she will be to vote in favor of the states and against the Indians whenever a jurisdictional conflict between the two occurs. Just as the Court has become markedly more oriented toward states' rights over the last two decades—beginning with the appointments of Justices Burger and Rehnquist—so has it become correspondingly less supportive of American Indian tribes in the water cases. Since 1970 the tribes have lost six of the seven water-related cases to come before the High Court—mostly on jurisdictional grounds.[22]

Quantity of Water Reserved

The *Winters* decision and most of the reserved-right cases following it in the first half of the twentieth century held that the Indians' right should not be quantified, enabling the entitlement to expand with tribal needs. As competition for water has increased, a more recent trend has been toward placing an outside limit on the precise quantity subject to Indian claims. The 9th Circuit experimented with quantification in *Walker River* in 1939[23] based on the "reasonably forseeable needs" of the tribe, but the quantification criterion most frequently discussed currently is the "practicably irrigable acreage" test proposed by the Special Master and adopted by the Supreme Court in *Arizona* v. *California* in 1963.

Although the use of this criterion proved to be relatively generous in that case, potential pitfalls are involved in its future use to resolve the claims of other tribes. First, when *Arizona* v. *California* was recently reopened to adjudicate additional Indian claims, the new Special Master made it clear that determining what lands were "practicably irrigable" for the purposes of Indian water-rights quantification would be accomplished through the use of classic cost-benefit analysis.[24] Analysts familiar with the use and misuse of this technique in evaluation of water projects have been quick to point out that in the hands of an untrained or hostile fact-finder, an Indian right could be quantified at drastically reduced levels through a failure to distinguish between economic and financial feasibility, an insufficiently narrow consideration of costs and benefits, or the choice of an inappropriate discount rate.[25] Even using this analysis, the Special Master found that additional allocations to lower Colorado River basin tribes were in order. However, in March of 1983 the U.S. Supreme Court rejected the master's report and refused to grant the tribes more water—not because of faulty methodology but because they did not wish to rehear the quantification issue.[26]

A second drawback to the use of the "practicably-irrigable-acreage" test is that though it may work to the advantage of tribes inhabiting alluvial plains or other relatively flat lands adjacent to a watercourse, forest and mountain-dwelling tribes are severely penalized by such a criterion since agriculture will never have the primacy in their economies that timber, minerals development, or recreation could have, given an adequate water supply.[27] In these situations, more appropriate quantification criterion must be developed, if quantification is attempted at all.

Relatively little case law exists on the extension of *Winters*-doctrine rights to groundwater supplies. The Supreme Court did rule in 1976 in *Cappaert* v. *United States* that once a federal reservation has been created (in this case, it was a national monument), a reservation of groundwater may be implied if there is a "hydrological connection" between ground and surface waters and if a nonfederal diversion of the groundwater supply subsequent to the reservation's founding is thwarting the purpose for which the reservation was established. Ten years later the U.S. Court of Claims expressly acknowledged groundwater resources as impliedly reserved unto Indian reservations if one purpose in founding the reservation was irrigated agriculture.[28]

Some tribes are now beginning to assert an "aboriginal" water right, based on the use of water from "time immemorial" rather than on its reservation by the federal government at the time an Indian reservation was created by treaty, agreement, or executive order. The aboriginal right has been recognized partially in at least one federal case,[29] but if quantified, an aboriginal right claimed by a traditionally agricultural tribe would probably be no larger than a *Winters*-doctrine claim (since most tribes historically have used less water than they hope to in the future).[30]

Indian leaders and tribal advocates hold mixed opinions as to the wisdom of agreeing to quantification of a *Winters* right.[31] The weight of opinion is probably against quantification because the sense of indeterminacy created by a legitimate, unquantified reserved-rights claim is one of the Indians' principal sources of bargaining power. Yet modern tribal leaders are realists who must continually balance what seems to tribal members a just and honorable solution to a water-rights dispute against what may be achievable in court or Congress.

Regarding quantification, litigants are also currently in conflict over consent decrees rendered much earlier in this century, when the federal government represented the tribes (sometimes over their objections) in settlement negotiations to end lawsuits involving federal and tribal water rights. The most notorious of these are the 1910 Kent Decree and the 1935 Globe Equity Decree, involving the adjudication of the Salt and Gila rivers in Arizona, respectively; and the 1944 Orr Ditch Decree, settling federal, tribal, and other rights to the Truckee River in Nevada. In 1973 the Pyramid Lake Paiutes sued to have the Orr Ditch Decree nullified on the grounds that the federal government acquiesced in quantification of Paiute rights at unreasonably low levels. But in 1983 the U.S. Supreme Court rejected the Indian claim, not because the Court disagreed with the tribe's assertion that it had been dramatically short-changed by federal government bargaining in 1944 but because the

Court did not want to set a precedent of reopening cases already settled by judicial-consent decrees, even if those settlements seemed unjust by contemporary standards.[32]

Uses of Reserved Waters

The essential theme of the *Winters* doctrine is that on the date of a federal reservation of land, enough previously unappropriated water is also reserved to fulfill the purpose(s) for which the reservation was created. In defining an Indian reserved right, determining why an Indian reservation was created is a necessary first step in identifying the specific purposes for which water is reserved and in estimating the amount of water necessary to fulfill those purposes. Critics of expansive *Winters*-doctrine claims assert that since the intent of ninteenth-century treaties was to encourage the tribes (particularly in the Plains area) to convert from hunting and gathering to farming, agricultural production should be the only use to which a reserved water right can be devoted.[33]

Regarding non-Indian federal reserved water rights, the Supreme Court in the late 1970s did indeed adopt a progressively narrower definition of the purposes of federal reservations, such as national forests,[34] in an effort to minimize the impact of federal claims on state systems of water-rights allocation. But in 1979 in a per curiam supplemental decree in *Arizona* v. *California*,[35] the Court stated that even though "practicably irrigable acreage" was the criterion for quantifying the Indian right and agricultural development was among the primary purposes of the reservations concerned, the tribes were not restricted in the use of their waters to irrigation or other agricultural applications.[36]

Since the general purposes stated in creating nearly all Indian reservations included assistance to the tribes in learning the "arts of civilization" and otherwise becoming economically self-sustaining, analysts for minerals developers have concluded that the courts will probably construe activities such as silviculture and logging, energy-resource extraction and processing, and recreation as among the legitimate uses to which tribes can devote water resources acquired under the *Winters* doctrine.[37] But efficiency of use is still a concern in the West, and controversy over what technologies the tribes use to apply their waters will doubtlessly continue since method of use affects quantities needed.

An important case in the 9th Circuit exemplifies the interrelationship between the quantity reserved and purpose-of-use issues. In *Colville Confederated Tribes* v. *Walton*,[38] the Indians appealed a federal district court decision denying them reserved rights to the minimum instream flow necessary to restore spawning grounds for a fishery appurtenant to their reservation in the state of Washington. The trial court had reasoned that since the Indians were being supplied with artificially propagated fish from a federal hatchery, an instream flow sufficient to support natural propagation was not necessary to fulfillment of the purposes of the reservation.[39] But the appeals court disagreed. In holding that the obligation of the U.S. government was to guarantee the tribes sufficient water to allow them to achieve their reservation's purposes rather than simply to meet the Indians' economic needs by other means,[40] the 9th Circuit's decision in *Walton* was also an important statement of support for tribal self-determination in resource management.

Sale of Reserved Waters

Currently the most heated controversy over the use of reserved waters concerns the Indians' ability to lease their water to non-Indians outside their reservation's borders. Advocates of tribal sovereignty argue that the tribes should be allowed to do so, just as large urban water providers like the Denver Water Department market excess supply to their suburban neighbors.[41] But critics of this approach[42] point out that retailing water supplies to non-Indians is nowhere mentioned in any of the treaties, acts, and executive orders that created the Indian reservations as a purpose for their establishment and therefore the tribes should not be allowed to use their water in this way.

Others have recommended a more balanced perspective that would allow the tribes the same marketing rights as other water-holding governmental entities but without inordinately infringing on existing non-Indian rights.[43] However, even though water marketing in the West is being vigorously advocated as a way of improving efficiency of use, the ability of Indian tribes to do so is being just as vigorously opposed by most non-Indian water-rights holders. Further, if enemies of tribal marketing rights are as successful in other state courts as they were in Wyoming in 1989 (in the state supreme court decision allowing the Shoshones to lease their water on but not off the reservation) and if the U.S. Supreme Court fails to intervene, tribes may see this right eroded by state judicial systems.

Unquestionably, the unfettered right of tribes to sell reserved waters off-reservation will result in a measurable degree of the redistribution of wealth in the American West as water becomes an ever more precious commodity. For western advocates of states' rights, there is something particularly galling about the idea of forfeiting water rights to the tribes either through litigation or a negotiated settlement and then having to buy back some of that same water at prices set by the tribes. Conversely, from the tribal perspective the ability of the Indians to sell some portion of their water may well be their last best hope for lifting their reservations out of the grinding poverty in which they have lain since their creation.

From the time of the 1921 circuit court decision in *Skeem v. United States*,[44] the ability of tribes to lease reserved water has been fairly well established when it is leased in conjunction with the lease of reservation land. A more frequent source of contention now is the breadth of the reserved water right acquired by a non-Indian successor to tribal lands which passed out of Indian control during the Allotment Era (i.e., non-Indian lands wholly within or adjacent to reservation boundaries which carry a reserved water right). The early case law on this issue was relatively generous to the non-Indian successors to title, ruling that they do indeed share in a tribe's reserved rights,[45] although not to the same unquantified extent.[46]

In 1981 the 9th Circuit clarified and slightly reduced the scope of the non-Indian reserved-rights claim. In *Colville Confederated Tribes v. Walton* the court held that although non-Indians do take a reserved water right in allotted lands with an appropriation date of the founding of the reservation, they appropriate only that amount of water actually being put to "diligent use" at the time of succession to title; but in no instance is the quantum to exceed that amount necessary to service the "practicably irrigable acreage" of the non-Indian lands. In settling a long-standing dispute over groundwater rights between the San Xavier district of the Tohono O'Odham Tribe (formerly the Papago) and the city of Tucson, Congress specifically empowered the Indians to market their water (i.e., to sell it back to Tucson and other local users). But it just as specifically disclaimed that this legislative provision either did or did not empower other Indian tribes to do so.

Tribal Sovereignty, Water-Resource Management, and Water Quality

As the tribes anticipate an era of greater functional control over water resources they previously have held only in theory, the question of the scope of Indian management authority—including rights and responsibilities vis-à-vis water quality—inevitably looms larger.[47] The more water the tribes are able to divert, the more dependent their economies will become on upstream users abiding by delivery agreements and the more dependent downstream users will become on wise practices of water-resource management by the Indians. The question of sovereignty in fact looms large over every aspect of tribal water rights. Some values attendant on a culture's relationship with water are simply not subject to categorization, calibration, and the vagaries of market forces—in short, to the relatively narrow perspective Euro-American society has traditionally brought to bear in water-resource decision making. To the extent that a tribe values its water in ways that are at variance with the dominant culture, we might reasonably expect to see that variance expressed in the ways the tribe seeks to manage its water.

Throughout the first half of this century, Indian water projects were usually planned and operated by agencies of the Interior Department on the tribes' behalf, so most open disputes over the scope of Indian management authority have occurred since the mid-1960s with the assertion of greater tribal self-determination.[48] Recent decisions of the 9th Circuit and the U.S. Supreme Court offer markedly different perspectives on the issue of Indian sovereignty over water resources. In *Colville Confederated Tribes* v. *Walton* and its companion, *Washington* v. *United States*,[49] non-Indian successors to allotted Indian lands and the state of Washington had argued for state water-rights administration on non-Indian land holdings within the reservation. But the 9th Circuit held that in watersheds wholly encompassed by an Indian reservation, it is within the power of the tribal government—not the state—to regulate water rights on privately held lands within reservation borders. This tribal regulatory authority was characterized as an "important sovereign power,"[50] abrogated neither by the McCarran Amendment nor by Public Law 280.

Although the Supreme Court denied certiorari in *Walton*, its decision in another case that same year was just as derogative of Indian sovereignty over water management as *Walton* had been supportive of it. The case was *Montana* v. *United States*,[51] a dispute over ownership of the beds of rivers flowing through an Indian reservation. Montana asserted the right to enforce its fishing regulations against non-Indians on allotted lands within the reservation, based on its claim of title to the riverbeds; in opposition, the federal government asserted title as fiduciary for the Indians. In a decision remarkable for its abandonment of traditional doctrines of treaty interpretation, the Court held that creation of an Indian reservation fails to establish riverbed ownership in the tribe unless the language of the treaty, agreement, or executive order establishing the reservation specifies such a transfer.[52] Thus, the Court abruptly countered one-and-a-half centuries of precedent laid down in *Worcester*, *Winans*, *Winters*, and subsequent decisions which ruled that ambiguities in reservation-creating documents are to be construed in the tribes' favor and that title to all resources not specifically conveyed by the Indians in such agreements should remain with the tribes.[53] Further, the Court denied inherent Indian sovereignty over the regulation of non-Indian behavior within the reservation or on its navigable waterways, unless such behavior directly imperils the "political integrity, economic security, or health and welfare" of the tribe.[54] Unclear from this finding is just how much residual authority the tribes now have for preventing the pollution of waters flowing into the reservation—indisputably a "health and welfare" problem.

Tribes in the American Southwest are now litigating this issue in actions triggered by the increasing scope and severity of the environmental impact of the development of energy projects. There are disputes now pending on the radioactive contamination of ground and surface waters by private uranium mining appurtenant to the Navajo Reservation and on the impact of geothermal development on the water resources of the Pueblos.[55] It remains to be seen whether the tribes, as semisovereign governmental entities, will be able to obtain remedies that are substantially superior to those available to aggrieved private parties.

The extent of tribal rights and responsibilities under federal statutes on water pollution control has not yet received a great deal of attention since the breadth of Indian water-management authority has previously not been great.[56] Predictably, the issue is complicated because many federal environmental-protection statutes, such as the Clean Water Act,[57] the Resource Conservation and Recovery Act (RCRA),[58] and the Safe Drinking Water Act[59] devolve major enforcement authority to state governments willing and able to implement their provisions. But state governments are now implementing their own programs at the same time that many tribal governments are trying to lure increased industrial activity onto reservation lands, and (over tribal objections) some states have been asserting authority to enforce their environmental programs on the reservations.

In 1985 the state of Washington in a RCRA action before the 9th Circuit asserted that the state should be empowered to enforce its RCRA implementation program on Indian reservations. The court ruled against the state, holding that the EPA rather than the state should develop an implementation program, working directly with tribes as sovereign governments.[60] This case represents only the tip of the iceberg. A survey commissioned by the EPA and published in the same year as the *Colville* decision found nearly twelve hundred hazardous-waste dumpsites on or proximate to Indian reservations, mostly in the western states. Some of them pose immediate and serious public health hazards.[61]

If non-Indian neighbors suspect the Indians of trying to attract polluting industries without adequately regulating the discharge of effluents, the tribes may face stiff legal opposition to any future development. Likewise, tribes are becoming more and more sensitive to the effects of non-Indian development on the quality of reservation water and are becoming ever more willing to take legal action when they perceive a threat to water-quality—as evidenced by the recent energy-related water-quality cases.

Representation of Indian Interests

Until passage of the Indian Reorganization Act in 1934, there was no confusion over who would represent the tribes in court; authority inhered solely in the federal government as the trustee of Indian interests. This arrangement engendered bitter resentment among many western tribes since if the United States failed to protect their water rights there was no other party who could. As early as 1910, tribes in Arizona were charging that the federal government, as putative guardian of the Indian right, was selling them down the river by bargaining away their water rights on terms highly advantageous to their non-Indian neighbors.[62] Although the Reorganization Act empowered them to retain their own counsel subject to approval by the Interior Department, most tribes continued to rely primarily on the federal government for protection of their interests because of the extraordinary costs involved in the independent sponsorship of water-rights litigation.

However, a sharp split has occurred and is now broadening between Interior and some tribes over the issue of representation of interests. The most dramatic example of the problem involves the White Mountain Apache Tribe, who inhabit a mountainous reservation in the upper Gila River basin of east-central Arizona. In accordance with the Reagan administration's interpretation of the 1976 Supreme Court ruling on water-rights adjudication jurisdiction, against the expressed wishes of the tribe the Interior secretary and attorney general in 1981 joined in state adjudication of the White Mountain Apaches' water rights, purportedly as representatives of tribal interests. The tribe itself has refused consistently to participate in state proceedings and mounted an unsuccessful effort in the federal courts to enjoin federal executives from defending their water rights in Arizona courts.[63] As of this writing, White Mountain Apache interests are still being represented in Arizona courts in a massive adjudication to the rights of the Gila River. Conflict of interest in the Interior Department regarding protection of Indian natural-resource entitlements is a familiar theme to students of Indian law;[64] the case in point is just an unusually graphic illustration. The severity of this conflict is likely to be greatest in presidential administrations that adopt as a consistent policy the devolution of authority over substantial resource management to state governments.

METHODS OF DISPUTE MANAGEMENT
IN CONTEMPORARY CASES

In June 1982 an extensive survey of disputes over Indian water rights throughout the western United States was completed by the Western Network, a regional research institute based in Santa Fe, New Mexico.[65] Investigators learned that about fifty major disputes were either in progress at that time or had just reached tentative settlement. The updated results of this survey are presented in Table 3.1. Information about each of these cases is organized according to (1) the state in which the controversy arose; (2) Indian and other parties to the dispute (including case names when litigation had been initiated and the titles of relevant legislative enactments); (3) the citations to cases and enactments; (4) principal issues raised in the dispute; and (5) the method(s) of dispute management resorted to by the parties. These categories of information deserve some elaboration since Table 3.1 contains the data base on which all subsequent research in this study has been developed.

Case Names and Citations. These refer in most instances to actions brought by the tribes or on their behalf in federal court. However, countersuits and related actions have also been filed by non-Indian disputants in state courts in many of these controversies. For each entry where the case name has been marked with a double asterisk and where the Issues column contains the symbol ''FJ'' (forum jurisdiction), it may be assumed that one or more concurrent actions have been filed by non-Indian litigants in the court systems of those states party to the dispute. In most of these cases the state action is a general-stream adjudication.[66]

Issues. Symbols were chosen to denote key issues in these controversies since the same issues are featured repeatedly in disputes within the same geographic region. For instance, forum jurisdiction—the question of whether an Indian water-rights case should be heard in state or federal court—is a procedural aspect of cases throughout this survey in which the principal substantive issue is the perfection of reserved rights, that is, the legal effort of a given tribe to put into practical effect the theoretical reservation of waters on its behalf by the Supreme Court's 1908 *Winters* decision. Geographically, these cases tend to be concentrated in arid regions such as the greater Rio Grande and Colorado river basins and the intermountain West.

In contrast, the issues most frequently contested in a water-rich area like the Pacific Northwest have less to do with entitlement to the consumptive use of water resources than with the maintenance of instream flow in a given watercourse, usually for the purpose of fisheries protection. The most common threat to unimpeded instream flow in this region is the construction of hydroelectric facilities, which along with other resource-development activities such as logging and transportation of energy minerals may also pose problems of water-pollution control. An additional means of asserting tribal jurisdiction over fisheries in public-land states where tribal fishing rights are in some doubt has been the tribal claim of riverbed ownership of streams flowing through or appurtenant to reservation lands. Other questions presented in Indian water-rights cases throughout the West include the extent of Indian authority regarding the conveyance of reserved rights to non-Indian parties and representation of Indian interests, which may involve challenges either to the adequacy of past representation by the federal government or to current federal representation of those interests in the absence of tribal consent.

Methods of Dispute Management. Four broad categories of these methods were adopted for this survey. Litigation is the most straightforward and simply refers to an original or appellate action filed by Indian or other parties in a state or federal court. Negotiation includes any formal gesture towards nonlitigated, consensual settlement of disputes made by one party and responded to affirmatively by an adversarial party; most of the negotiation efforts cited in this study have matured to the point where at least a draft settlement has been generated by the parties. Legislation refers to situations in which a negotiated settlement requires ratification by a legislative body but also encompasses situations in which one party unilaterally attempts to achieve ends through legislative action which appeared unobtainable by any other means of dispute management. Administrative adjudication occurs mostly in situations such as hydroelectric-licensing proceedings (where the courts require exhaustion of administrative remedies prior to judicial review) or in the contractual allocation of water resources from federal reclamation projects—a proceeding in which the Bureau of Reclamation has original jurisdiction.

Tabulation of the data in the dispute-management column of Table 3.1 yields some interesting results. Note first that among the options listed, litigation is by far the preferred method—it has been used or is being employed in forty-two of the fifty disputes surveyed. The six instances of administrative adjudication listed are for the most part hydropower licensing actions, which may be expected to ripen into federal court cases if either the tribes or the affected utility companies are unable to defend their cause successfully before the Federal Energy Regulatory Commission (FERC); the same holds true for allocation proceedings for reclamation projects before the U.S. Bureau of Reclamation.

Resorting to legislated solutions for problems of water rights has been primarily for the purpose of putting into effect large-scale negoti-

Table 3.1. Contemporary Indian Water Rights Disputes*

State	Indian and Other Disputants (and case names, if applicable)	Citations	Issues	Dispute Management Method(s) Lit.	Nego.	Ad. Adj.	Legis.
Arizona	1. Lower Colorado River tribes party to *Arizona v. California*, on AZ side of the River; US; AZ; CA.	460 U.S. 605 (1983)	PRR to lower Colo. River	X			
	2. Hopi & Navajo tribes; US; local irrigators; municipalities (*Navajo Nation et al. v. US*)**	463 U.S. 545 (1983)	FJ, PRR to Little Colorado River	X			
	3. *Arizona v. San Carlos Apache***	463 U.S. 545 (1983)	FJ, PRR to Salt River	X			
	4. Apache, Maricopa, Papago, Pima, & Yavapai tribes; US; AZ; municipalities, local irrigators, mining cos. (*US v. Gila Valley Irrigation Dist.*)**	454 F.2d 219 (9th Cir. 1972)	FJ, PRR to Lower Gila River	X		X	
	5. *Salt River Pima-Maricopa Indian Community v. State of Arizona***	rev'd. 463 U.S. 545 (1983); P.L. 100-512	FJ, PRR to Salt River	X	X		X
	6. *Fort McDowell Mohave-Apache Indian Community v. Salt River Valley Water Users Ass'n.***	rev'd. 463 U.S. 545 (1983)	FJ, PRR to Verde River	X			
	7. Gila River Pima-Maricopa Indian Community; Kennecott Copper Co. (*Water Rights Settlement & Exchange Agreement*)	private agreement, signed 1/1/77	private bilateral PRR to limited area in lower Gila Basin		X		
	8. Papago tribe; City of Tucson; local irri-	Civ. No. 75-39	PRR(G) to upper	X	X		X

	Citation	Issue			
gators; mining cos.; several hundred private water users; US (*US v. City of Tucson; Southern Arizona Water Rights Settlement Act of 1982*).	TUC (D. Ariz. 1975); PL 97-293 (1982).	Santa Cruz River Basin			X
9. Ak Chin Community of Indians; local irrigators; US (*Ak Chin Indian Community Water Rights Settlement Act*).	P.L. 95-328 (1978); P.L. 98-530 (1984)	PRR(G) to lower Santa Cruz River Basin		X	X
10. White Mountain Apache v. William French Smith & James Watt	463 U.S. 1228 (1983)	IIR	X		
California 11. Lower Colorado River tribes party to *Arizona v. California* on Calif. side of the river (same as case no. 1)	460 U.S. 605 (1983)	PRR to Lower Colorado River	X		
12. Various Mission Indian bands; US; municipalities, utility cos. (*San Pasqual, La Jolla, Rincon, Pauma, and Pala Bands of Mission Indians v. FERC; US v. Escondido Mutual Water Co.*)**	692 F.2d 1223 (1982); P.L. 100-675 (1988)	IIR, PRR, M1F hydropower licensure on San Luis River	X	X	X
13. Agua Caliente Band of Mission Indians; utility co.; US (*In the Matter of So. Cal. Ed. Co.*).	20 F.E.R.C. Rep. 61,349 (Sep. 23, 1982)	MIF hydropower licensure on White River in Coachella Basin		X	

*Survey completed 3/82; updated 4/90. **One of several suits filed in this dispute. †J. Folk-Williams, *What Indian Water Means to the West* (Santa Fe, N. Mex.: Western Network, 1982). *Key to issue symbols:* FJ = forum jurisdiction; FP = fisheries protection; G = groundwater; IIR = Indian interest representation; MIF = maintenance of instream flow; PC = pollution control; PRR = perfection of reserved rights; RO = riverbed ownership.

Continued.

Table 3.1, continued.

State	Indian and Other Disputants (and case names, if applicable)	Citations	Issues	Dispute Management Method(s)				
				Lit.	Nego.	Ad.	Adj.	Legis.
California, continued								
	14. Karok, Tolowa, & Yurok tribes; US; environmental groups (*Northwest Indian Cemetery Protection Ass'n. v. Peterson*).	764 F.2d 581	PC(FP) on tributaries to Klamath River	X	X			
Colorado	15. Ute tribes; US; CO; local irrigators; environmental & recreation groups (*In the Matter of the Application for Water Rights of the U.S., Water District No. 7, Colo.*)	P.L. 100-585 (1988)	PRR to tributaries of the San Juan River, construction of the Animas-La Plata Proj.	X	X			
Florida	16. Seminole tribe, Florida, US.	P.L. 100-228 (1987)	MIF in wetlands	X	X			X
Idaho	17. Kootenai bands; US; utility co.; environmental & recreation groups	See Folk-Williams†	MIF(FP)—hydro power licensure on Kootenai River	X			X	
Montana	18. Northern Cheyenne tribe; US; MT; local irrigators (*Montana v. Northern Cheyenne Tribe*)**	463 U.S. 545 (1983)	FJ, PRR to Tongue River	X	X			
	19. Crow tribe; US; MT; local irrigators (*US v. Big Horn Low Line Canal et al.*)**	rev'd. 463 U.S. 545 (1983)	PRR to Big Horn River	X	X			

	Citation	Issues			
20. Crow tribe; US; MT (*Montana v. US*)**	450 U.S. 544 (1981)	RO Big Horn River	X		
21. Blackfeet, Assiniboine, Sioux, Gros Ventre, & Chippewa-Cree tribes; US; MT; local irrigators (*US v. Aageson*)**	rev'd. 463 U.S. 545 (1983)	FJ, PRR to Milk & St. Mary Rivers	X	X	
22. Assiniboine & Sioux tribes; US; MT; local irrigators (*US v. Aasheim*)**	Id.	FJ, PRR to Big Muddy & Poplar Rivers	X	X	
23. Salish & Kootenai tribes; US; MT; local irrigators (*US v. Abell*)**	Id.	FJ, PRR to Flathead River System	X		
24. Blackfeet tribe; US; MT; local irrigators (*US v. AMS Ranch*)**	Id.	FJ, PRR to Marias River system	X		
25. Salish & Kootenai tribes; US; utility co. (*In the Matter of Northern Lights Inc.*)	See Folk-Williams†	MIF(FP)— hydropower licensure on Kootenai River			X
Nevada 26. Pyramid Lake Paiute tribe; US; NV; municipalities; utility cos.; local irrigators (*US & Pyramid Lake Paiute v. Truckee-Carson Irrigation Dist.*)**	463 U.S. 110 (1983); S.1554 (1989)	IIR, MIF(FP), PRR to Truckee & Carson Rivers, Pyramid Lake	X	X	
New Mexico 27. Navajo, Ute, & Apache tribes; US; NM; municipalities (*New Mexico v. US*)**	*cert. denied* 429 U.S. 1121 (1977)	FJ, PRR to San Juan River	X		

*Survey completed 3/82; updated 4/90. **One of several suits filed in this dispute. †J. Folk-Williams, *What Indian Water Means to the West* (Santa Fe, N. Mex.: Western Network, 1982). *Key to issue symbols:* FJ = forum jurisdiction; FP = fisheries protection; G = groundwater; IIR = Indian interest representation; MIF = maintenance of instream flow; PC = pollution control; PRR = perfection of reserved rights; RO = riverbed ownership.

Continued.

Table 3.1, continued.

State	Indian and Other Disputants (and case names, if applicable)	Citations	Issues	Lit.	Nego.	Ad.	Adj.	Legis.
New Mexico, *continued*								
	28. *Jicarilla Apache Tribe v. US***	*cert. denied* 444 U.S. 995 (1979)	FJ, MIF(FP), PRR to Navajo River	X				
	29. Several Pueblo tribes; US; NM; private water users (*New Mexico v. Aamodt*)**	*cert. denied* 429 U.S. 1121 (1977)	FJ, PRR to tributaries of Rio Grande	X				
	30. Mescalero Apache tribe; US; NM; local irrigators (*New Mexico v. Lewis*)**	88 N.M. 636, 545 P.2d 1014 (1976)	FJ, PRR to tributaries of Pecos River	X				
	31. Several Pueblo & Jicarilla Apache tribes; US; NM; local water users (*New Mexico v. Aragon*)**	Civ. No. 7941 (D.N.M., filed 3/5/69)	FJ, PRR to Chamas River	X				
	32. Navajo tribe; US; several energy devel. cos. (*Peshlakai v. Schlesinger*)	CV No. 78-2416 (D.D.C. 1978).	Impact of proposed uranium devel. on surface & G; PRR(G)	X				
	33. Navajo tribe; US; NM; uranium devel. co.	See Folk-Williams†	PC(S&G) from uranium tailings spill into Rio Puerco	X				
	34. Acoma & Laguna Pueblo tribes; US; NM; municipality (*Pueblo of Laguna & Acoma v. City of Grants NM et al.*)	Civ. NO. 1540-HB (D.N.M., 12/30/82).	PC(S)—municipal sewage pollution of tribal water supply from Rio San Jose	X				

State	Case	Citation	Issue		
Oregon	35. Klamath tribe; US; OR; private water users (*US v. Adair*)**	478 F. Supp. 336 (D. Ore. 1979).	FJ, PRR(FP) to Williamson River		X
South Dakota	36. Several Sioux tribes; US; SD; municipalities; local irrigators (*South Dakota v. Rippling Water Ranch*)**	531 F. Supp. 449 (D.S.D. 1982).	FJ, PRR to Missouri River basin in western SD		X
	37. *Yankton Sioux Tribe v. Nelson*	*cert. denied* 107 S.Ct. 3228 (1987)	RO, Lake Andes (tributary to Missouri River)		X
Utah	38. Ute Indian tribe; US; UT (*Ute Indian Deferral Agreement of 1965; Ute Indian Water Compact*)	Utah Code Ann. L&SC Title 73-21-2 (1980); S.536 (1989)	PRR to waters of Uinta Basin, facilitating Central Utah Project	X	X
Washington	39. Yakima Indian tribes & bands; US; WA; local irrigators & private water users (*Holly v. Yakima Indian Nation*)	*cert. denied* 108 S. Ct. 85 (1987).	FJ, PRR to Yakima River		X
	40. Colville Confederated tribes; US; WA; private water users (*Colville Confederated Tribes v. Walton*)**	*cert. denied* 454 U.S. 1092 (1981).	FJ, PRR to No Name Creek, limits on conveyance of reserved rights		X

*Survey completed 3/82; updated 4/90. **One of several suits filed in this dispute. †J. Folk-Williams, *What Indian Water Means to the West* (Santa Fe, N. Mex.: Western Network, 1982). *Key to issue symbols*, 1982). FJ = forum jurisdiction; FP = fisheries protection; G = groundwater; IIR = Indian interest representation; MIF = maintenance of instream flow; PC = pollution control; PRR = perfection of reserved rights; RO = riverbed ownership.

Continued.

Table 3.1, *continued*.

State	Indian and Other Disputants (and case names, if applicable)	Citations	Issues	Dispute Management Method(s)			
				Lit.	Nego.	Ad. Adj.	Legis.
Washington, *continued*							
	41. Spokane tribe; US; WA; lumber co. private water users (*US v. Anderson*)**	*cert. denied* 450 U.S. 920 (1981).	FJ, MIF(FP), PRR to Chamokane Creek	X			
	42. Lummi tribe; US; WA; local water users (*US v. Bel Bay Community & Water Ass'n.*)**	See Folk-Williams†	FJ, PRR(G) in Nooksak River Basin	X			
	43. Swinomish, Sauk-Suiattle, and Upper Skagit tribes; US; WA; Seattle (*Swinomish Tribal Community v. FERC*)	627 F.2d 499 (D.C. Cir. 1980)	MIF(FP)—hydropower licensure on Skagit River	X	X		
	44. Muckleshoot tribe; US; utility co. (*Puget Sound Power & Light v. FERC; Muckleshoot Tribe v. Puget Sound Power & Light*)	*cert. denied,* 454 U.S. 1053 (1981)	FJ, MIF(FP), PRR & damages—hydropower licensure on White River	X			
	45. 19 tribes & bands inhabiting Olympic Peninsula & mainland west of Cascade Mtns.; US; WA; commercial & sports fishermen (*US v. Washington*)**	*cert. denied* 454 U.S. 1143 (1982)	FJ, MIF(FP), PC PRR to watersheds draining western Cascade Mtns. & Olympic Peninsula	X			
	46. *Puyallup Tribe of Indians v. Port of Tacoma*	*cert. denied;* 465 U.S. 1049 (1984).	PC, RO(FP), Puyallup River	X			
	47. Skokomish tribe; US; WA; utility co.	See Folk-Williams†	MIF(FP)—hydropower licensure on south fork, Skokomish River			X	

	48. 8 tribes & bands inhabiting Puget Sound area; US; pipeline developers (*Lower Elwha Tribal Community et al. v. Reagan*)	520 F. Supp. 334 (W.D. Wash. 1981)	PC(FP)—impact of oil pipeline const. & maint. on Puget Sound fishery	
Wyoming	49. Shoshone & Arapaho tribes; US; WY; private water users (*In re Adjudication of the Big Horn River Basin*)**	753 P.2d 76 (1988); 109 S.Ct. 2994 (1988).	FJ, MIF(FP), PRR of Wind River Reservation to Big Horn River Basin	X

*Survey completed 3/82; updated 4/90. **One of several suits filed in this dispute. †]. Folk-Williams, *What Indian Water Means to the West* (Santa Fe, N. Mex.: Western Network, 1982). *Key to issue symbols:* FJ = forum jurisdiction; FP = fisheries protection; G = groundwater; IIR = Indian interest representation; MIF = maintenance of instream flow; PC = pollution control; PRR = perfection of reserved rights; RO = riverbed ownership.

ated agreements with Indian tribes to which the U.S. government or a state government was a party. Negotiation has been attempted in fourteen of the fifty disputes surveyed, prior to or in conjunction with litigation in ten of these instances. As case studies in Chapter 4 will demonstrate, this updated survey has discovered a total of seven examples of successfully negotiated settlements of Indian water-rights disputes—almost half of which occurred in 1988 alone.

THE QUEST FOR NONLITIGATED SETTLEMENTS

The dilemma of Indian water rights now facing the American West—and indeed, the entire nation—has not come upon us overnight and in fact has been the subject of serious governmental study for quite some time. One of the more concise analyses of the problem, accompanied by concrete proposals for its resolution, is in the final report of the National Water Commission (NWC),[67] a study group established by Congress in 1968 to make recommendations on the content and implementation of a comprehensive policy for national water-resource management. The commission soon recognized the gravity of the Indian water-rights situation. It dubbed the United States' failure to protect Indian water rights from non-Indian appropriation as one of our national history's "sorrier chapters"[68] and then set about to formulate some remedies.

Regarding jurisdiction over water-rights adjudication, the commission recommended that Congress clearly designate the federal district courts as having primary jurisdiction over all Indian water-rights cases in order to avoid the "suspicion of bias" in adjudication of those rights by elected and appointed state officials.[69] Quantification and adjudication of all rights were also recommended,[70] along with liberal construance of reservation purposes and recognition of the prerogatives of tribal water-resource management.[71]

However, in the nearly two decades since publication of the NWC final report, Congress has not adopted one of these general recommendations as national policy. The commission also suggested policies and procedures which would have perfected the Indian right in a relatively friendly forum and obligated the federal government to finance development of those rights, even to the extent of condemning (with compensation) the rights of some non-Indian users whose entitlements the Interior Department had assured under state law.[72] But such a solution, while substantially honoring the federal obligation to the tribes, would be both costly and contrary to the interests of many western senators and congressional representatives whose non-Indian constituents have no wish to see Indian water rights developed at their expense. Since the

1908 *Winters* decision the western state governments, municipalities, agricultural conservancy districts, land developers, and other major water-rights holders opposing the tribes in court have been combating American Indians with equal vigor in the halls of Congress. Perceiving in the *Winters* doctrine a very real threat to the rights they have established—sometimes at great expense—under state prior-appropriation doctrines, they have fought the tribes to a standstill legislatively every time some proposal was put forward which in some way would have curtailed prior-appropriation rights on the Indians' behalf.

As a result, a routine has developed in Congress: Supporters of the Indian cause (generally, the same legislators who sponsor bills for the benefit of other traditionally disadvantaged social groups) submit fairly generous legislation for Indian water-rights settlement.[73] This is blocked or deflected by a coalition of western congressmen—who in turn have submitted their own measures for the uniform state adjudication and/or condemnation of Indian reserved rights, which the civil-rights coalition and others then reject as inherently unfair.[74] The result has been a legislative stalemate over the comprehensive recognition and fulfillment of Indian water-rights claims.

Congress has continued to play its more limited traditional role of ratifying individual large-scale agreements involving the disposition of Indian water resources. Measures such as the Navajo Indian Irrigation Project Act, the Ak Chin and Papago groundwater-settlement agreements, and the Mission, Ute, and Pima settlements were bargains either ratified or authorized by Congress and were all situations in which the tribes agreed to limit or defer *Winters* rights in return for guaranteed water delivery. Most of these acts also authorized funding to accomplish the purposes of the agreements. Although not approximating a comprehensive solution, these acts for limited, situation-specific, incrementally funded projects may well prove to be the only achievable response from a divided Congress to the controversial and expensive question of what to do about tribal *Winters*-doctrine claims.[75]

Beset by a wavering court on one side and a deadlocked Congress on the other, nearly everyone now seems to be either guardedly or enthusiastically urging negotiation as the preferred method of settling Indian water-rights disputes—everyone, that is, except the Indians. The Reagan and Bush administrations (as did Carter before them) have touted negotiation as the best means of curbing the onslaught of litigation over Indian water-rights which has "stalled essential economic progress";[76] some conservation groups seem intrigued by the idea,[77] as are academic advocates of Indian resource rights[78] and even some tribal litigators.[79] Since 1978, several large-scale agreements requiring either congressional ratification or authorization have been negotiated. In

these settlements, the Indians agreed to quantification of their entitlements and waiver of their *Winters* rights in return for the delivery of
specified quantities of water.

Although the tribal councils who were party to these agreements
apparently concluded that more is to be gained through present
negotiation than future litigation, the majority of tribes surveyed in
Table 3.1 so far have reached the opposite conclusion. Either way, Indian
representatives are taking something of a gamble. If the tribes indicate a
willingness to forego *Winters* claims as the price of project development,
a waiting game ensues while Congress annually determines the rate at
which it will appropriate funds for the Indian project. If appropriations
are not forthcoming at the rate specified in the agreement, the tribes'
only real option is to go to court to perfect their original claims—their
position having been weakened by the subsequent non-Indian appropriation of water resources the tribes had traded away in negotiations.
However, if all the western tribes adhere exclusively to a course of
federal court adjudication of their *Winters* rights (as the NWC final report
recommended), it is possible that in addition to shouldering the great
financial burden of independent water-rights litigation, they will also
incur the wrath of enough western congressmen to force passage of
retributive legislation condemning Indian reserved-water rights.[80]

The Indians are thus in a delicate position. The western tribes do
not have enough friends in Congress to finance the perfection of their
Winters rights or enough enemies (at the moment) to take them away.
The Interior Department is most eager to negotiate on behalf of or with
the tribes, as are state governments and corporate developers. Meanwhile, the Supreme Court seems to be on the verge of undermining the
sovereignty of Indian water rights. It is little wonder that while tribal
leaders are not wildly enthusiastic about negotiation, many of them are
reluctant to reject that alternative unequivocally.

Given the High Court's rapidly eroding support for tribal water
rights, the increased incidence of negotiated settlements in the late 1980s
is understandable. The tribes entering into these agreements obviously
sensed that their chances of prevailing in court—especially in state
court—were diminishing rapidly. Furthermore, by the end of the decade
the federal bench from the Supreme Court on down had been remade
largely in the Reagan image; the hopes that a right-wing federal
judiciary oriented toward states' rights would fulfill its trust obligation
in protection of Indian treaty rights were becoming dimmer and
dimmer. Thus, the agreements entered into by the tribes during this
period of changing orientation in the federal court deserve special
attention. The continuing question in examining these agreements is
whether these pacts represent the ushering in of a bright new era of

cooperation and compromise among traditional adversaries or whether instead an older, darker, and much more familiar tale—that of pressuring the Indians into making lopsided deals that they will not have the power to enforce—is simply being retold.

At the beginning of this century, the U.S. Supreme Court reasoned in *Winters* v. *United States* that once the framers of the Constitution had acknowledged the Indian tribes' right to exist and the supremacy of federal agreements with them, the federal government is obliged to honor those agreements; and further, that once a treaty or agreement in furtherance of that acknowledgment has been adopted, the resources on which the tribes' continued existence depends are not to be considered as having been bargained away unless the terms of the agreement specifically divest the Indians of such entitlements. It is important to remember that in the three quarters of a century since *Winters* was written, while Congress has never ordered the Justice Department to perfect all Indian reserved water rights nor even clearly specified the forum for the adjudication of those rights, neither has it ever passed legislation nullifying or even substantially limiting the *Winters* doctrine as applied to the tribes. I suggest this results from a fundamental ambivalence in the halls of Congress where the status of Indian tribes is concerned.

The *Winters* doctrine may sound just and honorable in the abstract, but because of earlier congressional and executive inattention, the costs of its implementation are now substantial. Justice and honor are most easily identified and ardently embraced when their cost is not high—whether that price is paid in racial unrest or by a substantial outlay of federal tax dollars (or both). As it became apparent that Indian water rights might have to be perfected at the partial expense of non-Indian rights and that Indian water projects might have to be developed at the partial expense of non-Indian projects, the congressional sense of justice on the subject of Indian water rights was heavily offset by financial and political considerations. Further, perhaps Congress has not hastened to perfect the Indians' *Winters* rights over the course of this century because the federal courts have so consistently defended those entitlements. The nation has enjoyed the moral satisfaction of just decisions without the social and fiscal inconvenience of having to implement them.

This situation is changing. With just one exception, since 1976 the U.S. Supreme Court has steadily become less of a guardian of Indian water rights than at any other time in this century. With the addition of ardent advocates of states' rights to the Court (some of whom hail from the very states seeking to limit Indian rights) the current Court has at times rejected the Indian position on issues such as court jurisdiction,[81] quantification,[82] and tribal-government jurisdiction over waterways within reservations.[83] Just as Congress has chosen to leave well enough alone as long as the federal courts were protecting the *Winters* doctrine, the time may be overdue for Congress at least to correct the imbalance created by changes in High Court philosophy on the water rights of Indian tribes relative to the states. To designate the federal district courts or a specially created Indian Water Rights Commission as having primary jurisdiction and to finance the perfection of *Winters* rights— either by tribal counsel or the Justice Department, depending on the wishes of each western tribe—would be clear signals to the Supreme Court of our nation's continued willingness to honor the Indian water right. And this Court is in need of clear signals.

Given the congressional deadlock on the comprehensive resolution of claims, however, and given the Supreme Court's increasing hostility to the Indian position, tribal willingness to take a more active interest in negotiation is understandable. The Court gaveth (in *Winters* v. *U.S.*), and the Court tooketh away (mostly throughout the 1980s). Congress never did give much, and—with the exception of the tribes fortunate enough to be within House Interior Committee Chairman Morris Udall's geopolitical sphere of influence (i.e., the Southwest)—it is unclear whether it will be willing to give much more in the future. American Indian tribes may indeed be experiencing the limits of law.

CHAPTER FOUR

The Peril and Promise of Negotiation: A Closer Look

Given the flurry of interest in the negotiated settlement of disputes over American Indian water rights arising in the late 1980s, it is easy to get the impression that negotiation represents a novel, contemporary innovation in the resolution of these long-standing conflicts. In fact, just the opposite is true. For as long as there has been a *Winters* doctrine, there have been concerted efforts to get the tribes to relinquish a reserved-rights entitlement in return for the guaranteed provision of a lesser quantity of water. Officials in federal and state government agencies, local water users, and (more recently) neighboring municipalities have all sought to convince the tribes that their best interests lay in surrendering a theoretical paper water right in return for a smaller quantity of wet water delivered to the reservation.

A comparative review of all these cases reveals both a great diversity of circumstances and some unsettling similarities. From the earliest settlement in 1910 to the agreements awaiting ratification by Congress eight decades later, the promise of improved tribal economy and the peril of very real threats to tribal welfare have coexisted. The case studies in the comprehensive settlement of Indian water-rights claims fall into three distinct eras: (1) agreements negotiated on the tribes' behalf (but in some cases without their consent) in the first half of the twentieth century; (2) waiver and deferral agreements negotiated during the era when the adjudication of *Arizona* v. *California* was reinvigorating the *Winters* doctrine in the 1960s; and (3) the contemporary settlements being negotiated in the wake of distinctly anti-Indian decision making by the United States Supreme Court and the release of federal tax dollars to implement these increasingly expensive compacts.

EARLY TWENTIETH-CENTURY SETTLEMENTS

The Kent Decree (1910). This dispute arose between the Salt River Pima-Maricopa Indian community and neighboring non-Indian water users in the early days of this century. In 1902, just one month after passage of the Reclamation Act, the Interior secretary withdrew lands for reclamation-project development at the confluence of the Salt and Verde rivers, just east of present-day metropolitan Phoenix, Arizona. Engendering a tension between the reclamation service and the Bureau of Indian Affairs that would last from that day to this,[1] the reclamation project was not designed to service any Indian lands but instead would take water the Indians had formerly been using.

In 1905, the U.S. attorney filed suit in state court to adjudicate the rights of the Salt River and Fort McDowell reservations under the prior-appropriation doctrine but unfortunately did not amend the complaint in 1908 subsequent to the Supreme Court's decision in *Winters* v. *U.S.*[2] In 1910 the federal government entered into a stipulated settlement of the lawsuit on the tribe's behalf in which the Indians were limited to natural-flow rights in the river with no right to store water and no rights whatsoever under the reserved-rights doctrine established two years earlier by the U.S. Supreme Court. The tribes attempted unsuccessfully to have the case reopened to adjudicate their *Winters* rights following the court's decree. In 1917 the Interior Department transferred operation and maintenance of the newly completed Salt River Project to local government authorities, with no requirement that any water at all be delivered to the Pima Indians.

This negotiated settlement of a suit adjudicating tribal rights on terms that left the tribes with far less water than they had previously used and with no rights to participate in local water-project development sowed the seeds for decades of costly litigation. The Salt River community filed suit for damages against the federal government in the 1940s and against the Salt River Project, the state, several cities, and dozens of local water users in the 1970s and 80s. In the late 1980s the bulk of these disputes once again became the subject of a comprehensive negotiated settlement.

The Mission Indians Settlement (1914, 1924). The Mission Indian bands were established on a reservation in San Diego County, California, by act of Congress in 1891. Over the next two decades the federal government granted rights of way across Indian lands to a succession of water and power companies, one of which entered into a contract with the United States in 1914 to deliver a certain amount of water and power to the reservation in return for permission to site a hydroelectric facility, power lines, and access roads on the Rincon Reservation.[3]

In 1924, without tribal consent, the Federal Power Commission granted much broader water and power rights to non-Indian utility companies operating on the reservation and throughout the middle years of the twentieth century continued to withdraw for consumptive use substantial quantities of water from the San Luis River. Finally, in 1969 the Rincon and La Jolla bands filed suit in federal court to void the utility companies' water and power contracts with the federal government and to restore water rights to the tribe. The litigation dragged on into the 1980s, when negotiated resolution of this long-standing dispute was once again attempted.

The Globe Equity Decree (1935). To settle a lengthy water-rights dispute over flow rights to the Gila River in east-central Arizona, the federal government in 1935 entered into a stipulated decree on behalf of the San Carlos Apaches and Gila River Pima-Maricopa Indian commu-nity. Negotiating on the tribes' behalf but without their consent, the federal government established rights for the tribes on condition that non-Indian farmers would receive "a major share of the Indian right."[4] The tribes have never accepted the decree as determinative of their rights and have been engaged for decades in litigation challenging the allocation of Gila River water to their non-Indian neighbors.[5] A dispute over state versus federal jurisdiction in this conflict finally reached the U.S. Supreme Court in 1983, resulting in the *Arizona* v. *San Carlos Apache* decision affirming state-court authority to quantify tribal water rights in general-stream adjudications.

Orr Ditch Decree (1944). For much of this century, the Pyramid Lake Paiutes in Nevada have been ensnared in a complex web of litigation with local, state, and federal agencies and other water users over the flow of the Truckee River, which drains into Pyramid Lake. The problems first arose in 1913, when the federal government sued to clarify both its own water rights and those of the Pyramid Lake Paiute Tribe to the Truckee River in conjunction with completion of the first major irrigation project authorized by the federal government under the 1902 Reclamation Act.[6] This case dragged on for years in Nevada's federal district court until the U.S. government finally negotiated a water-rights settlement on its own behalf and the Indians' with all non-Indian water users on the Truckee in Nevada; the court ratified this settlement as the Orr Ditch Decree in 1944. However, in 1973 the tribe successfully intervened in a new action brought by the United States to enhance its rights to the Truckee River; the tribe was primarily inter-ested in guaranteeing an annual minimum flow into Pyramid Lake sufficient to protect the Lahontan Cut-throat Trout Fishery on which the tribal economy largely depends. The tribe was (and is) of the opinion that the federal government's 1944 settlement on its behalf was overly generous to non-Indian interests. However, the Indians were ultimately unsuccessful in getting their rights readjudicated because of a U.S. Supreme Court decision against them in 1983;[7] by the end of 1989, another negotiated settlement was in the offing.

In each of these cases two characteristics are worth noting. First, the tribes were either pressured into accepting these settlements—all of which were negotiated for them by the federal government—or these agreements were simply imposed on the tribes without their consent. Second, as a result of the duress to which the tribes were subjected and the generally unfavorable terms (for the Indians), every one of these settlements engendered deep resentment within the tribes involved and later became the subject of costly, protracted, and highly disruptive water-rights litigation. Thus there is a fairly direct correlation between the level of coercion to which the tribes were subjected and the lack of durability of the ensuing agreements.

Water and sovereignty—the tribes' turning water to their own uses and their freedom to determine those uses—were issues as central in the first quarter of this century as they are today. The tribes' relative inability to exercise sovereign powers then and the water they lost as a result does much to explain the modest circumstances of the residents of these reservations today compared to their non-Indian neighbors. It also explains why they have been in court off and on for most of the last half-century, seeking redress from the disadvantages they suffered in these early settlements.

WAIVER AND DEFERRAL IN THE 1960S

As the legal status of the tribes evolved during the middle years of the twentieth century, so too did the circumstances under which their water-rights claims were settled through negotiation. Of particular significance were the Indian Reorganization Act of 1934 and *Arizona* v. *California* in 1963. Three of the four Indian water-rights settlements just discussed were fashioned at a time when the tribes had no standing to represent their own interests independently in court; as trustee for tribal resource rights, only the federal government was empowered to enter into binding agreements concerning the use and disposition of reservation resources. But in the 1934 Indian Reorganization Act,[8] Congress authorized the tribes to hire their own legal counsel and assert their own interests in legal proceedings. This new-found independence was not total and not without significant limiting conditions, of course. Under the act, the hiring of independent counsel by a tribe was subject to approval by the Interior Department in each instance, as was the tribal budget from which the attorney would be paid.[9] The increased sense of tribal self-determination provided by the Reorganization Act took on particular significance in the 1960s, with the Supreme Court's expansive interpretation of tribal reserved-water rights in *Arizona* v. *California*.[10] Even as the Special Master in this case was receiving evidence from the many parties concerned—preparatory to the Court's 1963 decision—it became apparent that the tribes along the lower Colorado River stood a good chance of perfecting claims to a significant portion of the river as a result of the federal government's advocacy on their behalf.

Navajo Indian Irrigation Project (1962). It was in the context of this uncertainty over the scope of Indian rights to the Colorado that the Navajo tribal council was induced to waive its rights to the San Juan River, a tributary of the upper Colorado. The tribe agreed to waive its priority rights to diversions from the San Juan and to share shortages proportionately in dry years, rather than to assert its senior *Winters* rights to the river. In return, the tribe was promised the delivery of 508,000 acre-feet of water via an irrigation project to be constructed by the Bureau of Reclamation.[11]

However, the state of New Mexico objected even to this allocation unless the authorizing legislation included a companion project to divert water out of the San Juan basin into the upper Rio Grande basin to service non-Indian agricultural lands in northern New Mexico. Appropriations for the Navajo and New Mexico projects did not proceed apace: eight years after authorization the state project was two-thirds completed and the Navajo irrigation works were only seventeen percent finished. The delay was due in part to complaints over the relative inefficiency of the NIIP as originally conceived. The Interior Department in 1974 concluded that with increased technological efficiency, the tribe could irrigate the lands in question with only 370,000 acre-feet of water instead of the 508,000 written into the NIIP agreement and should therefore be entitled only to that amount of water.[12] Then a year later the state of New Mexico became embroiled in water-rights litigation with another Indian tribe (the Jicarilla Apaches) over the flow of the San Juan, named the Navajos as a necessary party, and proceeded to adjudicate everyone's rights in New Mexico state courts.

Fifteen years after New Mexico's legal assault on the Navajos' rights to the San Juan, the promises made in the original NIIP agreement and legislation remain unfulfilled;[13] a heated controversy over project efficiency remains unresolved, and the future of the project is still in doubt. Thus the NIIP also remains one of the more discouraging modern examples of negotiated Indian water-rights limitations conditioned on the assurance of government-built projects that somehow were never completed.

Ute Tribe (Uintah and Ouray Reservations) Deferral Agreement (1965). After the Supreme Court's 1963 decision in *Arizona v. California*, politicians throughout the Colorado River basin scrambled to secure federal funding for the entrapment and distribution of their share of the river.

As home to some sizable Indian reservations, the state of Utah was concerned that the issue of rights would interfere with its ability to attract the funding necessary to complete its Central Utah Project.

In 1965 the state convinced the tribe to defer the diversion of water onto more than 15,000 acres of arable reservation land until the twenty-first century, by which time—according to assurances in the agreement—an Indian unit of the Central Utah Project would be constructed to serve the reservations.[14] But in 1977 tribal leadership changed, and the terms of the original deferral agreement came to be seen in a much more unfavorable light.[15] At the same time, it became increasingly clear that federal funds for completion of the CUP would not be forthcoming until a more comprehensive and permanent settlement of the Ute Tribe's reserved rights in the Green River system were clarified. Accordingly, in 1980 the Utah legislature sought to achieve this greater certainty, negotiating a proposed permanent Ute water compact and then enacting it into law.[16] But one prominent Indian water-rights advocate immediately denounced the proposed compact—which would quantify the tribe's *Winters* rights and subject them to state adjudication—as a virtual giveaway of tribal water-resource entitlements.[17] By the end of the 1980s the tribe had still not ratified the compact,[18] apparently holding out for a better deal possibly obtainable through legislation pending in Congress.

Navajo Generating Station Agreement (1968). Six years after Congress passed the Navajo Indian Irrigation Project Act and during a period when the project still seemed to be more or less on schedule, the Navajos entered into another agreement limiting their rights to the major rivers flowing through their reservation in return for promises of economic development. In this case the tribe joined in the implementation of a plan devised by a consortium of utility companies and the U.S. Department of the Interior for the construction of a huge coal-burning power plant on the Navajo Reservation. In return for the anticipated economic benefits accruing to the tribe from the construction and operation of the plant, the Navajos consented to relinquish all but 50,000 acre-feet of their reserved rights to the upper Colorado River for a fifty-year period.[19]

The Interior Department holds a major interest in the plant, which is now causing such serious particulate pollution of the air in the Four Corners/Grand Canyon National Park area that it may either have to be retrofitted with enormously expensive scrubbing equipment or else have its use curtailed; either option could cut significantly into tribal revenues. In addition, engineers and attorneys later retained by the Navajo Nation have calculated that the Navajo Generating Station agreement limited the tribe's *Winters* rights to about one percent of the huge reservation's theoretical entitlement to the upper Colorado River (the Navajo Nation is the largest Indian reservation in the United States, and most of it lies in the upper Colorado basin). Tribal attorneys in the late 1980s were preparing a case to adjudicate the Navajos' reserved rights to the upper Colorado River;[20] when it is filed, some observers expect the claim to be for about five million acre-feet of Colorado River water.[21] This is more than was allocated to the state of California in the Supreme Court's 1963 *Arizona* v. *California* decision and almost twice as much as was awarded to Arizona. Even if a more modest amount is eventually awarded—more conservative estimates of provable Navajo reserved-rights claims have been set at about two million acre-feet[22]— that still represents nearly a third of the entire apportionment of 7.5 million acre-feet to all four of the upper basin states.

The two Navajo waivers and the Ute deferral were not imposed on the tribes with the same unilateral disregard for their provable rights as were the decrees entered into on the Indians' behalf but against their will earlier in this century; the degree of tribal volition in each of these settlements was certainly greater. But at the same time, these agreements were all struck at a time when the full measure of tribal empowerment under the 1963 *Arizona* v. *California* decision had not yet been taken.

It appears in retrospect that the tribes either deferred or surrendered potent, senior, and superior rights to a great deal of water in return for promises made but not yet fulfilled (as in the NIIP and Ute Deferral agreements) or for economic development that has proved largely illusory (the Navajo Generating Station). The 50,000 acre-foot limitation in the NGS agreement is so utterly out of keeping with provable Navajo rights to the upper Colorado that quite probably it will fail if legally challenged. Although the Ute agreement is now a quarter of a century old, none of the promised water has yet reached the lands for which it was promised. Thus, the question to keep in mind while evaluating more contemporary agreements is whether these hold the hope of being notable improvements over government treatment of the Utes and Navajos in the 1960s—agreements that at the time seemed better than nothing to the tribes but that now resemble delaying actions rather than just and durable solutions.

CONTEMPORARY COMPREHENSIVE SETTLEMENTS

The era of contemporary, comprehensive negotiated settlements differs from the waiver and deferral agreements of the 1960s more in scope and degree than in kind. The basic structure of most of the settlements achieved in the last decade or so has been tribal surrender of reserved-rights claims to substantial amounts of water in return for government-funded delivery of a smaller quantity of water to the reservations. In reviewing these settlements, the principal focus is on major agreements requiring congressional ratification and a substantial infusion of federal tax dollars to resolve those disputes peacefully, but two interesting state-tribal pacts not involving the federal government (the Montana-Fort Peck and Florida-Big Cypress) are also examined. The presentation is chronological, beginning with the Ak Chin and Tohono O'Odham (Papago) settlements in south-central Arizona. Because these two acts are in many ways prototypical of those which were to follow and because they have a longer history of implementation than any of the contemporary settlements, Chapter 5 is devoted to a more detailed study of these cases.

The Ak Chin Agreement (1978, 1984). The Ak Chin community is located on a reservation comprising mostly developed agricultural lands at the base of the Santa Cruz River basin, approximately fifty miles south of Phoenix, Arizona. Like the neighboring Papago Tribe to the south, the Ak Chin community watched in growing frustration as adjoining non-Indian irrigators rapidly increased the rate of ground-water withdrawals from the underlying aquifer throughout the 1960s. When it became obvious that the rates of withdrawal were far exceeding the rates of recharge in the area and that reservation groundwater resources were indeed being depleted to some extent by neighboring irrigators, Ak Chin community leaders sought legal advice on the most effective means of protecting their groundwater rights.[23]

Eventually, they opted to forego litigation in favor of a contract with the federal government, whereby the Indians agreed to waive all present and future reserved groundwater claims against neighboring irrigators and others in return for a federal promise to deliver annually about 60,000 acre-feet of water to the reservation from adjoining federal-well fields or to accept money damages in lieu of water if the agreement did not prove technically feasible. The general terms of the agreement were drawn up in legislation sponsored by Congressman Morris Udall and adopted by Congress in July of 1978.[24] However, serious problems of technical implementation developed after the act's adoption, owing to an insufficiency of groundwater supplies on nearby federal lands. As the project fell further behind schedule, the Reagan administration refused to request a supplemental appropriation to honor the federal commitment to the tribes by other means, and in 1983 the tribe threatened to sue the federal government for damages.[25]

To remedy the situation, in 1984 Congress amended the original agreement to provide for the delivery of waters promised to the Indians through the uncompleted Central Arizona Project (CAP).[26] In addition to the $40 million spent to implement the original agreement, Congress authorized the expenditure of nearly $50 million more to put into effect the 1984 amendments; this was in addition to funds already appropriated by Congress to complete CAP construction. The Ak Chin community was not limited by the 1984 amendments to specific uses of the water it was promised but neither was it specifically authorized to market water off-reservation.

Since the CAP has played such a pivotal role not only in the Ak Chin settlement but also in the resolution of several southwestern tribal water-rights disputes, some background on how and why the Central Arizona Project came into being in the way it did may help set these agreements within the larger context of southwestern water-resource development. Subsequent to the state's victory in *Arizona* v. *California* in 1963, Arizona's congressional delegation set about convincing their colleagues to authorize a reclamation project on the lower Colorado River to divert their share of the river into the arid central portions of the state (much as California had done a half-century earlier in the Imperial Valley). However, though California may have lost in court, its delegation was big enough to keep Arizona from winning anything in Congress. It took five years of intense bargaining to convince California to support the project—the price being that the authorizing legislation[27] guaranteed that California's full share of the river would be delivered to it first, even in times of extreme drought or other exigencies.[28]

The CAP—its costs now measured in the billions of dollars and still uncompleted as of 1990—diverts Colorado River water first to the greater Phoenix area in the desert floor of the south-central region of the state and then up the lower Santa Cruz valley 120 miles south to Tucson; this is by far the largest federal reclamation project designed and operated explicitly for municipal as well as agricultural use. Since the CAP also passes through the vicinity of several Indian reservations whose water rights were in dispute, promised allocations from the project would become a powerful inducement to several tribes to settle their lawsuits.

The Papago (Tohono O'Odham) Groundwater Settlement Act (1982). It had long been apparent to the Tohono O'Odham (formerly the Papago) Tribe of southern Arizona that increasing rates of groundwater withdrawals by mining companies, irrigators, and the city of Tucson near the eastern border of the reservation were resulting in the depletion of groundwater resources beneath tribal lands; but the extent of tribal jurisdiction over groundwater was an issue which had never been tested judicially. Then in 1974 a federal district court in Nevada and the 9th Circuit Court of Appeals (which has federal appellate jurisdiction over Arizona) both held that the federal reserved water right (the *"Winters"* right on which most Indian water entitlements are based) was applicable to groundwater supplies necessary to fulfill the purposes of the federal reservation of the overlying land when a hydrological connection between surface and groundwater could be demonstrated.[29]

A year later the U.S. government (and later, the tribe itself) filed a federal court action against the city of Tucson, mining companies and irrigation districts, and several hundred private water users to enjoin the continuing withdrawal of groundwater from beneath the eastern districts of the Tohono O'Odham Reservation. During the lengthy and complex identification of necessary parties, joinder of claims, and service of process, the attorney for the tribe let it be known that a negotiated settlement of the suit might be a possibility. An ad hoc advisory commission comprised of counsel for the tribe, tribal leaders, and representatives of several major defendant groups was convened in 1977 in an effort to achieve a bargained settlement of this massive groundwater dispute.

The Tucson and Washington, D.C., staff of Congressman Morris Udall, whose congressional district encompasses the disputed groundwater basin, gradually assumed some responsibility for facilitating negotiations; Congressman Udall chairs the House Interior and Insular Affairs Committee, which has subject-matter jurisdiction over the required congressional ratification of major Indian water-rights settlements. The service phase of litigation and other related preliminary actions proceeded concurrently with negotiations until Udall was able to obtain tribal and defendant consent to, congressional adoption of, and a presidential signature on a far-ranging groundwater-settlement agreement for the Santa Cruz River basin in the autumn of 1982.[30]

The tribe agreed to abandon its *Winters* doctrine claims to the groundwater underlying the eastern districts of its reservation in return for the delivery of close to 40,000 acre-feet of agricultural-quality water to its lands through the uncompleted Central Arizona Project and/or through the Interior secretary's purchase of water and water rights from willing sellers. The Indians also agreed to accept money damages instead of wet water in the event the Central Arizona Project was not completed or the agreement otherwise proved infeasible.[31] The tribe is allowed to market water to non-Indians off the reservation, but it is simultaneously subjected to the jurisdiction of state groundwater law.

To avoid problems like the Reagan administration's bad-faith refusal to seek supplemental appropriations for the Ak Chin agreement (which was already in trouble by the time the Tohono O'Odham settlement was being drafted), Congressman Udall structured in a funding mechanism that relied on interest from a trust fund to finance implementation of key elements of the act rather than on continuing appropriations from Congress.[32] President Reagan vetoed the act as originally drafted because of his view that it represented an expensive federal solution to a ''local problem.'' The Interior Department joined in negotiations over revision of the bill; in its final form the legislation required a significant contribution from defendants in the groundwater litigation to the implementation fund established by the act.[33] The bill escaped the veto in revised form also because Congressman Udall attached it as a rider to a piece of legislation the president wanted—an amendment to the reclamation act allowing large landholders (e.g., agribusiness interests in California's Central Valley) easier access to cheap water from federal reclamation projects.[34] And although President Reagan and his Interior Department representatives complained about costs at the time,[35] the initial $35 million price tag on this agreement[36] would soon be dwarfed by Indian water-rights settlements waiting in the wings of the legislative stage in the late 1980s.

Salt River Pima-Maricopa Indian Community Settlement (1988). The precedent set by the Ak Chin and Tohono O'Odham settlements, combined with the U.S. Supreme Court's 1983 *San Carlos Apache* decision requiring the adjudication of most Indian water-rights claims in state courts, precipitated something of a rush to the bargaining table by litigants in the Indian cases throughout the latter half of the 1980s. Further north in the Arizona desert, a settlement closely resembling the terms of the Ak Chin and Tohono O'Odham agreements took legislative form in 1988. This situation involved the Salt River Pima-Maricopa Indian community, whose water rights had been the subject of the ill-fated Kent Decree in 1910. Once some of its lawsuits had been removed from federal to state court after the *San Carlos* decision,[37] both the Indians and their adversaries faced a higher-risk game. If the Arizona courts held the Kent Decree to be binding, the Indians' rights could be quantified at disastrously low levels (since *Winters* doctrine rights played no part in the original decree). But if the courts did allow new *Winters* claims to be adjudicated, the result would be significant prior and superior rights accruing to the Indian community.[38]

With this sword of uncertainty hanging over everyone's head, the Central Arizona Project continuing in the neighborhood of the Salt River valley, and Congress providing major money to satisfy Arizona Indian claims with CAP water (i.e., Ak Chin and Tohono O'Odham), litigants negotiated a settlement ratified by Congress in 1988.[39] This exceedingly complex agreement provides for water exchanges among various user groups in the Salt River valley, involving Central Arizona Project water and a variety of other sources. The Indians are guaranteed a CAP allotment, which they are also compelled to make available to surrounding cities in return for other waters. Under the agreement, water resources accruing to the Indian community total just over 120,000 acre-feet per year. In exchange, the Indians agreed to state court jurisdiction for the administration of some water resources subject to the agreement. Although the payment of money damages to the tribe in lieu of water is contemplated in the event the agreement fails,[40] the tribe is not barred from relitigating its rights in the event the federal or state governments fail to honor the bargain.[41] The tribe is specifically empowered to sell water at a rate fixed in the agreement to surrounding cities in the metropolitan Phoenix area[42] and is just as specifically prohibited from selling water to anyone else off the reservation.[43] The federal government agreed to contribute a total of $58 million to implement the settlement, some of which will be deposited in a $29 million trust fund, with the interest also used to implement the act, a feature of the agreement borrowed directly from the Tohono O'Odham settlement. Also patterned after the 1982 act is a substantial required local contribution to the settlement; the state and Phoenix-area cities will contribute $28 million to implementation of the agreement (the Indians will contribute $2 million) and as much as an additional $96 million worth of water.[44]

The Colorado Ute Settlement (1988). Once the rights of the lower Colorado River basin states and Indian reservations had been determined in the Supreme Court's 1963 decision in *Arizona v. California,* intense competition ensued among the congressional delegations of upper and lower basin states over the development of federal reclamation projects to divert and use their share of the river. To avoid the protracted litigation that plagued the lower basin states, in 1948 the upper basin states negotiated a separate compact among themselves for the definition of their respective allotments of Colorado River water.[45] As a result of these negotiations, Utah succeeded in the authorization of its Central Utah Project as early as 1956.[46] But the single most significant project-authorization bill in the history of the river was the prodigious Colorado River Basin Project bill, enacted into law by Congress in 1968. The cornerstone of the bill was the Central Arizona Project, designed to deliver Arizona's portion of the river across the desert basin to the metropolitan Phoenix area and then up the Santa Cruz valley to Tucson.[47]

Arizona had to do a lot of horse-trading to lay claim to its portion of the Colorado. First it had to agree to California's demand that in dry years the entirety of the golden state's share of the river would be delivered, even if it meant Arizona would receive less than its full allotment. Second, Arizona had to allay the well-grounded fears of the upper basin states that—since the drafters of the 1922 Colorado River Compact had erroneously over-appropriated the river—once the lower basin states had captured their full share of the river through reclamation projects, there would not be enough left to fulfill the terms of the upper-basin compact. To assuage upper-basin anxieties, drafters of the 1968 project act agreed to write in five major reclamation projects for the upper basin states, including the Animas–La Plata Project in south-western Colorado.[48] When the Colorado Basin Project Act finally rolled over the legislative finish line in September 1968, this gigantic porcine edifice contained over a billion dollars worth of authorized projects.[49]

Since project authorization is only the first step in actually diverting water, interstate competition then moved from authorizations to an annual struggle over the appropriations necessary to actually construct the authorized projects. And one of the projects that did not fare well in this competition was Colorado's Animas–La Plata—at least not until the federal government filed suit to perfect the Colorado Ute Indians' reserved water rights in 1976. Even though the U.S. Supreme Court's decision in *Colorado River Conservation District* v. *U.S.* in that same year would mean the Indian right would be adjudicated in Colorado courts, the Utes nevertheless stood to gain a substantial entitlement from the lawsuit and also tie up everyone else's rights in the region for years to come. But in the mid-1980s Congressman Ben Nighthorse Campbell of Colorado—himself the only American Indian in Congress—followed in Congressman Udall's footsteps by seeking to get the Utes to drop their suit in return for the delivery of water from the as-yet-unbuilt Ani-mas–La Plata Project.

However, there were two key differences between the legislation under which the Ak Chin, Tohono O'Odham, and Salt River Pima-Maricopa communities abandoned their reserved-rights claims in return for Central Arizona Project water and the swap being contemplated in Colorado for project water for the Ute reserved rights. First, the CAP was about half finished when the deals with the southern Arizona tribes were struck; planners simply rerouted the canals to service the reserva-tions before they were constructed. In contrast, work had not even begun on Animas–La Plata; absent the Indian claims it was unlikely the project would ever see the light of day. The second difference lay in the measurable merits of the two projects. Compared to the CAP, the cost-benefit ratio of the Animas–La Plata Project was far more dubious and its environmental impact far more negative.

Animas–La Plata, as reauthorized in 1988 in conjunction with the settlement of Ute water-rights claims,[50] is a complicated system involv-ing the pumping of several thousand acre-feet of water up and out of one watershed and into another, primarily for the benefit of non-Indian growers of livestock feed. Although the Ute tribes will unquestionably be aided by the legislation (e.g., it will for the first time bring running water to a reservation town as well as facilitate Indian agriculture), it is just as unquestionable that the primary beneficiaries will be non-Indian farmers. Comparative analysis of all the Indian water-rights settlement acts by officials in the Interior Department shows that the construction costs of water delivered through Animas–La Plata will total about $6,000 per acre-foot, more than twice the federal cost of CAP water to the Tohono O'Odham, more than three times the cost of CAP water to Ak Chin, and more than twelve times the cost of CAP water to the Salt River Pima-Maricopa community.[51] Congressman Campbell successfully advocated the project not on its quantifiable merits but on its being the only real hope for providing desperately needed economic benefits for the Utes and simultaneously dispelling the cloud cast over Four Corners–area water rights by their lawsuit.[52] His critics fought the bill on the grounds of inefficiency, huge energy costs, limited benefits to the tribes, and significant environmental damage (the storage reservoir would wipe out deer and elk habitat).[53]

As adopted in September of 1988, the act provided for 70,000 acre-feet of water to the Southern Ute and Ute Mountain tribes through the partially completed Dolores Project and the as-yet-unconstructed Animas–La Plata Project, in return for which the Utes would drop their reserved-rights suit. The tribes were granted a limited right to market water off the reservation but with the proviso that such waters would be subject to comprehensive regulation under state water law.[54] As in the Tohono O'Odham and Salt River settlements, the funding mechanism for the Indian portion of the project was interest from a $60 million trust fund, about $50 million of which is to be provided by the federal government and the remainder from state and local interests. Congress also obligated the federal government itself to come up with $380 million to build the Animas–La Plata Project. And as with the Tohono O'Odham and Salt River settlements, the agreement compels a hefty state and local contribution to the project—nearly $70 million during phase one of the construction period and an additional $132 million over the construction life of the project.

Mission Indians Settlement Act (1988). One of the earliest settlements negotiated on the Indians' behalf resulted from the Interior Department's acquiescence in non-Indian water and power development on Mission Indian lands in southern California in 1914 and 1924. The tribes sued to void these contracts in the late 1960s, initiating litigation that would last for the next two decades.[55]

Defendant water and power companies and the Mission Indians fashioned a proposed settlement in the late 1980s, which would have required the satisfaction of Indian claims through the federally constructed Central Valley Project.[56] However, congressmen representing other powerful CVP customers objected strongly to committing CVP water in this way, with the result that the proposed settlement had to be amended to cover tribal water claims by other means. These turned out to be the conservation retrofitting of existing irrigation facilities and the use of some of the water saved to substitute for the Indians' rights to the San Luis River. Specifically, the agreement in its final form called for local water users—not the federal government—to pay for the lining of deteriorating portions of the eighty-year-old All American Canal. Congress enacted this settlement into law in November 1988.[57] The only federal contribution to the agreement was authorization of a $30 million trust fund to finance the fulfillment of tribal administrative responsibilities under the act.[58] In return for the assured delivery of 16,000 acre-feet of conserved water, the tribes surrendered their disputed reserved-rights claims to the San Luis River. The agreement does not empower the tribes to market their water off-reservation, although it does authorize water-sharing arrangements with non-Indian entities.[59] Thus, with an emphasis on the more efficient use of existing facilities rather than on the construction of new ones, the federal government emerged from this settlement with far less of a financial obligation than from most of the other federally sponsored agreements examined in this study.

One of the problems involved in examining a rapidly evolving area of law and policy is that the only constant is change. Like a photograph of a river, the captured image cannot fully portray the current reality. Thus the emphasis in this study is more on the patterns and themes established by this succession of agreements on Indian water rights than on the specifics of each settlement. By the end of the 1980s, in addition to the federally sponsored settlements enacted into law by Congress, two more agreements had matured to the point of legislation proposed to Congress (and several more are rapidly headed in that direction).[60] These two pending settlements represent renewed attempts to resolve disputes in which negotiation was seriously attempted earlier in this century but without satisfactory results. The first is an agreement negotiated in the wake of an anti-Indian Supreme Court decision and the second an effort by Utah's congressional delegation to get Congress to uphold an agreement the state made with the Utes in 1965.

Pyramid Lake Paiute Ratification Bill (1989). In the 1944 Orr Ditch Decree, the federal government negotiated a settlement of its own claims and those of the Pyramid Lake Paiute Tribe to the flow of the Truckee River in eastern California and Nevada. The Paiutes were interested primarily in keeping enough water in the Truckee to maintain fishery habitat in Pyramid Lake, into which the river flows; operation of the fishery was the tribe's principal means of economic sustenance.

In litigation begun in 1973 the tribe sought to enlarge its entitlement, arguing that the 1944 decree represented an unreasonably small quantification of its reserved rights (the "practicably irrigable acreage" quantification standard would not be instituted by the Supreme Court until 1963). But the U.S. Supreme Court disallowed the Paiutes' claim in 1983, not because of the merits of the quantification argument but because the Court did not want to set the precedent of reopening any of the other water-rights cases previously settled by consent decrees.[61] Thereafter, the federal government, the Paiutes, and the defendants in this suit began to pursue a negotiated resolution of the dispute. By 1989 a settlement had been fashioned that would empower the Interior secretary to buy up water rights from willing sellers in the Truckee and Carson river basins and to use those resources (along with effluent from the Tahoe basin) to maintain habitat in state and federal wildlife preserves as well as in Pyramid Lake. As embodied in legislation submitted to Congress in 1989,[62] the agreement also authorized water-rights exchange and sharing arrangements. The tribes would dismiss their major pending lawsuits, and the federal government would restore the Paiutes' fisheries habitat. The Interior Department could spend up to $16 million to buy up water rights;[63] Congress would also set aside a $75 million trust fund for tribal economic development.[64] Since one of the purposes of this settlement is restoration of a badly depleted lake-terminus watershed in the most arid region of the nation, off-reservation marketing of tribal water is not discussed per se although there is provision for upstream shared uses and exchanges among all parties to the agreement.

Utah Ute Water Rights Settlement Bill (1989). Since the mid-1960s the government of Utah has pursued a negotiated settlement of water-rights entitlements with the Ute Indian reservations within its borders—first by securing a deferral of those claims, pending the construction of irrigation works to divert Indian water through the Central Utah Project. The Utah congressional delegation and the Utes from the Uintah and Ouray Reservation are now attempting to get Congress to honor promises the state made to the tribes a quarter of a century ago.

It now turns out that these were expensive promises. The preamble to the bill proposed in 1989 to fulfill pledges to the Utes asserts that the original commitment would "cost in excess of $2 billion" to implement,[65] but drafters of the new settlement estimate that these assurances can now be honored for only $515 million[66] (the most expensive single Indian bailout discussed in this book). Major construction projects would be authorized by this settlement, as would a $150 million trust fund for tribal administrative purposes and as compensation to the Utes for having deferred perfection of their water-rights claims. The "Ute Indian Tribe and others" would receive a consumptive annual water allotment of just under 250,000 acre-feet as specified in the water-rights compact this bill would ratify.[67] In return, the tribes would approve the major provisions of the agreement first offered to them by the Utah legislature in 1980, including the waiver of reserved rights and subjection of rights quantified in the compact to state water law.

In addition to the preceding settlements, involving substantial federal action both in sponsoring negotiations and (in most cases) in funding their implementation, other pacts were negotiated in the 1980s in which the federal government played little or no role but that nevertheless represented settlements of significant water-rights disputes.

Fort Peck Sioux and Assiniboine-Montana Compact (1985). Water-rights litigation involving these tribes began over a decade ago, and resulted— among other things—in the U.S. Supreme Court's 1983 decision reaffirming its position that most Indian water-rights disputes must be adjudicated in state courts.[68] Two years later the Sioux and Assiniboine tribes of the Fort Peck Reservation negotiated a compact, ratified by the state and the tribal governments, in which the tribes waived their reserved-rights claims in return for consumptive-use rights to over a half million acre-feet of water from the Missouri River and its tributaries.[69] The water can be used on the reservation for any purpose; up to 50,000 acre-feet per year may be marketed to non-Indians off-reservation, subject to state law. The tribes are empowered to promulgate their own water code, subject to approval by the secretary of the Interior.[70] Observers have noted that the tribes and the state of Montana probably structured their compact so as not to require congressional approval, in order to prevent downstream states along the Missouri River from blocking ratification of the compact on the floor of Congress, although it did receive the approval of the U.S. attorney and secretary of the Interior.[71]

The federal executive branch was probably willing to acquiesce in tribal involvement in this agreement partly because it did not cost the federal government anything. Unlike other settlements, in which hundreds of millions of federal tax dollars have been obligated to deliver irrigation-project water to the reservations, the Montana agreement is nearly costless to the federal government. And although the Montana Compact represents the largest Indian settlement in this study (the 525,236 acre-foot consumptive allotment is in excess of any other settlement discussed here), no money is provided to tribes for the construction of diversion facilities to bring water to their lands.

Seminole-Florida Land and Water Claims Settlement (1987). This agreement is unique among those surveyed here in that it is the only one resolving a dispute that implicates riparian water rights. The dispute arose out of actions in which the state designated lands as a flood-control easement that had originally been set aside for Indian use under state law. The Indians brought a quiet title action against the state and neighboring land-use groups in 1978. But as discovery proceeded in this litigation, the surface-water rights of all parties concerned were clearly implicated as well, in that the natural-flow rights of the Seminoles were being seriously impaired. Nine years later the disputants negotiated a settlement of the land-use and water-rights conflict. The tribe relinquished some of its land-title claims and entered into a cooperative agreement for local management of riparian water rights in return for money compensation and a limited recognition of its water-rights claims.[72] Since the agreement also implicated title to federal trust lands, congressional ratification was required and achieved in 1988.[73]

A comparative review of contemporary settlements demonstrates the ways in which these agreements are both similar to and different from those generated early in this century and in the 1960s. First, the similarities, beginning with quantification and deferral. The doctrine of prior appropriation, which governs the allocation of water resources in all the arid western states, is essentially an effort to impose legal certainty on gross climatic uncertainty. In a region characterized by wild fluctuations in the quantity, form, and timing of generally scarce precipitation, water policy makers have prized above all the values of an allocational scheme that would give everyone some reasonable, reliable expectation of how much water they could expect to receive, and when. The absolute quantification of rights, the specification of the beneficial uses to which the water could be put, the loss of the right through non-use, and an absolute hierarchy of user rights based on the seniority of appropriation are all features of a doctrine that places extraordinary emphasis on the certainty of a water right.

Thus the *Winters* doctrine is anathema to non-Indian western water users; every settlement discussed in this chapter includes a provision whereby the tribes agree to the receipt of absolute quantities of water in return for relinquishing legal claims to much larger and sometimes unspecified amounts. From the early unilateral settlements through the Navajo waiver agreements of the 1960s to all the contemporary settlements, the most sought-after goal of non-Indian negotiators has been a cap on the upper limits of Indian entitlements. Only if the Indians are barred from claiming more water in the future can non-Indians proceed with some confidence to develop what little water there is in the West that remains unappropriated or to sell existing rights whose seniority and quantity have been called into question by tribal reserved-rights litigation.

Diminution of the original claim is a second similarity: In all the settlements from 1910 to 1989, the tribes (or the federal government on their behalf) have settled for less in terms of quantity than they would have been entitled to had their *Winters* doctrine claims been perfected in court. This feature of the settlements most closely resembles the reservation-creating treaties and agreements of the latter half of the nineteenth century, in which the tribes forfeited possession of millions of acres of land in the Indian Country of the nineteenth-century Great Plains, West, and Southwest in return for much smaller parcels accompanied by federal promises of assistance in making these smaller reservations economically self-sufficient.

In most instances the tribes have relinquished a large claim in return for assurance of a smaller quantity of water, accompanied by promises of economic assistance in developing this smaller quantity for productive use. To some extent, then, the tribes have traded a historic—though legally unproven—right for token wealth, continuing a tradition initiated on Manhattan Island a third of a millennium ago: the "glass bead effect."

In some settlements, such as the Ak Chin and Tohono O'Odham, the tribes actually agreed to accept money damages instead of wet water if the federal government fails to keep its promises. In the Salt River agreement, a remedy of money damages is implied although not compelled. In others, there is the acknowledgment that the tribes can simply return to court if governmental obligations are not honored. But in all of these bargains, some portion of a heritage of natural resources has been let go in exchange for the promised ability to make a better living from remaining resources. There are diverse views on the question of whether such trades are a good idea. From one perspective, the mechanism of money damages is an extremely dangerous feature of settlement legislation, since if the federal government chooses, it can fail to deliver any water to the tribes and simply pay them damages instead. This essentially would be the same as a condemnation of the Indian right, just as land is condemned by government in eminent-domain proceedings for devotion to a public purpose such as highway construction.

The two settlement acts containing explicit damages clauses address the rights of two reservations in southern Arizona's Santa Cruz valley, one of the driest areas of the United States. Until the Central Arizona Project is completed, Tucson will remain the largest city in the nation totally reliant on groundwater resources; it is now withdrawing groundwater from the Santa Cruz basin more than three times faster than it is being recharged. If the water crisis in the area grows significantly worse—a likely scenario, if the size of the city continues to expand at its post–World War II pace—partial or total condemnation of the Indian right might begin to appear economically attractive.

However, others point out that it was probably only the threat of the money-damages clause in the original 1978 Ak Chin settlement that convinced the Reagan administration to sign the 1984 amendments to that agreement, once the terms in the 1978 act proved technologically infeasible. From this point of view, the damages clause was a political masterstroke; for if Congress and the administration chose to ignore the promise made to the Ak Chin community in the 1978 act—as indeed the administration did in 1982—the government still bore a powerful, binding financial obligation to the Indians, enforceable in the U.S. Court of Claims. Further, the legislation was written in such a way as to make the liability of federal damages open and continuing; damages were owing for every day water was not delivered. However, under the settlement agreement, the federal liability ends once CAP delivery facilities are constructed and as long as water is actually supplied. Moreover, the Ak Chin was a model contemporary settlement. To have forfeited on its terms would have demonstrated graphically to other tribes considering negotiation that the federal government was lying to them and had no intention of keeping the promises it was making in other pending settlement negotiations.

In contrast, if some of the other recent agreements are not kept, the tribes' only recourse will be to return to state water-resource commissions and state water courts to resume the costly and time-consuming litigation of their rights. And in the interim period between the tribes' dismissal of their suits pursuant to contemporary agreements and the possible future refiling of those actions if the agreements are not kept, non-Indian water users will have begun to appropriate and put to use the water assigned to them in the original settlements.

In sum, any form of negotiated settlement carries risks—for the Indians, the risk that future presidential administrations and Congresses will not keep the promises made by current ones. And the last two hundred years of U.S./Indian history are littered with the carcasses of failed treaties and unfulfilled federal promises, as the tribal resource base steadily diminished. The tribes thus have plenty of reasons to be suspicious of contemporary federal promises.

However, there are risks for non-Indian water users as well. American society's conception of substantive justice (and more important, American courts' conception of it) is a somewhat ephemeral phenomenon; it evolves and changes over time. When the U.S. attorney settled Indian water-rights claims in the 1910 Kent Decree, the 1914–24 Mission Indian agreements, the 1935 Globe Equity Decree, and the 1944 Orr Ditch Decree, the government evidently felt at the time it was the best it could do on the Indians' behalf. The *Winters* doctrine was still relatively untested, and both the Justice Department and the Bureau of

Indian Affairs also feared the political repercussions of litigating Indian reserved rights too actively and too successfully; a concerted western congressional backlash might have resulted in federal legislation that either destroyed or severely limited tribal *Winters* rights.[74] But these early settlements have triggered fresh litigation in the late twentieth century because by contemporary standards some of those early decrees seem manifestly unfair. The certainty those agreements were designed to establish proved altogether illusory.

The same is true of the waiver and deferral agreements of the 1960s. Stewart Udall, who was secretary of the Interior at the time they were all created, commented when the Navajo Generating Station agreement came into being that it at least established certain, deliverable benefits for the Navajos (jobs and revenue) that the tribe could otherwise contemplate only in theory.[75] Something, in other words, was better than nothing. For the last quarter-century, non-Indian neighbors of the Navajo Nation have counted on the certainty that the agreement was supposed to have created. But now the tribe is on the verge of filing a suit that may claim a hundred times as much water from the Colorado River as the Navajos agreed to limit themselves to in the 1960s. Non-Indians in the upper Colorado River basin therefore have ample reason to wonder how much confidence they should reasonably place in the durability of agreements on water-rights limitation with Indian tribes. Trying to make these present settlements more durable than previous ones has in fact been a major preoccupation of the political leaders who have fashioned the contemporary reserved-rights compacts, and these bargains consequently contain features that clearly distinguish them from those gone before.

Most of the nineteenth-century treaties failed because Congress refused over time to continue appropriating the funds necessary to keep them in effect and because the tribes did not have any means of forcing Congress to keep its word. The architects of contemporary agreements have addressed this problem of congressional forgetfulness quite directly by instituting the trust fund construct.

Instead of relying on continuing congressional appropriations, those aspects of settlement implementation requiring tribal action are being underwritten by the interest accruing on trust funds established by the settlement legislation. The Ak Chin, Tohono O'Odham, Pima, Mission, and Colorado Ute settlement acts all contain this provision, as do the proposed Paiute and Utah Ute agreements. Once the original fund-establishing appropriations have been made, a significant portion of the bargain has been honored. What these trust funds generally do not cover is the additional federal financial commitment necessary to construct water-delivery facilities. However, in most of these agreements, neighboring non-Indian water users will actually reap greater financial benefits from reclamation-project construction than will the Indians, and the impetus toward project completion is therefore entrusted to the traditional pork-barrel politics of the reclamation lobby. Indian projects are tied to powerful non-Indian westerners' thirst for the region's remaining water.

The Navajo Indian Irrigation Project demonstrates how non-Indian westerners traditionally have been much more successful in convincing Congress to fund reclamation-project development than have the Indians or the Bureau of Indian Affairs acting on their behalf. When the westerners did run into opposition from eastern congressional delegations decrying what they saw as wasteful pork-barrel subsidies, western congressmen sometimes resorted to a new tactic: wrapping the proposed project in what BIA officials came to refer to as an "Indian Blanket."[76] Proponents would add to the disputed proposal a feature calling for the delivery of water to an Indian reservation in the vicinity of the desired reclamation facility. Then anyone in Congress opposed to the project would also be positioned against aiding a desperately underprivileged minority group for whom Congress holds trust responsibility.

Arizona's congressional delegation used this prime strategy in getting Congress to renew the flow of appropriations into the Central Arizona Project, which the Carter administration in the late 1970s had refused to request funds to complete. The success of the Ak Chin, Tohono O'Odham, and Salt River Pima-Maricopa settlements are all entirely dependent on completion of the CAP; the damages clauses in the first two of these acts compelled Congress to pay up whether the CAP was built or not, so why not complete the project and do a good turn for the Indians at the same time?

Perhaps the most blatant contemporary example of this maneuver is Animas–La Plata. The extraordinary expense of the water delivered relative to other projects and the demonstrable inefficiency of its operating design render it highly suspect; Interior Department analysts have alleged that it would never have been reauthorized had the provisions for the Colorado Utes not been added.[77] Local non-Indian farmers will also realize far greater economic advantages from the project than will the Indians.

Yet no one can dispute Colorado Congressman Campbell's assertion that the impoverished, isolated Ute tribes in the region will benefit economically from its construction, which will also extinguish the powerful, worrisome Indian reserved-rights claims pending in Colorado water courts. If Animas–La Plata opponents subsequently seek to block its appropriations, they will probably have to find some other—albeit less expensive—means of assisting the Indians economically if they are to succeed.

Another prominent feature of contemporary settlements is local cost sharing. President Reagan vetoed the original version of the 1982 Tucson–Tohono O'Odham groundwater-settlement act because of his finding that it represented a costly federal solution to what he saw—with a characteristic ignorance of historical fact—as an exclusively "local problem." The revised version of the bill therefore contained provisions obligating some of the major defendants in the original groundwater suit (such as the city of Tucson, the state of Arizona, and agribusiness and mining interests) to make substantial contributions to the trust fund established to implement the settlement. Likewise, in southern California, it is local water users (including the powerful Metropolitan Water District) and not the federal government who must bear the construction costs of water availability although Congress is obligated to provide most of the implementing trust fund.[78] Phoenix, Arizona, and its suburbs must contribute heavily to the Salt River Pima-Maricopa settlement (they have been using what was arguably Pima water for most of this century anyway). If Colorado's Animas–La Plata Project is built as planned, state and local jurisdictions may have to bear nearly forty percent of its eventual construction and operating costs.

The clear signal from Congress and the administration seems to be that if the West is going to continue to petition the nation for funds to develop its water, the region will have to match that federal commitment with ever greater measures of its own wealth. The West, so long accustomed to burying both hands deep in federal pockets to finance the quenching of its thirst, is now being compelled to reach into its own as well. This twist in policy is particularly irksome for some westerners since a portion of this cash layout is then going straight into the pockets of their historically less powerful adversaries—their American Indian neighbors.

As we turn to a more detailed examination of the prototypical Ak Chin and Tohono O'Odham settlements and then to concluding recommendations for a comprehensive settlement policy, some themes and patterns are worth keeping in mind. First, the federal government is historically not very good at keeping its word. Second, the majority of bargains struck either with the Indians or on their behalf have in retrospect come to be seen as distinctly ungenerous to the tribes and have therefore generally lacked durability. Third, these agreements have all resulted in a net loss of resources for the tribes; to a greater or lesser extent and in one form or another, the Indians traded resources for glass beads whose value would later prove illusory. In all these respects, then, twentieth-century agreements over water-rights settlements closely parallel the nineteenth-century trail of broken treaties insofar as the loss of tribal resources has been concerned.

Yet some aspects of these contemporary agreements are different. Skilled legislators have sought to offset Congress's historic inattention to promises made to the Indians by resorting to the trust fund construct to finance tribal implementation activities. The Indian Blanket has linked the quenching of western thirst to the honoring of trust responsibilities to the tribes; environmental avarice has been clothed in noble purpose. Moreover, some of these agreements are by most measures fairly generous to the tribes. The half-million acre-foot allotment to the reservations in the Fort Peck–Montana agreement is by far the largest American Indian water-rights settlement agreement in the history of the United States to date.[79] And although most tribes have been compelled to limit their water marketing powers somewhat in contemporary agreements, as the value of water in the American West continues to increase, so will revenues accruing to the tribes.[80] Also encouraging is the early track record on appropriations to implement the contemporary agreements. With the glaring exception of Ak Chin, when the Reagan administration hoisted a warning flag in 1982 by refusing to seek additional implementation funding and Congress just as quickly lowered that flag by amending the settlement act in 1984, the current agreements are generally on schedule at least insofar as appropriations are concerned.[81] In fact, the Ak Chin incident taught Congress as well as the tribes that if other Indians are to be induced to surrender *Winters* rights for wet water, adequate implementation of previous agreements is critical.

CHAPTER FIVE

Groundwater Rights, Planning, and Bargaining in South-Central Arizona

The Ak Chin and Tohono O'Odham groundwater settlement acts of 1978, 1982, and 1984 in many ways provided the template for the other contemporary agreements to follow. Durability, marketability, enforceability, equity, and perpetuity (of tribal entitlement to the resource base) are therefore instructive criteria for judging the viability of contemporary settlements and the fairness of future ones. The question intriguing interested observers is "Will these agreements prove to be history making or history repeating?" Are we now embarking on a new era of U.S./Indian relations distinguished by consensual dispute settlement and a continuing federal financial commitment to the honoring of such bargains, or have we simply exhumed our nineteenth-century legacy of convincing the Indians to forfeit theoretical resource rights in exchange for promises of development made by one Congress but ignored by later ones? Have these southern Arizona Indian communities shrewdly made the best of a complex and difficult legal/political situation, or have they just been had?

By the end of the century we will be able to answer these questions with considerably more confidence than we can now. In the meantime, a close look at (1) the circumstances giving rise to the Tohono O'Odham and Ak Chin disputes, (2) the negotiation processes aimed at resolving them, (3) the substance of the agreements, and (4) some of their early problems of implementation can at least begin to tell us how to answer these questions, if not what those answers will be.

HUMAN SETTLEMENT AND GROUNDWATER MANAGEMENT IN SOUTH-CENTRAL ARIZONA: A HISTORICAL SKETCH

There is archeological evidence of an established Desert culture maintained by hunting and gathering peoples in the lower Salt, Verde, Gila, and Santa Cruz river basins of south-central Arizona by about 10,000 B.C.[1] By 300 A.D. a highly defined cultural group almost wholly dependent on irrigated agriculture—the Hohokam—was occupying this region,[2] and was responsible for developing perhaps the most extensive and sophisticated irrigation system to be found in North America prior to European colonization.[3] Although the combined effects of siltation of the irrigation system, increasing soil salinity, and erratic climate changes apparently triggered cultural decline and the retirement of much culti- vated land by the fifteenth century, the latter-day Pima and Tohono O'Odham tribes are generally conceded to be among the direct cultural descendants of this ancient agricultural population.[4]

By the time of first contact with the Spanish in the early 1500s many Pima communities were clustered along the lower Gila River in the general area of present-day Phoenix, Arizona. The natives whom later Euro-American settlers would come to refer to as the Papago (now the Tohono O'Odham)[5] were well established in the more southerly and slightly more elevated basin of a Gila River tributary, the Santa Cruz.[6] Although the unevenness of the terrain made most of the O'Odham territory less suitable for large-scale intensive agriculture than the Pima lands to the north, crop raising remained crucial to O'Odham survival in areas where surface water was plentiful and the alluvial soil fertile, as in the upper Santa Cruz basin near the present-day city of Tucson.

This fortuitous combination of soil and water, along with a densely settled Indian population adjacent to the Santa Cruz, held great appeal for the Spanish missionaries visiting the area in the 1690s. Under the leadership of the Jesuit Eusebio Francisco Kino, in 1696 they established their northernmost mission at the Indian settlement of Bac, inhabited at the time by a population of about one-thousand natives.[7] Kino's men donated a herd of cattle to the settlement in return for permission to build a mission, eventually named San Xavier del Bac. The mission still stands today within the San Xavier O'Odham Reservation on the southwestern outskirts of the city of Tucson.

Spanish presence ebbed and flowed in the area throughout the 1700s, but profound disruption overtook the region during the first half of the nineteenth century with the coming of Mexican independence and that young nation's military defeat by the United States in 1848. The tribes' problems were caused less by these warring governments than by the failure of any military presence to aid in defending their settlements from raids by the Apaches, who stole livestock, enslaved women and children, and killed the men. The situation did not improve significantly with the U.S. acquisition of southern Arizona from Mexico through the Gadsden purchase of 1853 since the United States was soon to become embroiled in its own civil war.

A joint military force of O'Odham and newly arrived Anglo- American settlers in Tucson finally succeeded in bringing the Apache raids to an end in the 1870s. The generally cooperative relationship between Tucsonans and the tribe endured throughout most of the decade and was marked by a federal executive order creating the 69,200-acre San Xavier Papago Reservation and the more northerly Gila Bend Papago Reservation on the Gila River in 1884.[8] However, only about four-hundred of the estimated six-thousand O'Odham were actually settled on these lands. The rest lived in small villages scattered throughout the tribe's traditional three-million-acre range, stretching roughly from Tucson southwest to the northern tip of the Gulf of California, in Mexico. And by the 1880s, Anglo/Indian relations had taken a decided turn for the worse.

Euro-American prospectors discovered copper and silver at the very center of the Tohono O'Odham's traditional range, and by 1884 an Anglo mining town of about ten-thousand inhabitants had developed there (this boom town—Quijotoa—was abandoned a few years later when the ore veins ran out).[9] To support this and other instant new towns in the desert west of the Santa Cruz basin required more water than surface supplies could provide, so mining engineers dug wells and began to pump groundwater. By the time these early mines were played out, West Texas ranchers had settled in the area, with vastly larger herds of cattle than the Indians had been maintaining. Since important limiting factors on herd size were water, forage, and labor, competition for the first two resources soon developed between tribal and Anglo cattlemen. The incoming ranchers appropriated many of the existing surface-water supplies, and, following the example of the miners, also began to withdraw groundwater to support their herds. By the mid-1880s there were sporadic incidents of armed conflict between Indian and non-Indian ranchers; the first actual Anglo/Indian battle over a water hole was reported in 1885.[10]

As elsewhere in the West, cattle-raising in southern Arizona fell on hard times in the late 1880s and early 1890s. A combination of chronic overgrazing and two consecutive years of drought killed as many as three fourths of the cattle in Arizona in 1893.[11] Eroding soil stripped of native grasses was eventually revegetated mostly by sage and mesquite (which the U.S. Forest Service is still trying to eradicate), but this combination of erosion and altered vegetal cover caused a long-term impairment in the southern Arizona landscape's ability to retain precipitation. Hence, the reliance on groundwater resources was to become even greater,[12] at the same time that the groundwater recharge capability of the land surface was being diminished.

By the time Arizona was admitted to the Union in February 1912, Tucson had evolved from quiet Indian village (with a population of about eight-hundred in 1697),[13] to Spanish presidio, to southern Arizona cow town and military outpost, to regional trading and distribution center, boasting a population of more than thirteen-thousand.[14] The

Southern Pacific Railroad had laid track through the town in March 1880,[15] putting Tucson on a southern route which would one day stretch from Los Angeles to New Orleans. But an equally significant development, from the San Xavier Reservation's point of view, had been the formation of the Tucson Water Company, which in 1881 sank a series of wells along the western banks of the Santa Cruz River near the reservation to withdraw a municipal water supply. By the end of the decade the company had augmented its supply with a reservoir created by a low dam across the river.[16] And by 1885—the same year Tohono O'Odham and Anglo ranchers started shooting it out over water holes in the desert west of town—occurred the first significant litigation over competing water uses in the Tucson area of the Santa Cruz basin.[17]

Subsequent to statehood, the federal government tried to reduce Anglo-tribal tensions by formally reserving for the Indians a large portion of their traditional range and encouraging all tribal members to settle there. First, an effort was made to accommodate the wishes of the Maricopa band of O'Odham, who had migrated north from their traditional territory with the arrival of Anglo ranchers in the 1870s. This band was agriculturally oriented, so on May 28, 1912, the federal government by executive order established the 21,840-acre Ak Chin Indian Reservation[18] in low-lying desert land about fifty miles south of Phoenix, just north of where the lower Santa Cruz basin flattens out to join the lower Gila basin. Except for sparse water supplies, the area could with a modicum of effort be made suitable for sustained commercial agriculture. Then by executive order in 1918 the federal government created most of what is today the main body of the Tohono O'Odham Reservation, setting aside a two-million-acre tract of desert land west of the Santa Cruz basin, ranging from the Mexican border on the south about halfway to the city of Phoenix on the north. Since this area does not feature any major surface-water supplies, the federal government also began a program of groundwater pumping on the Indians' behalf and by 1933 had drilled a total of thirty-two deep wells on reservation lands (see n. 18).

Thus, by the end of World War I, the U.S. government had established for the O'Odham a main reservation located sixty miles west of Tucson (the two million acres reserved in 1918, later to be expanded), with unconnected satellite reservations at San Xavier del Bac eight miles southwest of Tucson and out near the town of Gila Bend, southwest of Phoenix.[19] The Ak Chin community, about midway between Phoenix and the main body of the Tohono O'Odham Reservation, was formed as an entirely separate tribal entity, not subject to the jurisdiction of the Tohono O'Odham Tribal Council. Irrigated agriculture had from its inception been the economic mainstay of the Ak Chin community. By the mid-1970s more than 5,000 acres were planted to cotton, wheat, and maize; further agricultural development awaited only the resolution of legal conflicts over groundwater supplies.[20] A 1976 Bureau of Indian Affairs census counted 312 Ak Chin community residents.[21] However, the Tohono O'Odham, on the higher, uneven lands of the main reservation, came to rely more heavily on ranching, at least to the extent that dwindling water supplies would permit. The 1976 BIA census recorded 8,707 O'Odham living on the reservation.[22]

Although Indian populations and land-use patterns remained relatively stable from statehood in 1912 until authorization of the Central Arizona Project in 1968, the changes Tucson underwent were nothing short of phenomenal. The state had established its land-grant college there in 1886, and the institution soon began to produce many of the hydrologists, mining engineers, agricultural advisors, and ranch managers who would accelerate the pace of southern Arizona resource development.[23] By the mid-1920s large-scale commercial agriculture had become a prominent feature of the Santa Cruz basin landscape; nearly 15,000 acres were under cultivation (the figure would later more than triple), all irrigated by large deep wells pumping from the same aquifer on which both the city of Tucson and the San Xavier Reservation depended for their water supplies.[24]

World War I brought military installations to the city;[25] in September 1927 Charles Lindbergh flew there to receive a hero's welcome and to dedicate what would later become a principal training facility of the Strategic Air Command, Davis-Monthan Air Force Base. World War II triggered another military-induced population explosion; the air bases bracketing the town comprised the world's largest pilot-training center during the wartime era. Many veterans returned after the war, and aerospace and electronics firms began to locate testing and manufacturing centers there. The humble land-grant technical school of the 1880s became the sprawling thirty-thousand-student charter campus of the University of Arizona. From 1950 to 1960 the city's population grew nearly four hundred percent, from forty-five-thousand to two-hundred-thirteen-thousand. In the next decade an additional fifty-thousand people would become Tucsonans.[26]

Changing Status of the Groundwater

The two case studies discussed in this chapter concern the depletion of groundwater resources in the Upper Santa Cruz basin: in the aquifer underlying the San Xavier district of the Tohono O'Odham Reservation and the well fields of the city of Tucson; and in the south-central Arizona desert in the immediate area of the Ak Chin Indian community, at the foot of the lower Santa Cruz basin at its geomorphologic confluence with the lower Gila River basin. The net loss of groundwater in both these areas over the course of the mid-twentieth century has been extraordinary.

Although the groundwater system was in equilibrium (withdrawals roughly equaling surface recharge) as late as 1923, from then until 1964 the water table in the area of Ak Chin Farms fell more than three-hundred feet.[27] The same analysis projected an even greater and more rapidly accelerating decline from the 1960s through the 1980s, two decades that saw the development of large-scale commercial agriculture in the area around the Ak Chin community.[28]

A similar situation obtained in the aquifer underlying Tucson and the San Xavier Reservation. From 1940 to 1964 the rate of groundwater withdrawal there more than tripled.[29] Water use also shifted markedly away from agriculture and toward municipal and industrial applications. The water table plunged to a depth of more than 700 feet in some places[30] (making groundwater extraction extremely expensive); and by the time the O'Odham filed suit against Tucson in the mid-1970s, groundwater was being withdrawn from the Santa Cruz River basin aquifer between two and three times faster than it was being naturally recharged.[31]

True to western historical tradition, the development of legal doctrines and policies to cope with rampant competition for groundwater in Arizona followed at a respectful distance behind the problem. The Arizona legislature, which bears the constitutional responsibility for setting policy for resource distribution in the state, has for most of this century been so deadlocked by fiercely competing agricultural, municipal, and industrial interests that until quite recently no effective legislative guidance in the development of groundwater policy ever came forth. As a result, the state courts were left to piece together ersatz doctrines from old common law remnants as they moved along from case to novel case.[32] As a result, from territorial times through most of the twentieth century the "American reasonable use doctrine" prevailed: a landowner could withdraw any amount of water capable of being devoted to a "reasonable beneficial use" on the overlying land without being liable for damages caused to neighboring landowners as a result. Damages were payable only for the injurious withdrawal of waters which were transported away from the overlying land; injunctions might not be available under any circumstances.[33]

The legislature made uniformly unsuccessful attempts to enact a groundwater code during the early 1940s, as the wealthier landowners sank bigger, deeper wells and those of small-time ranchers and farmers began to go dry. Only when the federal Bureau of Reclamation intimated in 1945 that without more responsible groundwater management on Arizona's part it would be difficult to justify the construction of the Central Arizona Project was legislative action finally stimulated.[34] Even this modest groundwater code, which required only the record keeping of wells and (after amendment) sought to restrain increasing withdrawal rates in critical overdraft areas, was not warmly received by the Arizona courts. The statute had been passed largely to appease federal reclamation bureaucrats and small farmers fearful of encroachment by well-financed land developers. The prohibition on new drilling in critical overdraft areas written into the code had a sunset provision; when the law expired in 1955 the legislature did not renew it,[35] and in 1960 the Arizona Supreme Court swept away its restrictive debris.[36]

Thus the "race-to-the-pumphouse," anticonservationist American reasonable-use doctrine resumed its domination of Arizona groundwater-management policy; it was substantially reaffirmed by the Arizona Supreme Court as late as 1976.[37] And it was in this climate of legally sanctioned, unrestrained, unrelenting competition for groundwater that the federal government and Tohono O'Odham filed their water-rights suit in the mid-1970s.

THE SAN XAVIER RESERVATION GROUNDWATER CONTROVERSY

By the time that Congress in 1968 authorized its multi-billion-dollar project to bring Colorado River water to central Arizona,[38] the Indians on the San Xavier Reservation were acutely aware of their groundwater problems. Not only was Tucson feeding its seemingly exponential growth on the ever-sinking water table of the upper Santa Cruz basin, but the tribe also had contributed to the overdraft problem through ambiguities in its own business dealings.

During the 1960s the Indians had leased some San Xavier Reservation lands to the American Smelting and Refining Company (ASARCO) for copper mining and ore reduction. Apparently unclear to the tribe at the time was the amount of water the mining company would deem necessary to fulfillment of the lease. In 1928 the San Xavier O'Odham were farming 2,000 acres, watered by fifteen commercial-size wells. Because of water table drawdowns, half a century later the tribe had only five producing wells and was capable of cultivating no more than 500 acres.[39] Tribal executives took the position that ASARCO groundwater pumping on Papago land was substantially in excess of that which the tribe was originally given to believe would be necessary and that the Indians were being forced against their will by hydrologic circumstance to retire farmland for the sake of minerals production.[40] This matter arose in legal action between the tribe and ASARCO during the late 1960s and early 1970s. But by then it had become obvious that in considering the upper Santa Cruz aquifer as a unified groundwater storage system, withdrawals by the city of Tucson, agricultural interests, and other mines were having nearly as substantial an impact on the San Xavier Reservation water table as the pumping which ASARCO considered legitimately incidental to its mining lease.[41]

Groundwater depletion by the city of Tucson was particularly worrisome. As a result of Arizona Supreme Court rulings on the reasonable-use doctrine as applied to the groundwater needs of municipalities in relation to private interests,[42] the only way Tucson could acquire additional groundwater rights was to purchase in fee simple additional private lands overlying the aquifer which carried those rights. The city was buying these agricultural lands—some near the reservation—retiring them from production, and using the groundwater formerly devoted to crop raising to supplement the municipal supply. (By 1978, Tucson had purchased and retired a total of 12,000 acres of farmland for the sake of its groundwater supply and had budgeted $20 million to acquire three times that much land by 1985.)[43]

Under the groundwater-rights doctrine in effect in Arizona at the time, it was obvious that the pace of withdrawal would only increase. As Tucson grew, so would its moat of fallow farmland. Thus in 1975 the U.S. attorney filed an action on behalf of the O'Odham in federal district court, claiming reserved rights to the groundwaters of the Santa Cruz basin beneath the San Xavier Reservation and other reservation lands overlying the aquifer. Defendants included the city of Tucson, mining companies, and agricultural interests. Later the tribe filed its own amended complaint, which was consolidated with the original Justice Department action.[44]

At an early stage in the litigation, defendants started meeting on a regular basis to explore the possibility of coordinating their responses to the federal/tribal suit. By 1978 Bill Strickland (the tribe's general counsel in this litigation) had begun to attend these meetings to let defendants at least know "when the next shoe was going to drop."[45] Also by this time, the federal government had expended close to $200,000 on the case; the Bureau of Indian Affairs reported to the General Accounting Office that federal funds which could otherwise be spent on assessments for tribal water-resource needs and supply planning were having to be diverted to meet litigation expenses.[46]

What is not known is the exact extent to which the Indians' reluctance to spend their own scarce revenues on the groundwater suit made them amenable to negotiation. What is known is that the tribe's

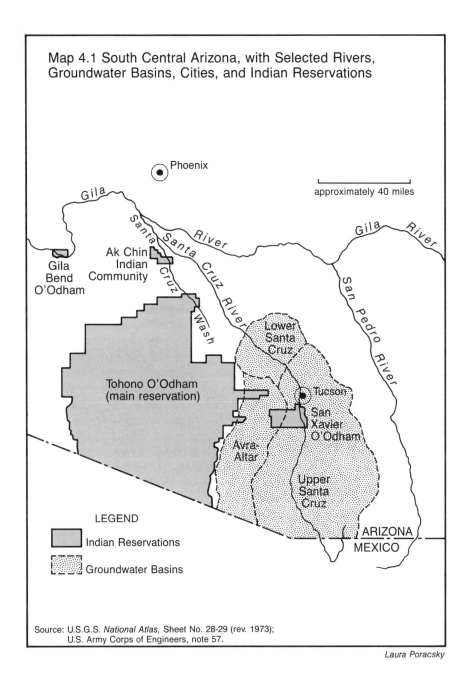

Map 4.1 South Central Arizona, with Selected Rivers, Groundwater Basins, Cities, and Indian Reservations

Phoenix

approximately 40 miles

Gila

Santa Cruz River

River

Gila River

Gila Bend O'Odham

Ak Chin Indian Community

San Pedro River

Wash

Lower Santa Cruz

Tohono O'Odham (main reservation)

Tucson

San Xavier O'Odham

Avra-Altar

Upper Santa Cruz

ARIZONA
MEXICO

LEGEND

Indian Reservations

Groundwater Basins

Source: U.S.G.S. *National Atlas,* Sheet No. 28-29 (rev. 1973);
U.S. Army Corps of Engineers, note 57.

Laura Poracsky

attorney formally initiated the negotiation process by telling the assembled defendants that the potential for a settlement might exist,
depending on their flexibility regarding Indian entitlements.[47] And the
defendants were in a bargaining mood. The suit had aroused mounting
apprehension among groundwater users in the upper Santa Cruz basin.
A year after the Indians filed their complaint, the U.S. Supreme Court
rendered its decision in *Cappaert* v. *United States*[48] and for the first time
extended the reserved-rights doctrine to groundwater.[49]

Cappaert had strengthened the Indians' position to the point where
one of the defendants would later estimate that the tribe would have
"probably stood about a sixty to seventy-five percent chance of winning
their case" if it had moved through the court system.[50] Nonetheless, all
parties to the dispute knew that nothing in *Cappaert* would lessen either
the time or the money involved in seeing the O'Odham case through to
its bitter and perhaps illusory end.[51] Although *Cappaert* may have
improved the Indians' chances of ultimately winning their case, rulings
on pretrial motions soon made it more difficult to conduct. The five
original defendants moved for a dismissal of the suit shortly after it was
filed, on the grounds that indispensable parties to the action had not
been named (i.e, all other groundwater pumpers in the upper Santa
Cruz basin). Rather than grant the motion, though, Judge Walsh
allowed the Justice Department and the tribe to file an amended
complaint, naming as defendants all commercial-capacity well operators
in the basin—about eighteen-hundred parties. So while the Indians'
case stayed in court, the cost of keeping it there rose dramatically.[52]

Once negotiation had begun, the ad hoc assemblage of disputants
began to take on an organizational life of its own. It adopted the name
"Water Resources Coordinating Committee" (WRCC), denoting its
intention to work out some sort of allocational scheme that all parties
could live with.[53] The group needed two things at the outset: a chairman
everyone could trust and numbers everyone could believe. It got both by
adopting as chairmen a succession of technical advisors from the
Phoenix regional office of the Army Corps of Engineers. The parties
generally perceived these federal officials as neutral insofar as the
question of groundwater rights was concerned and as capable of
providing much-needed data explaining just what was going on in the
groundwater basin of the upper Santa Cruz.

Soon after the Indians and the federal government had filed suit,
Congressman Morris Udall—whose district encompassed Tucson, the
lands of all defendants, and the reservation districts party to the suit—
had sponsored a resolution before the House Committee on Public
Works and Transportation, authorizing the Corps to conduct a major
study of water-supply problems and alternative solutions in the greater

Tucson area.[54] As a result of this ongoing federally funded project—the "Tucson Urban Study"—the Corps would eventually be able to provide, at no cost to the litigants, up-to-date research which the parties otherwise would have had to finance on their own during the discovery phase of the litigation. Negotiations chaired by Corps staff[55] and informed by Corps data began in 1978 and continued through passage of the second Papago groundwater-rights settlement act in 1982.[56] The Corps made Tucson Urban Study data analysis available to the WRCC as it was produced; the study itself first appeared in preliminary draft form in 1981.

The parties needed reliable figures on annual natural recharge (replenishment) of the upper Santa Cruz basin and on the rate of consumptive use (waters withdrawn and not replaced) by major categories of groundwater users in the basin. Subtracting recharge from consumptive use would yield figures for annual overdraft. Once the overdraft rate had been established with some degree of confidence, it could then be compared to the water-rights claims of the O'Odham in order to get some idea of which parties would have to relinquish how much water in order to try to satisfy the Indians' asserted entitlement.

Tucson Urban Study authors relied on the work of previous researchers[57] in defining the upper Santa Cruz basin and its hydrogeologic dynamics. Factoring in newly acquired data, they concluded that the average annual natural recharge of the upper Santa Cruz basin was just under 60,000 acre-feet of water and that consumptive use withdrawals from the same area were totalling over 165,000 acre-feet per year. The result was an annual overdraft (net water loss) of about 100,000 acre-feet of water.[58] When presented with this information, WRCC negotiators knew for certain (as if they hadn't already) that they had a very serious problem on their hands. The Supreme Court in its 1963 *Arizona* v. *California* decision had chosen to quantify the Indians' reserved rights by estimating the duty of water necessary to service all "practicably irrigable acreage" on the various reservations along the Colorado River and then had awarded them that annual amount of water. It was likely that the same criterion would be used in the O'Odham case.

About half of the 22,000-acre San Xavier Reservation overlies the upper Santa Cruz basin. Assuming for the sake of argument (and the Indians did) that all of this relatively flat, fertile land was irrigable, about 10,000 acres of land would be eligible for water delivery under the *Winters* doctrine. Assuming also that the duty of water for crop irrigation in the area averages about 5 acre-feet per acre per year (popular crops in southern Arizona include cotton, which requires 3.43 acre-feet, and alfalfa, which requires 6.19),[59] the tribe's groundwater entitlement under the *Winters* doctrine for the San Xavier Reservation could come to approximately 50,000 acre-feet per year. Plainly stated, if the Indians could fully perfect their reserved rights in federal court, they could legitimately lay claim to almost the entire 60,000 acre-foot annual natural recharge of the upper basin, leaving everybody else to pray for rain or move to California.

No extremes of water conservation and agricultural-land retirement would ever satisfy the Indian claims and still keep Tucson from becoming a colossal ghost town. Everybody knew the situation demanded more water, and everybody knew where to look for it. All eyes turned north to the federal contractors toiling their way across the desert, building the Central Arizona Project.

The Central Arizona Project and
the Reformed State Groundwater Law

Two related events in 1980 had a profound influence on the course of the negotiations for O'Odham groundwater rights. The first was the signing of contracts between the secretary of the Interior and twelve of Arizona's eligible Indian tribes for delivery of water from the Central Arizona Project (CAP). The second was comprehensive reform of the policy for groundwater allocation by the Arizona legislature. Many of the same players were involved in both transactions, and the scores are still being tabulated.

The story of negotiations for the delivery of water from the Central Arizona Project to Arizona's eligible Indian reservations properly begins in November 1922. The drafters of the original Colorado River Compact had made no effort to quantify the rights of the numerous Indian tribes living in the upper and lower Colorado River basins, and the basin-state negotiators apparently considered those rights insignificant both in quantity and in law.[60] They probably would have ignored the issue altogether but for commission chairman Herbert Hoover's admonition that "You always find some congressman who will bob up and say 'What is going to happen to the poor indian?' "[61] Hoover's means of placating the congressional do-gooders was to include in the Colorado River Compact's final draft his "wild Indian article"[62]—a one-sentence proviso declaring that "nothing in this compact shall be construed as affecting the obligations of the United States of America to Indian tribes."[63]

Four decades later the ghost of negotiations past returned to haunt the lower basin states. In litigating compact terms before the U.S. Supreme Court in 1963, Arizona and California learned to their chagrin that Hoover's article in combination with the *Winters* doctrine would give all basin-state tribes senior rights to Colorado River waters. The Supreme Court quantified those rights (in the lower basin) as the duty of water for all "practicably irrigable acreage" on the respective reservations,[64] with the quantity of water allocable to each Indian tribe subtracted from the total allocation to that state in which the reservation was located. As Arizona was the home of nineteen Indian tribes, including the two largest reservations in the nation, this ruling put quite a dent in its share of the river.

Five years after the *Arizona* v. *California* decision Congress authorized the Central Arizona Project, designed to transport water Arizona had won in court to the parched interior of the state (specifically, to the greater Phoenix area and up the Santa Cruz valley to Tucson). When major water users in Arizona started queuing up for deliveries from the project, they learned that the combined effect of the *Winters* doctrine, the 1922 compact, and the *Arizona* v. *California* ruling put the Indians very close to the head of the line.

The 1922 Colorado River Compact was vague because its authors could agree on so little. They all wanted rights to and delivery of Colorado River water, and they all knew that Congress would be hesitant to invest heavily in reclamation projects if there were unresolved controversies over allocation. Hence, the agreement was very broad; the details of state-by-state allocation were left to subsequent negotiations in the upper basin and litigation (i.e., *Arizona* v. *California*) in the lower. Likewise, in terms of its vagueness on the subject of distribution, the 1968 CAP authorization act bore an uncanny resemblance to the 1922 compact. Every major interest group in Arizona had its own ideas about how the waters should be shared, but insofar as possible they wanted to avoid unseemly quibbling while Congress was still debating the measure. Traditional foes joined hands to pledge allegiance to the mutual benefits of reclamation funding. The details would be worked out later.

As a result, the 1968 legislation—in keeping with the U.S. Supreme Court's ruling in *Arizona* v. *California*—vested in the Interior secretary (who at the time was Morris Udall's brother Stewart) enormous discretion in the distribution of water from CAP facilities. The details of who would get how much water in what order of priority and how seasonal shortages would be shared were all left to the secretary to work out during the process of negotiating contracts with principal users for CAP deliveries.[65] The recommendations of the Arizona Department of Water Resources (DWR) would be taken into account, but they were not controlling. DWR made its first recommendations to the U.S. Interior Department in the early 1970s;[66] Acting Interior Secretary Frizzel published the first proposed allocations in 1976.[67] With a change in presidential administrations at the end of 1976, however, came a period of radical rethinking on the subject of funding for federal water projects.

The Carter administration's economically rational if politically suicidal effort to scale down or cancel several large projects (including the CAP) rallied the faithful in Arizona and elsewhere in the West to protect the gains they had made in earlier legislation. It was a time of stormy, uncertain relations between Arizona and the Interior Department, marked in 1979 by the secretary's threat to halt construction of the CAP until Arizona had adopted a more responsible, less wasteful system of groundwater regulation. This conflict over CAP management came to a head in the closing days of the Carter administration, in a fast-action sequence of events illustrative of the entertainment value of western water law. It started in August 1980, when Interior Secretary Cecil Andrus proposed a revision of CAP water allocations to Indian tribes in Arizona—allocations which were considerably more generous to the Indians than had been Acting Secretary Frizzel's proposals in 1976.[68]

Arizonans were stunned, since under the Supreme Court's 1963 *Arizona v. California* ruling, more water for the tribes meant less for the rest of the state. State government officials protested vigorously but to no avail.[69] On December 10, 1980 (after President Carter had lost his bid for reelection), Secretary Andrus made final his CAP allocations to the tribes, giving primacy to the federal government's obligation to the Indians in the distribution of CAP water—as opposed to the Arizona government's wishes regarding CAP allocations.[70]

State officials were furious, and Secretary Andrus anticipated (correctly) that they would take immediate legal action to halt the allocations. Therefore, late on the evening of December 11 (while the federal court was still considering Arizona's request for injunctive relief), Interior Department administrators quietly convened the chairpersons and legal counsel of each of the Arizona tribes agreeing to CAP allocations at the federal building in Phoenix. There, in an event some state-agency personnel still darkly refer to as the "midnight signing," the Interior Department signed CAP contracts for water delivery with each of the tribes (including the Tohono O'Odham and Ak Chin community). The next morning the state found itself in the position of trying to prevent something that had already happened. Subsequent legal efforts by the state to delay contract implementation were also ultimately unsuccessful.[71] And with the Indians thus assured of the delivery of water through the same project which would be supplying the city of Tucson, the disputants trying to resolve the controversy over the upper Santa Cruz basin groundwater began to sense the real possibility for a negotiated settlement.

Even though negotiators on the Water Resources Coordinating

Committee knew that CAP water would help alleviate their chronic overdraft problems, they also knew that it would not solve those problems entirely. The Tucson Urban Study projected that annual groundwater overdrafts in the Santa Cruz basin area would by the year 2000 exceed Arizona's most optimistic plans for CAP allocations.[72] The disputants in 1980 also realized that no CAP water would reach Tucson until the 1990s at the very earliest;[73] in the intervening decade overdrafting could proceed unabated, and the damages suffered by the Indians would increase. In addition, research conducted by the state of Arizona would soon show that the long-term overdraft problem was probably more serious than the Corps had at first estimated. In other words, it was apparent that if Tucson's and the mines' increasing rates of groundwater consumption continued at the pace they had attained by 1980, the Central Arizona Project would only postpone the upper Santa Cruz basin's ultimate day of reckoning rather than obviating it.[74] Any durable agreement among upper-basin negotiators would have to include limitations on groundwater withdrawals—limitations the negotiators were loathe to impose upon themselves.

Interior Secretary Andrus was no less aware than any other observer that delivering expensive, federally financed water to locales which had proven themselves incapable of adequately managing the dwindling supplies they already had would be a tragic waste of both natural and fiscal resources. He intimated as much to Arizona Governor Bruce Babbitt in a written communication in the autumn of 1979, when he also let it be known that he would not press Congress for full funding and timely completion of CAP construction until the state of Arizona took affirmative steps to improve its groundwater management capability.[75] The Secretary wanted a better state groundwater law.

Arizonans were by now familiar with if not inured to such federal arm-twisting. Interior had done the same thing as far back as 1945 in refusing to support CAP legislation until Arizona improved its groundwater regulation policies.[76] The Arizona legislature substantially complied with Interior Department demands in 1945, but the state then got involved in litigation over the Colorado River Compact before CAP legislation cleared Congress. When state legislators surmised that there would be no CAP authorization until the U.S. Supreme Court rendered its *Arizona* v. *California* decision, they let the groundwater regulation statute die on the vine in 1955 by failing to renew its overdraft provisions.[77] But by 1979 the situation was different. Congress had authorized the Central Arizona Project in 1968; construction had begun in 1973, and—as the projected completion date receded into the late 1980s or early 1990s—total projected costs were rising into the billions of dollars.[78] Arizona's economic future had become heavily dependent on

CAP distribution of the state's share of the Colorado River, and it was beginning to look as if reform of groundwater law would be the purchase price of that future.

The legislature and the governor bit the proverbial bullet in June 1980 with adoption of the Arizona Groundwater Management Act.[79] Even in light of the federal threats involved, the statute represents such a dramatic reversal of past policy that it bespeaks no small measure of political courage and conciliatory talent on the part of its creators.[80] Key provisions of the act

- brought into being "active management areas" in the state, wherein all groundwater withdrawals are to be monitored by DWR personnel and new withdrawals are allowable subject only to permit;
- mandated progressively stricter conservation measures intended to bring consumptive uses into balance with recharge by the year 2025;
- provided for the permanent retirement of agricultural land without the transfer of groundwater rights accompanying that land to other uses; and
- prohibited the future residential subdivision of land in active management areas absent the subdivider's proved acquisition and development of a 100-year water supply adequate to sustain the development.

The law levied a pump tax on all groundwater withdrawals to finance its implementation and measures for water conservation. Further, it mandated progressively more effective techniques for water conservation among all categories of existing groundwater users—a sort of best available conservation technology for municipal, industrial, and agricultural uses. Since the law designated most of the Santa Cruz basin as an active management area subject to these comprehensive regulations, passage of legislation for state groundwater reform removed a major impediment to settlement of the groundwater dispute in the upper Santa Cruz basin. A strict conservation-oriented limitation on groundwater withdrawals, which disputants had been unable or unwilling to impose upon themselves, had been locked in by the Arizona legislature and the governor. Settlement of the Papago groundwater conflict was one step closer.

Once the provision of CAP water to the O'Odham had been contracted for and nonfederal groundwater pumpers in the upper Santa Cruz basin were subjected to comprehensive state regulation of groundwater withdrawal, negotiators were in a position to discuss what specific terms an agreement should contain. The Indians wanted an assured, reliable supply of high-quality water suitable for agricultural and other development on their reservation; Tucson, the mines, and the farmers wanted the Indian cloud permanently removed from their groundwater rights. The Tucson City Council and mayor were especially anxious to settle the dispute since in their bond offerings they were required to disclose that the rights to the water supplies nourishing Tucson's immediate economic development were being seriously jeopardized by the reserved-rights suit. The city's legal problems with access to water were beginning to affect its access to capital.[81]

An upper-basin settlement agreement had to be embodied in federal legislation for several reasons. First, the Indians wanted all federal assurances regarding CAP deliveries, water quality and quantity, and financing guaranteed in writing by the ultimate authority capable of making such guarantees—the U.S. Congress. Second, implementation of an agreement was going to cost money—money Congress would have to authorize and appropriate. And third, in return for these assurances and expenditures, the "permanent settlement" of disputes over Indian groundwater rights in the upper Santa Cruz basin would probably require that the tribe not only dismiss its current suit but also waive rights to bring such suits in the future, if the federal government upheld its end of the bargain.

The waiver of such a fundamental and valuable Indian right had to be authorized by the U.S. government, as fiduciary for tribal interests. Previous interior secretaries had created terrible legal problems for the Indians, the federal government, and other western water users by making such waivers without congressional consent, as exemplified by the era of the first Indian water-rights settlements in the early twentieth century. The logical sponsor for such dispute-settling legislation was Congressman Morris Udall of Arizona. Not only was the upper Santa Cruz basin in his district, but he was also chairman of the House Interior and Insular Affairs Committee, which has legislative jurisdiction over Indian Affairs and reclamation project authorization bills. Staff members of Congressman Udall's office had monitored but not taken an active part in WRCC negotiations from 1978 to 1980, but as the bargaining action began to gravitate from the legal to the legislative arena, congressional staff got more directly involved.

A generally worded bill obligating the Interior secretary to deliver water to the San Xavier Reservation was submitted by Congressman Udall at the WRCC's request in 1980, but the House Interior Committee never considered it.[82] In July 1981 he introduced a second bill,[83] resulting in legislative hearings before the House Water Resources Subcommittee in Phoenix and Tucson during August of that year.[84] By the time the hearings ended, WRCC negotiators had agreed in principle to the terms in this legislation but had not reached consensus on specific terms regarding CAP and groundwater allocation.[85] However, the hearings were never published and the second bill also never came to a full House vote.[86]

Throughout this process, frustration and tension mounted on all sides. The Indians would not settle without the support of Congress; the non-Indian disputants would not compensate the tribe for past withdrawals; and there was no multilateral agreement among non-Indian parties as to how large a tribal allocation of groundwater, CAP water, and recycled water they were willing to support in legislative form.

Then in late 1981, counsel for a House Interior subcommittee, the attorneys for the Indians, and certain other WRCC members began to meet frequently to discuss the specifics of new settlement legislation.[87] Another bill was drafted, which conformed more closely to Congressman Udall's and subcommittee-staff estimates of what Congress would find palatable than had the previous bills. The House Interior and Insular Affairs Committee reported favorably on this measure—H.R. 5118—in November 1981. The House of Representatives adopted it in March 1982 by a vote of 311 to 50; it received unanimous consent in the Senate on May 11.[88] The Papago Tribal Council had ratified the agreement prior to a final vote in Congress. There was restrained jubilation in congressional offices and those of many WRCC negotiators over the fruits of their four years' labor at the bargaining table. Thanks to the CAP, responsible state groundwater regulation, effective congressional leadership, and an eventual spirit of reasonable compromise among negotiating parties, history had either just been made or repeated in southern Arizona. Tucson, the mines, and the farmers were off the legal hook, and the Indians might get as much water as they would have by perfecting their *Winters* rights in court (at far less cost).

The warm glow of success lasted from May 11, 1982, when the Senate unanimously adopted the bill, until the morning of June 1, when President Reagan vetoed it. He cited two reasons for rejecting the measure: (1) The "United States Government was never a party to the negotiations" but would (2) "bear almost the entire financial burden of the settlement"—an arrangement he termed a "serious misuse of federal funds."[89] Reagan vowed never to approve "legislation implementing a settlement to which the federal government had not been a major party," and he criticized H.R. 5118 as a "federal bailout" of a local problem.

This was a startling announcement, in that the first of the president's reasons for vetoing the bill had no basis in fact. The U.S. Army Corps of Engineers had chaired the WRCC negotiations; other "major parties" had included representatives of U.S. Senators Dennis DeConcini and Barry Goldwater and the Interior Department's own Bureau of Indian Affairs. Interior's Bureau of Reclamation had provided plans for

CAP implementation alternatives, and the U.S. Attorney's Office was representing the Tohono O'Odham in the ongoing litigation. A powerful congressional committee chairman and his staff had drafted the final agreement in legislative form, and the U.S. Congress had ratified it.

But there had not been policy-level coordination of the administration's position on Indian water-rights settlements. Many observers consequently interpreted this rationale of lack of federal involvement as another salvo in the ongoing political duel between Interior Committee Chairman Udall and Interior Department Secretary Watt. In the last line of the president's veto message he had announced, "I am asking the Secretary of the Interior to coordinate participation by my Administration in any such negotiations" aimed at resolving the Papago or other Indian water-rights disputes in the future.[90] The clear message was that only those settlements would be signed into law which the Interior secretary's office had authorized prior to their being drafted into legislation.

Three days after the veto, Interior Committee Chairman Udall wrote a long letter to the president. He pointed out the substantial degree of federal involvement in the settlement negotiations, and he flatly contradicted Reagan's legally and historically fallacious assertion "that the federal government has no obligation or duty to participate financially in the settlement of the Indian water rights claims."[91] Udall devoted a good portion of the letter to recounting the Interior Department's historically ambivalent role in protecting Indian water rights and to describing the federal government's trust responsibility to the tribes. He closed by urging the president to appoint a federal negotiator as soon as possible to sit down with WRCC representatives and rework H.R. 5118. The administration complied in July 1982 with the appointment of William P. Horn, deputy undersecretary of the Interior, as the leader of a federal negotiating team assigned the mission of settling all pending Indian water-rights claims.[92] Undersecretary Horn announced that the Papago case would receive first priority.[93]

Late afternoon negotiations (to accommodate everyone's schedule) resumed with Horn in attendance in Tucson in August. The site was a federal office building where the air conditioning system was shut off every afternoon at 5:00 P.M. to conserve energy—a time of day when the average temperature in the shade exceeds 100° Fahrenheit. Initially, tempers around the bargaining table topped the late afternoon temperature in the room.[94] Water Resources Coordinating Committee negotiators were angry, frustrated, and once again very mistrustful. Many of them felt betrayed by a process which had exacted major concessions in their bargaining positions and then had ultimately rejected those concessions.

This ill will notwithstanding, the administration's representative hammered away at the second point in the president's veto message: The federal government would not bear sole financial responsibility for satisfying the Indians' groundwater claims. Those local entities who had contributed to the tribe's groundwater problems would be required to contribute to their solution.[95] As negotiations progressed, Horn made it clear that the administration had in mind some sort of cooperative funding arrangement whereby the city of Tucson, the mines, Arizona state government, and agribusiness interests would have to share the expense of providing water to the San Xavier Reservation. The city of Tucson soon agreed because of its bond-rating jeopardy and its belief that passage of the Papago bill would hasten construction of the Tucson Aqueduct portion of the Central Arizona Project. The mines and farmers were more reluctant, but as it turned out their share of the financial burden would also be smaller.

A more significant problem was the acquiescence of the state of Arizona. The legislature eventually would have to authorize any major financial contribution, but it was not assembled for the consideration of such a proposal during these rapidly moving August negotiations. The state's representative on the WRCC was Wesley E. Steiner, director of the Arizona Department of Water Resources; he was convinced that without a state contribution there would be no Papago groundwater-settlement bill.[96] And without a bill, Congress might further delay completion of the CAP while the Indians, the mines, Tucson, and the farmers fought over CAP deliveries and groundwater withdrawals. Thus at a late stage in the negotiations on a day when Governor Babbitt happened to be in Tucson, he and the DWR director held a hastily scheduled meeting at which the governor agreed to a cooperative-fund contribution on the state's behalf.[97]

However, Wes Steiner (and, as it developed, some western states' congressional delegations) wanted two concessions in return. These were provisions in the Papago bill which would bar construance of the legislation as either affirming or denying (1) that the *Winters* doctrine applies to groundwater, or (2) that the act by implication granted off-reservation water use and sale rights to other Indian tribes. Although this finding stands in curious contrast to the U.S. Supreme Court's 1976 *Cappaert* decision, it was embodied in the final legislation.[98] Without these concessions, Steiner was concerned that Congress would not ratify the Papago act, since several western congressmen and state government leaders had told him they were afraid the rights which the Tohono O'Odham were obtaining in the legislation (liberal quantification, off-reservation sale and use rights) might by implication transfer to other tribes when they adjudicate their rights in court. The tribal council ratified this and other sections of the bill prior to its being submitted to Congress.[99]

A compromise bill cleared the House on August 17, 1982, and the Senate on August 20. For reasons which are still debated,[100] at its point of origin in the House, Congressman Udall attached the Papago settlement bill as a rider to an important reclamation reform measure the Reagan administration very much wanted—an act raising to 960 acres the amount of farmland in individual private ownership eligible to receive inexpensive, heavily subsidized water from federally funded reclamation projects.[101] This legislative freight train emerged from conference with final congressional approval (and a few surprises) during the last week of September; President Reagan signed the whole package into law on October 12, 1982.

An assessment of the more prominent features of the Southern Arizona Water Rights Settlement Act is of necessity to some extent subjective, based on an interpretation of whether a given feature of the legislation will benefit or limit Indian interests; only those aspects of Public Law 97-293 which seem to represent a plus or minus are reviewed here. A comparison of Public Law 97-293 with H.R. 5118 (the bill President Reagan vetoed in June 1982) shows little change in benefits gained by the Indians; there is merely a partial shift from federal to local financial responsibility for implementing the agreement. In general, the O'Odham were promised the following benefits:

- The Interior secretary must deliver to the San Xavier Reservation and Schuk Toak district of the main reservation 27,000 a-f. and 10,800 a-f. respectively, on an annual basis, subsequent to completion.[102]
- Tucson will provide the secretary with 28,200 annual a-f. of "reclaimed water" (treated effluent) suitable for agriculture for distribution to the Indians. Unlike H.R. 5118, P.L. 97-293 stipulated that Tucson shall provide this water free of charge.
- The tribe may use its waters for any purpose, and may use or sell its water off-reservation.
- A $15 million trust fund is established, the interest from which will be expended on the preparation of Indian lands for irrigation and maintenance of their irrigation works; and a $10.5 million-minimum "cooperative fund" is also created to finance the Interior secretary's delivery obligations other than direct CAP costs.[103]

These non-CAP responsibilities include a federal obligation to deliver non-CAP, noneffluent water to the Indians in the event that the CAP is never completed or other disabilities intervene and an obligation to pay money damages if none or only a portion of the water is delivered.

Most of the concessions made by the Indians were in H.R. 5118 (the earlier legislation), but some of those with the greatest impact appeared only in the final bill signed by the president. First, the original concessions:

- In return for CAP deliveries to the San Xavier Reservation and Schuk Toak district, the O'Odham agreed to be bound by a water management plan devised by the Interior secretary which would have the same substantial effect as if the tribe were subject to state water law, especially as related to activities such as water conservation practices.[104]
- The O'Odham Tribe agreed to limit groundwater pumping to 10,000 a-f. annually on the San Xavier Reservation and to withdrawal rates in effect on January 1, 1981, at the Schuk Toak district on the main reservation.
- The tribe agreed to accept money damages in lieu of water in the event that the Interior secretary is unable to meet the federal obligations set forth in the act. If for some reason CAP water can not be delivered, the secretary is first to acquire "alternative supplies" from local willing sellers; otherwise the tribe will accept money damages equal to the "replacement cost" of the waters. All non-CAP water transfers can be made pursuant only to state law.[105]
- The secretary retains veto power over all off-reservation sales of water by the tribe to non-Indian buyers, and the tribe is prohibited from permanently alienating its water rights.[106]
- The tribe agreed to limit its water rights solely to the terms set forth in the act. That is, the tribe cannot claim a water right exceeding the acre/feet allocations of CAP, effluent, and alternative water quantified in the law, or groundwater withdrawals exceeding 10,000 a-f. per year at San Xavier and January 1, 1981, withdrawal rates at the Schuk Toak district of the main reservation.[107]
- The tribe agreed to drop its pending groundwater suit and not to bring future actions except to enforce the terms of the act.
- Individual Indians who are successors in interest to allotted lands on the San Xavier Reservation (i.e., lands to which some individuals acquired title in fee simple during the Allotment Era) are also bound by the act, and—after the statute of limitations has expired—may not claim damages against non-Indian groundwater pumpers. Any water-rights claims of individual allottees within the San Xavier Reservation must be satisfied out of waters the tribe was granted in the act.

• Regarding administration of the trust fund, the tribe is limited to the expenditure only of interest and may therefore not expend or borrow against the principal for capital improvements of irrigation facilities for which it is responsible.

These concessions were written into H.R. 5118, which Congress passed in May and the president vetoed in June 1982. But at the Tucson negotiations in August of that year, several parties requested—and the Indians agreed to—terms barring construance of the new agreement as either affirming or denying (1) the applicability of the *Winters* doctrine to groundwater rights, and (2) the right of Indians to sell or use reserved waters off-reservation. Both of these waivers appeared in Public Law 97-293.[108]

Whether an analyst perceives the *Winters* doctrine disclaimer as an Indian concession or a gain depends on an estimation as to whether the Indians could have fully perfected their reserved-rights claims in federal court. For example, if the O'Odham had fully established a reserved right to groundwaters sufficient to serve all ''practicably irrigable acreage'' on their lands within the Tucson Active Management Area, they would have become the dominant holders of groundwater rights of Southern Arizona; the U.S. Supreme Court's 1976 *Cappaert* decision had held that senior federal reserved rights to groundwater were superior to those granted under state law. The Indians could have claimed damages for past withdrawals and perhaps made future withdrawals by Tucson, the mines, and agribusiness subject to periodic tribal consent and continuing financial compensation. However, if the tribe had failed in court, this Indian OPEC scenario would not have unfolded; the tribe might well have wound up with a less certain right, much less water, and much higher legal costs than resulted from the negotiations culminating in Public Law 97-293.

But the most significant last-minute concession demanded of the tribe—the diamond bearing on which the great mass of Public Law 97-293 litigation (if there is any) may turn—is a clause in section 313 of the act which appears to limit the annual damages payable to the tribe by the federal government to only the interest generated by the Cooperative Fund. The opinions of respondents to this research diverge widely on this point, but the language of Section 313(f) holds that ''Payment for damages . . . [for secretarial nondelivery of CAP or other waters] shall not exceed in any given year the amounts available for expenditure in any given year from the Cooperative Fund established in this section.''

A few rough calculations may help illustrate the possible impact of this subsection. The Interior secretary is obligated under the act to provide the O'Odham with a total of 66,000 acre-feet of water per year (37,800 acre-feet from the CAP and 28,200 acre-feet of effluent). Assuming a scenario in which the CAP is completed but no water is delivered to the reservation and an average prevailing market value of agricultural-quality water of $75 per acre-foot, then the secretary would be liable for nearly $5 million in annual damages for each year of nondelivery. The act establishes the Cooperative Fund size at $10.5 million, although it may be augmented by subsequent appropriations if Congress so desires. Assuming an annual yield of ten percent, the amount of interest available in the fund in any given year would at most be just over one million dollars—about twenty percent of the secretary's presumed liability under the act. Furthermore, the secretary's liability could go much higher if the CAP is never extended as far south as Tucson.

If the CAP is completed to Tucson but no water is delivered to the reservation, the tribe must be paid the going rate for CAP water. However, if the CAP never reaches Tucson (and it had not by the end of the 1980s) the secretary must pay the tribe the "avoided cost" of supplying the water—that is, damages equaling the funds necessary to buy water from willing sellers at an agreed upon price and to construct a delivery system to the San Xavier Papago Reservation. Thus, to the $5 million annual damages would be added construction costs of a water-delivery system to transport 66,000 acre-feet of agricultural quality water—probably well in excess of $20 million. Yet no matter what the size of the secretary's theoretical liability, a reading of section 313(f) seems to indicate that the actual damages the secretary will be forced to pay may not exceed annual Cooperative Fund interest, which—depending on the fund's portfolio and market conditions—could not amount to more than about $1 million per year. Even these damages would be paid not out of the Interior Department's annual budget but out of a fund which otherwise would have been used to meet the operating expenses of systems delivering water to the Papagos; some maintenance is required even when systems are not fully utilized.

Naturally enough, the Reagan administration adhered to this reading of section 313(f) throughout the 1980s, although Deputy Undersecretary Horn acknowledged a certain degree of ambiguity regarding congressional intent to limit federal liability.[109] Equally understandable is the diametrically opposing position adopted by the tribe's general counsel.[110] He cited the language of the House Conference Report accompanying Public Law 97-293, which in regard to section 313(f) holds that "in the event available income on the Fund is insufficient in any given year to pay damages . . . , the Tribe may seek a determination of damages in excess of payments made in the Court of Claims under section 1505 of Title 28, USC."[111] Thus the Conference Report seems to conclude that damages payable to the Papago Tribe by the secretary are not limited to interest from the Cooperative Fund but extend to whatever actual liability is incurred by reason of nondelivery of waters. Additionally, the Report declares this full liability to be justiciable in federal claims court—a finding not reflected in section 313(f).

For the sake of all parties concerned, it may be just as well if this particular example of ambivalence of legislative intent never has to stand the test of litigation. The most charitable evaluation of this ambiguity is that Congress wanted to create such a dangerously uncertain situation around the issue of damages that all parties would be afraid to approach it in court.

Subsequent negotiations between the tribe and the Interior Department over implementation of the settlement act have resulted in a delivery contract[112] containing language on damages paralleling that of the Conference Report (that is, interpreted to the tribe's advantage). Thus, it may be that the damage control the tribe's attorney was able to perform in getting favorable language written into the Conference Report and the delivery contracts drawn up pursuant to implementing the act have offset the serious threats posed against the O'Odham's money-damages guarantee in the original act. At the same time, the fact that such weakening, ambiguous language made it into the final act at all stands as a major warning of the mysterious fate which can befall even the most carefully crafted agreements in the closing moments of the legislative process.

THE AK CHIN INCIDENT

The post–World War II population boom in Arizona's urban centers coincided with rapidly increasing rates of groundwater withdrawals for agricultural purposes throughout much of the south-central region of the state. U.S. Geological Survey research showed that from 1923 to 1964 the water table underlying intensively cultivated lands between the city of Phoenix and the main Papago Reservation dropped as much as 340 feet—perhaps the most extreme example of overdraft in all of Arizona. Usable water was more than 700 feet below the land surface at several wells. And the Indians at Ak Chin community knew from the USGS research and from independent surveys they commissioned that the groundwater underlying their lands was being depleted much faster than could be accounted for by their own pumping, which served about 5,000 acres.[113]

Indeed, by the late 1970s the effects of unregulated overdrafting in south-central Arizona had become something of a national joke, although local residents found little to laugh about. Because of massive groundwater removals, the land surface actually had begun to sink, like a slowly deflating inner tube. From 1950 to 1980, this sinking, or "subsidence," at the town of Eloy (about 25 miles southeast of Ak Chin Farms) was measured at more than 10 vertical feet, causing large cracks in building foundations, pavement, and an interstate freeway which passes nearby.[114] The landscape was (and is) literally sinking into the sunset along with the water table.

While the Ak Chin community members watched in frustration as their lands sank and their wells began to go dry, they also noted with interest the filing of the Papago groundwater suit in 1975. When the Supreme Court in *Cappaert* extended federal reserved rights to groundwater, tribal leaders decided that some kind of legal action would probably be necessary to protect their rights. However, the community was quite resistant to filing a groundwater suit, for fiscal and other reasons.[115] The community's legal counsel suggested as a less expensive alternative a direct appeal to congressional leaders who might be capable of providing legislative relief. A proposal was drawn up which would obligate the federal government to ensure an adequate, quantified water supply for the Ak Chin community in return for which the Indians would waive all past, present, and future water-rights claims against all parties in its groundwater basin. Congressman Udall sponsored legislation to that effect in the House, and Senator DeConcini introduced it in the upper chamber. The act cleared both houses of Congress with little fanfare, and President Carter signed it on July 28, 1978.[116]

The Ak Chin settlement agreement preceded the final Papago legislation by about four years. The first of several differences one notices between the two is that while the 1982 Papago agreement is relatively lengthy and detailed, the earlier Ak Chin act is by contrast quite general and quite brief. It consists of only four substantive sections in addition to its introductory clauses.

In terms of Indian gains, in Section 2 of the act the Interior secretary was directed to deliver to the Ak Chin community a total of 85,000 acre-feet of water suitable for agriculture within four years. The water was to be withdrawn from nearby federal-well fields to be developed for that purpose or partly from those fields and partly from other surface supplies the secretary might obtain.[117] The law directed the secretary to fulfill this annual obligation of 85,000 acre-feet by any feasible interim means by the four-year deadline, but within twenty-five years he was responsible for providing facilities and resources to make permanently available that annual supply to the Ak Chin community. The bill authorized an appropriation of $42.5 million to enable the secretary to meet this interim obligation and to make plans to satisfy that delivery requirement permanently.

Regarding concessions, the Ak Chin community agreed to waive all past, present, and future water-rights claims against all public and private parties in its groundwater basin.[118] Additionally, the Indians agreed to accept less than the full amount promised them during the interim period if no feasible means of honoring the 85,000 acre-feet commitment could be developed without damaging non-Indian interests. The secretary's responsibility for providing a permanent supply within twenty-five years was undiminished by this concession. Finally, the Indians assented to money damages in lieu of water in the event of secretarial nondelivery; damages were to be calculated as the "replacement cost" of the water.

Public Law 95-328 ran into trouble almost as soon as the Interior Department tried to put it into effect. Some attributed its lack of viability to a premature birth (insufficient detail and inadequate authorizations in the act), and others cite foot-dragging by the Reagan administration (failure to request or expend necessary appropriations). At any rate, problems with the Ak Chin agreement's implementation began to unfold.

In May 1980, Interior Secretary Andrus and the Ak Chin community (represented since passage of the 1978 act by William Strickland, who was also general counsel for the Papagos) signed a contract putting into effect Public Law 95-328 that added considerable flesh to the bare bones of the act;[119] it established a timetable for the phased delivery of federal well water to Ak Chin Farms and provided for rehabilitation of existing wells on the reservation. However, preliminary survey work done under the contract showed that some of the federal well water alluded to in the legislation was of insufficient quality for agricultural purposes and that other federal wells to be developed shared an aquifer with northern districts of the Tohono O'Odham's main reservation. Fulfilling the secretarial obligation with these wells would amount to taking water away from one Indian reservation to give it to another. Interior Department hydrologists also concluded that developing the federal well fields not adjacent to the Papago Reservation would damage non-Indian groundwater interests, which the Ak Chin agreement forbade.[120] All this information had come to light by 1982, when the Reagan administration began to cut back on implementation of the Ak Chin contract. The Interior Department saw no way to continue the work without damaging the groundwater rights of either the Tohono O'Odham or non-Indian agribusiness interests.[121]

When the federal government started missing its delivery deadlines stipulated in the implementation contract, Ak Chin leaders threatened to invoke their damages clause in federal claims court. Subsequent to this sabre-rattling, Interior Secretary Watt agreed to meet with Ak Chin representatives and advisors in December 1982 to work out some compromise; Bill Horn, the undersecretary who had just renegotiated the Papago settlement on the administration's behalf, would be there also.[122] But on the day of the meeting, neither Watt nor Horn showed up; they had become involved in a summit conference among western states' governors, several western tribes with energy mineral resources, and some Indian rights organizations—a conference to which Ak Chin was not invited. Instead, they sent Assistant Secretary for Indian Affairs Ken Smith to inform Ak Chin leaders that the original $42.5 million appropriation for agreement implementation was considerably depleted and that because of the technical problems with the federal wells, the Reagan administration (or at least, the Office of Management and Budget) saw no point in requesting supplemental appropriations to implement an increasingly unworkable act.[123]

To the Ak Chin leaders and their advisors, it seemed that the worst fears of all Indians regarding negotiations with the federal government had just been reconfirmed. Gene Franzoy, the community's consulting hydrologic engineer, observed "At the same time Watt was upstairs saying how much help the federal government will give the Indians, we met downstairs to hear that they are not going to keep this project on line."[124] Ak Chin community Chairwoman Leona Kakar was more direct. "All we get are lies," she said. "If this law is not upheld, I will alert every Indian in the nation to be very cautious in any so-called settlement of water rights by negotiation."[125]

News accounts of the Ak Chin community's predicament and the threat to enforce legal guarantees of expansive money damages (which would ultimately come out of the Interior Department's hide) evidently had the desired effect. In September 1983, Secretary Watt signed a revised agreement with the community.[126] The Indians made some additional concessions in the new bargain. First, they agreed to accept $53.7 million in economic and agricultural development grants and loans in lieu of damages for undelivered interim water. Second, they agreed to lower their minimum required deliveries to 75,000 acre-feet annually in years of normal rainfall and 72,000 acre-feet in dry years; 85,000 acre-feet of water would still be delivered in years of surplus. In return, Secretary Watt obligated the Interior Department to deliver all of this water through the Central Arizona Project instead of from federal wells. In addition, this would be senior priority water; even in dry years, the Ak Chin community's water would be provided before deliveries to most other water users in the system. In an effort at least to satisfy the spirit of Public Law 95-328 and stave off a damages suit, Secretary Watt had ushered the Ak Chin community to the very head of the CAP allocation line.

As one might expect, this arrangement didn't play too well in Phoenix. To satisfy the increased commitment to Ak Chin (the community would now be receiving considerably more water through the CAP than they had contracted for at the midnight signing in December 1980), the secretary had to find more water in the lower Colorado River, which was already fully appropriated. In October 1983 the Interior Department proposed to do this by partially rescinding contracts for Colorado River water delivery held by the Arizona cities of Yuma and Kingman and by the Yuma-Mesa Irrigation District.[127] Deputy Undersecretary Horn inherited the unenviable task of trying to convince these CAP contractors and the State of Arizona to go along with the reallocation.[128]

Understandably, the government of Arizona was not in a very conciliatory mood. Most of the Colorado River water the Interior Department was planning to reallocate was contracted for but never used, and the director of Arizona's Department of Water Resources took the position that this water should therefore be available for reallocation to all CAP users and not just the Indians.[129] Undersecretary Horn's persuasive skills notwithstanding, the DWR director said he would be surprised if Yuma, Kingman, and the irrigation district didn't sue the secretary for breach of contract; if they did, he expected the state to join them.[130] The Ak Chin community's attorney conceded that the reallocation process would probably go more smoothly if Congress were to amend the Ak Chin settlement act to include these provisions; and in 1984, Congress did just that.

The 1984 amendments to the Ak Chin settlement act[131] for the most part codified the reworked 1983 agreement between the Interior Department and the community. In partial fulfillment of the federal government's obligation to Ak Chin, the 1984 act authorized the secretary to rescind contracts for 50,000 acre-feet of Colorado River water contracted for but never used in the Yuma, Arizona, area.[132] To mollify the non-Indian contractors who lost their Colorado River water allocations in this agreement through nonuse, the amendments authorized the payment of $9.4 million to help them upgrade their irrigation facilities.[133] And in contrast to earlier administration foot-dragging on implementation of the Ak Chin agreement, the assurances made in the 1984 amendments were actually honored ahead of schedule. Ak Chin Farms received its first delivery of CAP water in June 1987—almost a year before it was promised.[134]

When the Ak Chin agreement began to falter in the early 1980s, history appeared to be repeating itself, insofar as unkept promises to Indians was concerned. But having tied the fortunes of the community to the completion of the CAP—and thus the entire economic future of southern Arizona—the implementation of the 1984 amendments may have proven to be the greatest Indian water-rights settlement success story yet.

However, one important issue remained unresolved from the Indians' point of view. As originally drafted and agreed to by the tribe, the 1984 amendments would have granted the Ak Chin community the same off-reservation sale and use rights as the O'Odham.[135] But the final version of the bill adopted by Congress instead contains language holding that the water shall be "for the exclusive use and benefit of the Ak Chin Indian Community."[136] The executive director of the Ak Chin community believed this last-minute exclusion to be the work of state and local government leaders in Arizona and western congressmen who generally oppose off-reservation sale and use rights.[137] Another amendment to the Ak Chin settlement has since been drafted, however, which would grant the community the same sale and use rights as the O'Odham, and Arizona's congressional delegation (including Congressman Udall's office) has expressed its support for this measure.[138]

The Ak Chin Community was not the only group running into problems of implementation. Several difficulties have arisen with the act intended to settle the groundwater dispute between the San Xavier O'Odham and their Tucson-area neighbors—difficulties so serious that amendments to this legislation will probably also be required if it is ever to be implemented successfully. Problems include a lack of unity within the Tohono O'Odham Nation as to the acceptability of the terms and conditions of the original agreement, limitations on how the Indians can use the water, and serious ambiguities in the damages clause in the original act.

Like many Indian tribes in the American West (and the United States itself, for that matter), the O'Odham are not a tightly organized, hierarchically structured group. At the time the 1982 act was passed, each of the districts constituting the main body of the Tohono O'Odham Nation's reservation as well as the satellite reservations at Gila Bend and San Xavier del Bac were highly autonomous administrative units. As with many other Indian groups, the O'Odham have traditionally perceived themselves as much less homogeneous than their Mexican and Anglo neighbors or the U.S. government did. Some of their outlying districts were actually created because of those communities' desire not to be tied too directly to the government of the main reservation. But in 1986 the tribe adopted a new constitution giving the central tribal government increased authority—the net effect being in some ways to exacerbate rather than to alleviate tensions between tribal units.[139]

To complicate matters further, about 60 percent of the Indians in the San Xavier district are allottees; that is, they hold individual title to their land and the groundwater underlying it instead of those rights being held by the tribal government. Yet when the 1982 settlement act was drafted it was written as an intergovernmental agreement between the United States, state and local governments, and the Papago Tribe. The rights of allottees were subjected to the terms and conditions of the 1982 act[140] but without their explicit individual consent.

Well over 10,000 acres of San Xavier district land is irrigable. Using the "practicably irrigable acreage" criterion, theoretically the San Xavier reservation is entitled to close to 50,000 acre-feet of water per year, depending on how the criterion is applied. However, the 1982 agreement limited the San Xavier district as a whole (including allottees) to the withdrawal of no more than 10,800 acre-feet,[141] or less than a third of the allottees' theoretical PIA entitlement. Consequently, the allottees had not dismissed their groundwater suit against Tucson and their other agri/industrial neighbors as of spring 1990.[142] Thus, the terms and conditions of the agreement have not been fulfilled insofar as action by all tribal members is concerned.

Discord over use of waters is another obstacle. The 1982 act specifies that delivery of water through the Central Arizona Project or by other means to San Xavier lands need only be done if the Indians prepare their land for irrigated agriculture at no cost to the federal government.[143] Although the law elsewhere allows the tribe to use the water for other purposes,[144] forcing them to prepare lands for irrigated agriculture functionally compels them to use some portion of their water in that way. However, as the cost of water has skyrocketed and its availability has diminished, irrigated agriculture has become an increasingly marginal activity in southern Arizona. There are more profitable and far less environmentally damaging alternative uses for water in that region at present, yet the San Xavier O'Odham are statutorily compelled to transform their environment and engage in relatively unprofitable agricultural activities if they want to receive water.

The leadership of the main body of the Tohono O'Odham Nation has indicated a willingness to abide by these terms, but the San Xavier O'Odham are resistant.[145] As of spring 1990, San Xavier and main reservation leaders were trying to come to agreement over proposed language amending the 1982 act to relieve the San Xavier district of the obligation to prepare its land for agriculture.[146] If they can come to agreement, it will probably once again fall to Congressman Udall to guide these settlement amendments through Congress; his office has indicated general approval of changes tribal leaders are now considering.

The O'Odham are not the only parties seeking changes in the law, however. The 1982 act obligates the Interior Department to pay damages to the Indians if CAP or other water is not delivered on time. Yet Interior Department officials point out that any delay in water delivery—and as of 1990 the San Xavier project was far behind schedule—is mostly attributable to dissension between the San Xavier district and the main reservation over where the water should be delivered and how it should be used.[147] As a result, the Interior Department in 1990 was drafting its own amendment to the 1982 act, which would do nothing more than unilaterally relieve the department of its obligation to pay damages for late delivery of water.[148] As of this writing it is unclear which of any of the desired changes being sought by the San Xavier O'Odham, the main reservation O'Odham, or the Interior Department will find their way into law. It is becoming clear that a growing number of parties subject to the original agreement are not pleased with many of its provisions and very much want to see them altered.

The San Xavier O'Odham in particular are equally disturbed about the confusing, ambiguous, and potentially disastrous damages language in the original act. The law says one thing and the Conference Report and implementing contract quite another on the question of what quantum of damages should be paid if waters are not delivered. Should the 1982 act indeed be amended, San Xavier O'Odham are adamant in their view that the original act's language must be amended to conform with the Conference Report and contracts (that is, that damages shall be measured in terms of the replacement cost of the water instead of merely by the interest accrued in the implementation cooperative fund).[149]

LESSONS FROM THE AK CHIN AND O'ODHAM EXPERIENCE

The Indians in both the Ak Chin and Papago settlements traded paper water for wet water. They were willing to forego any groundwater entitlement they might have established and clarified through reserved-rights litigation in return for federal promises to deliver specified quantities of water by alternative means (in these cases, mostly via the CAP). As a consequence, they have also conditionally foregone reliance on the legal process (the federal courts) for reliance on the political process (the Congress) in order to obtain financing for the delivery of that water. Congress must now appropriate whatever funds are necessary to build the Tucson Aqueduct in order to provide the Papago with their CAP allocation. If the CAP is not completed, federal legislators must ensure that the Interior secretary requests, receives, and expends appropriations adequate to provide alternative water supplies to the O'Odham.

Provided that these initial appropriations are made, interest from the $15 million trust fund may supply a large enough annual operations and maintenance budget to sustain irrigated agriculture by the Indians. As a way to insulate tribes from future fluctuations in appropriations, this device has subsequently found its way into 1988 agreements involving the Mission, Pima, and Colorado Ute tribes. Legislators obviously hope such appropriations insurance will allay Indian suspicions that shifting political currents might erode gains made in settlement legislation. The O'Odham settlement act uses the interest-bearing fund concept both in its pure form (the trust fund) and in its hybrid form (the Cooperative Fund—with a floor of $10.5 million in federal and local contributions, which may rise to $16 million or higher if Congress chooses to augment it with additional appropriations). Crucial to the success of such an experiment in this and future legislation is the creation of a fund which generates enough interest to substantially cover the Indians' annual operating costs. Equally important is good fund management by the secretary (or the tribes, if they are so authorized) and good project management by the tribe.

The Ak Chin agreement does not contain such appropriations insurance, but it does have something the O'Odham act does not: more clarity on the subject of damages. One of the most difficult features of agreements such as the Ak Chin and O'Odham for all Indians to accept is that if the federal government fails utterly in its commitments to water delivery, the tribes will accept money damages instead of wet water. If water becomes scarce enough and valuable enough in the western states, this could conceivably amount to an inverse condemnation of the Indians' water right. The federal government could simply pay the damages instead of delivering the water.

In the Ak Chin and O'Odham acts the Indians' primary protection against this eventuality is that damages are keyed to the replacement cost or avoided cost of providing water, that is, the market value of the water at the time of federal default plus the cost of constructing facilities to deliver it, if such construction has not been completed when damages accrue. The tribes' attorney estimates that these costs would be so burdensome to the federal government that any responsible administrator would see the wisdom of delivering the water instead. He credits the damages clause in the Ak Chin settlement act and its implementing contract as the mechanism compelling Secretary Watt to come up with $54 million in federal aid and 75,000 acre-feet of CAP water when the Ak Chin act ran into problems of implementation in 1983.[150] Ambiguity in the Papago act on the question of damages is therefore troubling, although the implementation contract signed in October 1983 may have clarified this issue to some extent. Indeed, Undersecretary Horn acknowledged[151] that the Ak Chin community's ability to apply financial pressure on Interior on the question of damages was a principal reason the administration wanted language on limitation of government liability written into the O'Odham act.[152] The year the Interior Department first defaulted on its deliveries under the Ak Chin agreement—1982— was also the year the Interior secretary's office got involved in negotiations over the final O'Odham agreement.

Trust fund and Cooperative Fund interest may keep the O'Odham from having to go hat-in-hand to the Interior secretary and Congress every year for operations and maintenance money, but the last and most important line of defense for both the Ak Chin and O'Odham people is their ability to exact major, continuing damages from the federal government if it fails to honor its commitments. As a consequence, any feature of an Indian water-rights settlement bargain which threatens or impedes the Indians' ability to collect damages directly threatens or impedes their water rights as well.

The tribes are hoping to exchange paper water for wet water in these bargains; in worst-case situations, they are also agreeing by default to exchange wet water for paper money (damages). In a region of the country where a few unprepared hikers and motorists are still occasionally found dead of thirst, the acceptance of damages instead of water is in itself a major concession. It is hard to express to those who have not experienced desert life the primal attachment which any culture group—but especially a western Indian tribe—feels toward its water resources. Thirsty families, crops, and cattle cannot drink money, and most western tribal members would prefer devoting wet water to some use on their lands to collecting money damages while both they and their land lie idle.[153] The majority of western tribes no doubt will see the potential severance of the reservation/water connection by money damages as concession enough in any bargains they might make. If the federal government continues to insist on some limitations of its liability at a level below the replacement cost of the water it has promised to deliver, then the Indians will have even less incentive than they do now to negotiate comprehensive water-rights settlements.

Recognizing the importance of reliable hydrologic data is another lesson for negotiators in resolving water-rights settlements. Arizona's congressional delegation knew from the outset of the O'Odham groundwater dispute that a significant obstacle to its bargained resolution was the inadequacy of the geohydrologic data base. Litigants could not agree on data for rates of inflow and outflow in the upper Santa Cruz basin or on the rates of consumptive use by the Indians and the defendants. Realizing that the pie could not be divided consensually until everyone had some idea of how large (or small) it was, Congressman Udall and

Senator DeConcini moved to remedy the situation by obtaining authorization for the Army Corps of Engineers to undertake a definitive groundwater survey of the Tucson area.[154] The Papago suit was filed in 1975, and the Corps' Tucson Urban Study was authorized the following year. The Corps had preliminary unpublished findings available for use by negotiators for the upper Santa Cruz basin in 1981—findings which played an important role in apprising the parties of the magnitude of the problem of overdraft and of the degree of responsibility for that problem borne by each category of water user in the basin.

Also in 1981 the Arizona Department of Water Resources began implementation of the state's new groundwater regulation reform act. DWR established a Tucson Active Management Area office in that city and began to assemble its own comprehensive mathematical model of groundwater occurrence and use in the area. Successful implementation of the new groundwater code depends heavily on access to extensive, accurate geohydrologic information since the law mandates that the Tucson Active Management Area balance groundwater withdrawals with the safe yield of the groundwater basins in the area by the year 2025. How forcefully DWR must impose standards of conservation and use limits on Tucson-area groundwater pumpers is directly tied to what its groundwater model and well data reveal about changing overdraft conditions.

The Tucson Active Management Area encompasses roughly the same land mass as the Corps of Engineers' Tucson Urban Study, yet preliminary findings of the state's research published in 1982 painted a gloomier picture of the Tucson area's overdraft problems than had the earlier Corps study: The Corps of Engineers estimated a total overdraft of 175,102 acre-feet in the greater Tucson area (i.e., the Avra-Altar and upper and lower Santa Cruz basins) in 1980,[155] but DWR calculations indicated an overdraft of 238,000 acre-feet in the same area for the same year.[156] Several factors probably contributed to this discrepancy. First, the Corps study was in part predictive (not all 1980 figures were available when the Corps made its projections late that year), and the DWR research was retrospective (it was published more than a year after the requisite data had been obtained). Second, the Corps' access to groundwater-withdrawal data was limited to unverified voluntary contributions of such information by major users, but the later DWR study could benefit from access to information which users had to furnish on request. And third, state groundwater-basin modelers made assumptions regarding irrigation efficiency, rate of return flow from various uses, conservation, and basin recharge capability which differed in some respects from those made by the Corps.[157] The state also had access to a broader array of well data.

Beginning in 1984, all operators of commercial-capacity wells were required by law to report their quarterly withdrawal rates to DWR, so the state's model should become an increasingly accurate representation of the Tucson area's actual groundwater status over time. But the discrepancy between DWR and Corps overdraft figures for 1980 is of more than historical significance. If the overdraft problem is actually more critical than upper Santa Cruz basin negotiators thought it was in 1981 when the O'Odham agreement was first drafted, there may be several unforeseen effects on its future implementation.

For instance, no matter how stringent a standard of water conservation DWR imposes on Tucson water users to compensate for an overdraft emergency, the O'Odham act requires the Interior secretary to impose standards of equal stringency on the Indians, at least insofar as their use of groundwater is concerned. This in turn could drive their project operations and maintenance costs beyond levels which interest from the trust fund and Cooperative Fund could cover if they use groundwater as well as CAP water on their crops. Also, the provisions in the settlement act which set up the Interior secretary as a water banker—allowing him to purchase local private water supplies to satisfy Indian needs if the CAP fails to—are predicated on the assumption that such water will be available. But if southern Arizona's groundwater crisis is worse than previously thought, such alternative water may not be available from willing sellers, as the price of local water skyrockets, agriculture becomes totally unprofitable, and Tucson and the mines try to outbid each other for the remaining supplies. In this scenario, the secretary would then owe the O'Odham damages exceeding anyone's previous estimations.

The purpose of all this doomsaying is to underscore the importance of assembling the best possible data base on which to found negotiations. Without the Corps of Engineers' Tucson Urban Study, it is doubtful that upper basin negotiators could have achieved enough agreement on the facts of their predicament to allow any consensus on how to resolve it. How well the O'Odham act stands the test of time may depend in part on how well the Corps' original study approximated the geohydrologic realities of the Tucson area, which DWR now has the duty to define on a continuing basis.

Another legacy of these settlement negotiations has been the concept of ad hoc regional planning as a bargaining medium. One of the most unique features of the Papago groundwater negotiations was the attempt to build consensus through the planning process. Negotiations were chaired by planners (Corps technical personnel) with no immediate monetary stake in the bargaining outcome.[158] No one entity at the bargaining table had exclusive jurisdiction over the groundwater; state groundwater law did not define the Indian right, but the federal government had no authority to control groundwater management outside the confines of the O'Odham reservations and Davis-Monthan Air Force Base except through reserved-rights litigation.

Each party—the city, the state, the mines, the tribe, and agri-business—was accustomed to doing its own planning to meet its own needs. Negotiation chairmen were able in this instance to convince the parties of the necessity of enlarging their perspective sufficiently to regard the greater Tucson area's entire geohydrologic system as their planning unit.[159] As negotiators attained a more complete understanding of how water used consumptively by one party was lost to all others, the cause-and-effect nature of groundwater use came more clearly into focus. But planning in the absence of authority for implementation can soon become both fruitless and frustrating. Since only Congress had the ultimate constitutional authority to enact an Indian-related agreement and only Congress controlled the fiscal resources necessary to put it into effect, Congress dictated the final terms, and the Water Resources Coordinating Committee (WRCC) was eventually reduced to a purely advisory role. Once the major parties had agreed to the cooperative fund concept demanded by Undersecretary Horn and once the O'Odham agreed to waive all rights other than those outlined in the August 1982 negotiations, the affair was out of their hands.[160]

Is the transcultural, transjurisdictional planning effort which the WRCC represented replicable in Indian water-rights disputes elsewhere in the West? Like so many other features of Indian resource-management policy, the answer probably lies with Congress. WRCC planning may have been supported by its participants because they believed Arizona's congressional delegation could get the national legislature to adopt their suggestions. If would-be planner/negotiators have no confidence that Congress will implement their agreements, negotiation is a waste of time; a hot line to Capitol Hill should be standard equipment at all bargaining tables. Conversely, if Congress has any interest in fostering better Anglo/Indian relations in the western states, it should recognize that basin-wide, intercultural planning for water-resources might provide a useful vehicle for that improvement. A comprehensive water-rights agreement may or may not issue from a shared planning process, but at the very least it would provide an alternative institutional forum for discussing mutual problems of water management. In most of the West right now—with some exceptions—those discussions take place only in court.

CHAPTER SIX

Conclusion:
Improving the Prospects
for Negotiated Settlements

As they did on Manhattan Island three hundred years ago, American Indian tribes today stand at a historic crossroads. Euro-Americans are once again urging them to at least partially relinquish ancient title to a precious resource in return for immediate economic benefits. Because of the great variety of conditions under which negotiations over settlements of Indian water-rights disputes have taken place, it is simply not possible to declare that the tribes are being uniformly cheated out of all but a small portion of their heritage of water and should resist settlement, or conversely, that the deals being offered them now are the best they will be able to achieve and that further recourse to the courts would be strategically and economically inadvisable.

But at the same time, this very lack of consistency in circumstance—and therefore in the bargaining power of the parties and in the content of negotiated settlements—presents serious problems of fairness. Instead of a coherent, coordinated, and evenly applied federal policy of finding means to honor the reasonable claims of Indian tribes, the process of settlement has become a legislative free-for-all, with some tribes achieving markedly better terms of settlement than others.

Tribes fortunate enough to be in the service area of a large-scale water project whose primary purpose is to slake non-Indian thirst, such as the Central Arizona Project, have been able to convert threats to their neighbors' water rights into considerable quantities of delivered water. Yet even within this group of tribes one finds troubling variations in the settlements. The O'Odham, for instance, won off-reservation sale-and-use rights, but the damages language in their settlement is horribly mangled. Meanwhile, the Ak Chin community—less than an hour's drive to the north—cannot under their 1978 settlement or its 1984 amendments sell or use water off-reservation, but their damages protection has proved to be a potent enforcement tool.

The variation is even greater across the settlements elsewhere in the Southwest. The Pima can sell their water, but only to neighboring municipalities and at a fixed price. Agreements such as the Colorado

Utes' hinge on the future construction of a project of highly dubious merit, and their off-reservation use and sale would be subject to state law, implying waiver of all *Winters* doctrine protection for those waters.

The significant problems of equity raised by this situation-specific, haphazard settlement of Indian water-rights claims constitute perhaps the most serious single flaw in the current settlement process. Finding an effective remedy for this situation is one of the principal goals of this chapter.

POLICY OPTIONS FACING THE WESTERN TRIBES

American Indian tribes are now moving by various means to secure in fact the water resources they have previously held in theory. The choices in policy they face have been grouped under three headings for simplicity's sake: Option A (adjudication of rights), Option B (bargained resolution of individual cases), and Option C (comprehensive settlement legislation). In reality, of course, strategy is never this simple. Most of the tribes discussed in this study have been simultaneously adjudicating their rights and discussing possible terms of settlement, although some tribes have been conducting these discussions more openly and actively than others. A smaller number resolutely refuse to discuss water rights with anyone outside the courthouse.

Adjudication of Rights. The dozens of disputes over American Indian water rights now wending their way through state and federal tribunals throughout the western United States have been characterized as representing a "massively destabilizing collection of unresolved claims . . . [which] will, when adjudicated, at least cloud and perhaps eventually preempt many water rights under which non-Indian users have invested untold millions of dollars and on which their lives and livelihoods depend."[1] Little wonder, then, that the tribes are being severely pressured from every quarter to negotiate away their claims.

Until the 1980s, Indian water-rights disputes had been unusually resistant to negotiated settlement, for several reasons. First, the tribes have been largely successful in establishing the seniority of their claims in court. Second, the great majority of instances in which tribal water rights have been surrendered in the negotiation process either by or at the urging of the Interior Department proved in retrospect to be tactical disasters for tribal interests and sowed the seeds of subsequent protracted litigation. Examples include the 1910 Kent Decree, the 1935 Globe Equity Decree, the 1924 Mission Indian case, the recently litigated Orr Ditch Decree, and currently challenged agreements by the Navajo Nation to restrict profoundly its claims to the flow of the Colorado River.

But more recently, the tribes have begun to fare less well in litigation, in no small part because of an increasing orientation toward states' rights in the U.S. Supreme Court. Still, for the majority of tribes whose cases were reviewed in Chapter 3, adjudication of their rights remains the preferred option. Although expensive and time-consuming, the eventual outcomes of such lawsuits may leave the tribes with senior rights to a great deal of water. Even when the Indians have been compelled to litigate their rights in state court, they have so far done relatively well, at least in terms of quantities of water awarded. The most notable recent example is in Wyoming, where the state supreme court quantified tribal rights at a fairly high level, although the court simultaneously denied the Indians jurisdiction over groundwater.

As of 1990 the majority of tribes have preferred to stay in court for at least two reasons. First, they justifiably mistrust the ability and willingness of non-Indian governments to keep promises made in settlement negotiations. The nineteenth-century reservation-creating treaties, early twentieth-century water-rights consent decrees, and waiver and deferral agreements of the 1960s all proved ultimately detrimental to Indian interests, either because promises made were not kept or because the Indians were pressured into agreements clearly not in their best interests, or both. Second, either the threat or the reality of litigation is the Indians' principal source of power. The longer they can keep everyone else's rights in question (and thus forestall continued non-Indian economic development of the West), the better the deal they will be able to make if they eventually do agree to settle.

These two reasons for litigating water rights are also useful ways of differentiating the tribes engaged in litigation: those who are remaining in court on principle and because of well-founded historic mistrust, as distinguished from those who are litigating principally as a means of enhancing their bargaining power. The tribes in the latter group are the ones now most actively engaged in settlement negotiations.[2]

A question of real historic note at this point is whether the tribes in the first group are in the process of changing their minds. Are we in the early stages of a stampede to the bargaining table, in which all tribes will rush to make the best deal they can, and the vast majority of all pending cases will be settled before the turn of the century? Or conversely, is the current flurry of negotiating activity a temporary phenomenon? Has it been stimulated by a handful of relatively generous monetary settlements, and will interest in negotiation falter if federal funding commitments become less generous or are less consistently honored?

This question is important because the last tribes to agree to negotiate may be offered less favorable terms than the ones lining up to make a deal now, irrespective of the merits of their claims. The pie slices may become progressively smaller for the tribes closest to the end of the line, and the latecomers to the negotiation process may end up getting far less water than if they had stayed in court.

Bargained Resolution of Specific Cases. The contemporary settlements and pending agreements discussed in Chapter 4 are strikingly similar in some respects and just as noticeably different in others. The 1978 and 1984 Ak Chin legislation, the 1982 O'Odham settlement, the three 1988 settlement acts (Pima, Mission, Colorado Ute), and two of the three proposed 1989 legislative settlements (Utah Ute, Paiute) all involve making the pie larger (via CAP in Arizona, Animas-La Plata in Colorado, CUP in Utah, and water conservation in California). The federal government and local adversaries of the Indians are promising to spend major amounts of money to augment existing water supplies to address tribal needs and claims.

Another common feature of most of these agreements is a supposedly fail-safe funding mechanism: the use of interest-bearing trust accounts instead of continuing appropriations to finance agreement implementation. In most cases, however, these funds will cover only operations and maintenance costs; major additional appropriations will be needed to construct the projects to deliver the water.

Yet another common feature is the "Indian blanket": tying a water-delivery project for an Indian reservation to a proposed or in-process reclamation project undertaken to benefit non-Indian interests. The Central Arizona Project, Central Utah Project, Colorado's Animas-La Plata, and the proposed water exchange and development plans involving Nevada's Pyramid Lake Paiute are all examples of local interests' trying simultaneously to buy off the Indians and secure funding to develop their own water resources.

From the standpoint of intertribal equity, the differences between these settlements are the most troubling. Some tribes have retained off-reservation sale-and-use rights; others were forced either to severely curtail these rights or to bargain them away entirely. Some tribes (such as the O'Odham) agreed to waive all present and future reserved-rights claims; others did not. Some tribes are specifically empowered to collect money damages; others are not—and for those who are, there is substantial variation in how those damages will be calculated. Finally, some tribes will have vastly greater amounts of money either given to them or spent on their behalf than will others.

How can these variations be explained and accounted for? A great deal can be attributed to the individual political circumstances under which each bargain was struck. And even within this context, there are several variables at play. How strong was the tribe's legal position going into negotiations? How resistant were the tribe's non-Indian neighbors to conceding tribal points such as off-reservation sale-and-use rights? How capable is the congressional delegation within whose jurisdiction the dispute occurred of convincing Congress to authorize projects to deliver Indian water?

The single worst aspect of these ad hoc, case-by-case settlements has been the unequal treatment of the tribes in question. The relative abilities of their legal counsel, their ability (or lack thereof) to finance litigation, the degree to which a powerful member of Congress was willing to champion their cause, and the level of ambient racial tension in a given dispute[3] have all contributed to this inequity.

One political response to this lack of equal protection is "So what? Some tribes have more power than others, just as some cities and states have more power than others. Welcome to western water politics." But this approach completely ignores the fundamental legal and moral principles at stake in these disputes. Imagine, for instance, applying the same rationale of realpolitik to racial segregation—just as we as a nation did for the first half of the twentieth-century. Segregated public education, transportation, and accommodation were a local option; in those jurisdictions where it was thought morally repugnant or where minority populations had sufficient power to prevent it, it did not occur, but in other areas of the country such policies were the law of the land. It was not until the courts provided the principled moral leadership of the *Brown* v. *Board of Education* decision and its progeny, and Congress followed suit ten years later with the 1964 Civil Rights Act, that at least a threshold level of equal protection was guaranteed to minority groups otherwise subject to the whims of provincial social and political prejudice.

Although the parallel to American Indian water rights is not perfect, it is nevertheless apt. If the weakest, poorest tribes are compelled to bargain away fundamental rights that the more sophisticated and affluent ones have been able to protect in negotiations, we as a nation will in fact have replicated the worst features of the history of U.S./Indian relations—crushing the weak and rewarding the strong.

Quite apart from the loss of legal principle in the negotiation shuffle, the durability of contemporary agreements is as yet unproven. The 1978 Ak Chin settlement essentially failed, although the 1984 amendments apparently salvaged it. The 1982 O'Odham settlement act is in so much trouble that every respondent I talked to during the course of this research has acknowledged that if it is not substantially amended it will surely collapse. Further, most of the 1988 and 1989 settlements will require substantial appropriations to deliver water if not to fund operations and maintenance. If those continuing and significant financial obligations are not fully honored legislatively, the Indians will be considerably worse off than if they had never negotiated in the first place. If Congress does not provide the money to implement these settlements, everyone will be returning to court—and eventually perhaps to the bargaining table.

But if a more consistent, equitable, and reliable system of dispute resolution could be fashioned than the policy of ad hoc, case-by-case legislative bail-out we are struggling with now, these serious problems of fairness could be substantially resolved.

Comprehensive Settlement Legislation. At this point, Indian tribes have just as much reason to be leery of comprehensive, nationwide settlement legislation as they do of case-by-case agreements. When the National Water Commission in 1973 recommended that all Indian claims be adjudicated in federal court and that some existing non-Indian rights be terminated for the sake of honoring tribal claims, Congress never even pretended to take those recommendations seriously; none ever became law or even came close.

Other comprehensive settlements advocated by western congressmen hostile to Indian interests would have legislatively eliminated the *Winters* doctrine—wiping out all Indian water-rights claims. Such a prospect has made most tribal advocates reticent to propose comprehensive settlement bills for fear that once they are under consideration, enemies of Indian rights might succeed in legislatively decimating the doctrine the tribes and their allies have worked so assiduously in court to develop and protect.

Receiving little attention so far, however, are legislative proposals which would seek to make the negotiation process itself more fair, would provide environmentally sound means of supplying enough water to honor conflicting and mutually exclusive claims substantially, and would finance these activities in an equitable, reliable manner.

POLICY RECOMMENDATIONS: THE ELEMENTS
OF COMPREHENSIVE SETTLEMENT LEGISLATION

The policy recommendations reviewed here have been developed with three distinct objectives in mind: (1) to enhance the fairness of the negotiation process, (2) to ensure that the federal government will keep its promises to the tribes once they are made, and (3) to honor Indian claims substantially without disenfranchising non-Indian claimants who acquired their water interests in good faith either under state prior-appropriation doctrine or through contract with the U.S. Bureau of Reclamation. If these objectives can be attained, then negotiation could become a much more reliable, effective, and attractive means of settling tribal water-rights disputes than it is at present. Each of these issues is addressed in the hope of demonstrating how the prospects for negotiated settlement of these cases may indeed be measurably improved.

Reform of the Negotiation Process

The tragic and irreconcilable conflict of interest besetting the U.S. Department of the Interior regarding the dilemma of American Indian water rights is one of the best-documented features of what the National Water Commission has dubbed "one of American history's sorriest chapters." The problem has been that the department is charged with two missions which have proved to be wholly incompatible politically. On the one hand, since 1902 (with passage of the Reclamation Act) the Bureau of Reclamation has been ordered to impound and distribute the waters of the West for irrigated agriculture in accordance with state prior-appropriation doctrine; on the other hand, the Bureau of Indian Affairs has been equally responsible since 1908 (with the U.S. Supreme Court's holding in *Winters* v. *U.S.*) for defending the Indians' federally reserved water rights from non-Indian encroachment under state water law.

The department has been much more effective at achieving its former objective than its latter one. In the six decades immediately subsequent to the Reclamation Act's adoption, the Bureau of Reclamation developed and distributed hundreds of millions of acre-feet of water to the farmers and ranchers of the West (at Congress's instruction and with federal tax dollars); during the same period the Bureau of Indian Affairs (in conjunction with the U.S. Attorney's Office) rose to defend the Indians' federally reserved water rights in court only four times. Also during this period, the department negotiated agreements over Indian water-rights settlements with neighboring non-Indian water users against tribal wishes (the four early twentieth-century decrees). Every one of these settlements was an absolute calamity for the tribes and bred later litigation as well as profound mistrust of U.S. government motives and methods. As recently as 1983, tribes attempted (unsuccessfully) to prohibit the Interior secretary and attorney general from purporting to represent their interests in state water-rights proceedings.

It should therefore come as no surprise that the tribes are reluctant now to enter into negotiations sponsored and chaired by the Interior Department over the partial surrender of their water rights. The first of

the contemporary settlements—the Ak Chin and O'Odham agreements—were the result of negotiations in which the Interior Department
did not initially participate. President Reagan cited this lack of participation as his primary reason for vetoing Congress's initial ratification of
the O'Odham agreement. And when the Ak Chin agreement ran into
problems of technical implementation, the Reagan administration refused to ask Congress for additional funds to fulfill the terms of the
settlement. It took the public threat of a lawsuit against the Interior
Department by the Ak Chin Indian community and subsequent amendment of the original legislation to compel the federal executive branch to
honor its side of this agreement.

What most of the contemporary agreements have in common is the
collective expenditure of hundreds of millions of federal tax dollars to
return to tribal lands water resources which the federal government had
earlier neglected to protect from non-Indian appropriation under state
water law. Unfortunately, given the massive deficits now facing congressional budget makers, there is good reason to doubt whether the dozens
of still-outstanding tribal water rights cases will be settled in this
manner; the funds will be extremely difficult to obtain just to honor
agreements already made—much less to fund additional ones.

Despite the growing burden of federal debt occasioned by incidents
such as the savings and loan insurance debacle, if Congress fully funds
present and future negotiated settlements, the following suggestions
may have little appeal and appear to lack political viability. If, on the
other hand, appropriations for present agreements falter and the price
tag on future ones stalls their authorization, features of this structure for
comprehensive settlement may yet be seen as a realistic option. Successful resolution of the Interior Department's conflict-of-interest problems and some means of untying the Gordian knot of acquiring and
paying for adequate water supplies must be achieved.

Some of the information in the preceding chapters may have given
the impression that because the federal bench is becoming less respon-
sive to Indian arguments, legal adversaries of the tribes have less reason
to bargain with them. However, even in state court some tribes have
won huge quantities of water, perhaps more than they would have
settled for in negotiation—the 1989 Shoshone decision in Wyoming
being a relevant case in point. Further, the tribes currently in litigation
can easily keep most of these cases active through the end of the
twentieth century, holding all other affected applications for water rights
in limbo. Thus, strong incentives remain to seek a framework for
negotiation which does a better job of addressing basic concerns of
fairness than current ad hoc processes. If a process of negotiation can be
devised which avoids the conflict-of-interest problems inherent in the

Interior Department's role and if other substantive solutions can be found to the twin problems of acquiring and paying for adequate water supplies, the alternative of negotiation may yet prove to be a more viable and realistic policy.

In order to design a process in which the Interior Department can fully participate but cannot ultimately control, an alternative forum for the conduct of negotiations must be established: Thus the proposal for the creation of an American Indian Water Rights Commission. The proposed commission would be composed of six members: one from the Interior Department, one from the Justice Department's Natural Resources Division, one appointed by the president pro tem of the Senate, one appointed by the Speaker of the House of Representatives, and one tribal leader each from two different geographic regions of the western United States, appointed by the president from a list of nominees submitted by an organization such as the American Indian Congress.

Interior and Justice department participation is necessary because they can provide the greatest technical and legal expertise within the government regarding management of western water resources. Congressional participation is necessary because Congress will eventually have to ratify any agreements achieved through commission activities. American Indian participation is necessary because the tribes cannot be expected to support and participate in a process they do not have a major role in creating.

Potential problems of separation of powers with congressional appointment of commission members (problems of the sort identified by the U.S. Supreme Court in *Buckley* v. *Valeo*[4]) may be obviated since the commission's functions will be mediative rather than adjudicatory in nature. Further, in 1988 the Court has markedly liberalized its views on this issue and somewhat distanced itself from its earlier *Buckley* reasoning with its landmark ruling in *Morrison* v. *Olson*.[5] Because of the potential for Indian members of the commission being overruled by a non-Indian majority, major decisions would have to be subject to the rule that they could not stand if both tribal members objected.

The commission would perform five major functions, collectively intended to make negotiated settlement of disputes over Indian water rights more likely: intergovernmental water-resource planning, acquisition and analysis of data, the drafting and recording of model agreements, the standardization of guidelines and procedures for the negotiation process, and the provision of facilitators and sponsorship of negotiations.

Planning. Water-resource management in the western United States is an extraordinarily interdependent activity; hundreds of different management entities at every level of government are wholly dependent on the decisions of other entities for the successful achievement of their goals. The first major step in the settlement of the Tucson-O'Odham dispute was therefore the self-organization of disputants into an ad hoc regional water-resource planning commission—a function later partly subsumed by Arizona's groundwater-management act.[6] The proposed commission could provide a forum for the coordination of such planning in that any agreements arising from commission-sponsored negotiations would inevitably affect other holders of water rights in any given region.

Data Acquisition and Analysis. In water-rights litigation, the relevant hydrologic data must often be generated at the parties' expense through the discovery process. However, the proposed commission could act as a repository for the best currently available public information on hydrologic conditions in a region under dispute. It could also commission objective, reliable, site-specific studies to facilitate the settlement of disputes characterized either by high levels of disagreement over data or by substantial uncertainty over hydrologic conditions.

Repository for Model Agreements. Organizations such as the American Law Institute have over the last six decades performed an invaluable public service by the promulgation of model legal codes in specialty areas of the law, for possible use in the reform of policy by local jurisdictions lacking the capacity for performing such research themselves. Likewise, the proposed commission could act as an institutional memory for dispute negotiators in search of, inter alia, alternative means of calculating "practicably irrigable acreage," definitions of minimum stream-flow requirements, and present valuation of future resource allocation. In addition to helping negotiators avoid reinventing the wheel whenever such issues arise in resolving specific disputes, the evolution of a model of agreement could begin to establish substantive norms for what constitutes a fair and appropriate settlement.

Standardization of Negotiation Procedure. Procedural norms will be every bit as important as substantive ones if negotiation is to have a long-term future as an option for settling disputes in these cases. Guidelines for the definition of appropriate negotiating behavior, the timing and pacing of procedure, and criteria for the identification of progress (or lack of it) would all help to ensure that the good offices of the commission were being used rather than abused.

Enlistment of Facilitators and Sponsorship of Negotiations. For parties to disputes over American Indian water rights who do decide to explore the negotiation alternative and who have not been successful in doing so on their own, the commission can maintain a directory of experienced and respected intermediaries—as do the American Arbitration Association and the Federal Mediation and Conciliation Service—from which disputants can select a mediator whom they mutually determine to be appropriate to their needs. The commission could also make facilities available for the conduct of negotiations if necessary.

Substantive Suggestions for Honoring Conflicting Claims

In several regions of the United States where major Indian water-rights claims are outstanding (most notably the Southwest), supplies of surface water are already fully appropriated. If adjudicated outcomes of these disputes are attained, some parties will inevitably lose water at the expense of others—a classic zero sum game. Any negotiation-based alternative to an adjudicated resolution will have to provide a superior outcome and without coercive process. Two methods are being experimented with in some of the contemporary settlements: the voluntary reallocation of existing supplies and the conservation-based augmentation of existing supplies.

The first approach involves the Interior secretary acting in the capacity of water banker, purchasing water rights from willing sellers and transferring the rights to neighboring tribes. In order for this approach to be widely used, however, institutions for western-state water-resource allocation will have to become somewhat more receptive to the concept of the market-based allocation of water rights than they are at present. Although the idea has been under serious consideration as a policy alternative in the West for close to two decades,[7] strong political opposition from interests whose water-dependent economic activity is marginal at current prices and might be made unprofitable at higher ones has prevented widespread institutional experimentation with this alternative. To the extent that this practice is more commonly allowed in the future, the federal government may enter the market in that same measure to buy back for the tribes rights which they failed to protect on the tribes' behalf when those rights were first allocated under state law.

Even in the absence of a free market in water rights, the Interior secretary still has enormous latitude in western water-resource management. Modern federal case law, beginning with *Arizona* v. *California* in 1963, and the 1968 legislation authorizing the Central Arizona Project grant the secretary remarkably broad discretion in the operation of reclamation facilities for water and power distribution and also in the making and modification of contractual agreements for that distribution. Much to the consternation of the state of Arizona, in the early 1980s the Interior Department began to exercise this contractual discretion against irrigators along the lower Colorado River who either did not take delivery on waters contracted for or did not use those resources appropriately. The department then moved to use this legally reclaimed water to begin fulfilling tribal water needs within Arizona.

As a result of recent amendments to the Reclamation Act, maturing contracts for the delivery of water from federal reclamation projects are also being renegotiated at prices which more accurately reflect the true costs of impounding and delivering that water. Since about eighty-five percent of the water in much of the American West is used for irrigated agriculture and much of that agricultural activity (especially the growing of livestock feed) may become unprofitable if water prices begin to reflect the true cost of its delivery, a good deal of that water may soon become available for contractual dedication to other purposes. Political ramifications aside, the Interior secretary has no shortage of discretionary legal authority to begin reassigning to the tribes water resources made available by defaulted contracts or to grant them waters made available when new contract prices are unattractive to traditional users.

Another means of providing water is conservation-based augmentation of existing supplies. Making the pie larger is a time-honored approach to the political resolution of disputes over resource allocation when the additional resources are available. This method has evidently been used with some success in reaching accommodation with the Ak Chin community, the San Xavier O'Odham, the Ute Indians of southwestern Colorado, the Salt River–Maricopa Pima in central Arizona, and the Mission Indians in southern California.

There is no small degree of political irony in current efforts to secure federal appropriations for Indian water projects. For most of the twentieth-century, boosters of water projects in their headlong rush to develop the waters of the West all but ignored the reserved-rights claims of Indian tribes. But now that major new federal reclamation-project funding has slowed to a trickle, the reclamation lobby has suddenly developed a fervent dedication to the equitable treatment of the tribes.

More than one respondent to research I have conducted on settlements of tribal water-rights disputes has observed that the Tucson-O'Odham groundwater settlement act was probably crafted in the form that it took as a means of morally obligating Congress to fund completion of the Central Arizona Project. For Congress to deny appropriations sufficient to carry water up the Santa Cruz valley to Tucson would have meant also denying the San Xavier Reservation means of replacing the groundwater the city of Tucson was rapidly withdrawing from beneath Indian lands without permission or compensation.

But the rising tide of federal red ink facing every Congress through the end of this century will make the widespread use of this approach difficult in the future. Even the Tohono O'Odham and Ute agreements, as well as the Mission and Pima settlement acts, called for unprecedented levels of local and state financial contributions to the development of projects which in years gone by would have been funded totally by the federal government. And just as the Bureau of Reclamation has begun to preoccupy itself less with the planning of massive new projects and more with improving the operating efficiency of those already built, so too might this increasing interest in conservation partially begin to address the problem of finding new water supplies for the reservations in overappropriated areas without disenfranchising existing holders of water rights.

In the early 1980s, economist Zach Willey performed a thorough and intriguing analysis of water demand and supply in southern California and concluded that the giant, wealthy Metropolitan Water District could theoretically develop new supplies by financing the renovation of the Imperial Valley Irrigation District's eighty-year-old delivery system with state-of-the-art conservation technology. In return, the water salvaged could then be used to help meet MWD's ever-growing needs.[8] When municipal and agribusiness interests in southern California refused to support settlement legislation calling for allocations to the Mission Indians from the already fully committed Central Valley Project, the compromise position eventually enacted into law was drawn directly from Willey's analysis.[9] The act calls for locally financed conservation retrofitting of the All American Canal, with the water thus conserved devoted to Indian needs.[10]

Similarly, policy analysts for the Bureau of Reclamation, the Soil Conservation Service, and the Environmental Protection Agency have jointly concluded that major water savings in all regions of the country served by the reclamation program could be effected through conservation techniques.[11] In the arid region of the country defined in their 1979 report as the Southwestern irrigation characterization area (California's central valley and southern desert, the southern thirds of Arizona and New Mexico, and the southwestern rim of Texas along its border with Mexico),[12] analysts determined that total net depletions for irrigated agriculture (gross diversions minus return flow) could be reduced by a total of 3.1 million acre-feet per year if an aggressive program of conservation-oriented retrofitting of all facilities for existing distribution, application, and return flow were to be completed.[13] The report recommended off-farm conservation measures such as impervious linings of canals and laterals, piped conveyance systems, consolidation and/or realignment of delivery systems, improved accuracy of water measurement, inline water measurement and regulation structures, automation of regulating structures, better maintenance of facilities, better programs of weed control, better conveyance design, and more precisely scheduled water deliveries.[14] On-farm measures included ditch lining and piping, land leveling, improved structures for water control, devices for flow measurement, automated irrigation systems, and tailwater recovery systems.

Although many of these practices and techniques are commonplace in other arid regions of the world where water is at even more of a premium than in the American Southwest and although some of these measures are indeed already being undertaken here to a limited degree, such methods are not fully implemented here because of a relative lack of incentive to do so and of capital to undertake these admittedly expensive improvements. In the interagency report, the estimate for achieving the 3.1 million-acre-feet (maf.) reduction in net depletion in the Southwestern region was $6.1 billion in 1977 dollars.

Over the life of the renovated facilities, however, this figure may still begin to look like a sound investment. Ignoring for simplicity's sake both the possible future value of the funds invested and the water saved, the cost of the salvaged water may be calculated thus: Assuming that the work took place over a thirty-year period, the cost per year would be about $20.3 million. Assuming also that a 1/30 additional increment of the 3.1 maf. became available for each year that the retrofitting was done, the total water salvaged during the construction period would average 1.55 maf. per year (1/2 × 3.1 maf.), or 46.5 maf. for the thirty-year construction period. Finally, assuming at least thirty additional years of operation subsequent to renovation, water salvage of 3.1 maf. per year × 30 years yields additional water savings of 93 maf.; this added to the 46.5 maf. saved during construction totals 149.5 million acre-feet of water saved over the life of the renovated facilities. Dividing this figure into the $6.1 billion total price tag on conservation upgrading results in a cost of just under $41 per acre-foot of water saved (in 1977 dollars)—certainly well within present and future limits for the going rate for an acre-foot of irrigation-quality water.

An additional 3.1 million acre-feet of irrigation water would probably not totally satisfy the outstanding reserved-rights claims of the tribes in the American Southwest. Some observers have calculated that if the huge Navajo Nation is successful in nullifying the disastrous agreements under which it consented to limit its annual upper Colorado River withdrawals to 50,000 acre-feet for the next fifty years in return for energy-project development, it could probably legitimately lay claim to about 2 million acre-feet.[15]

But in combination with the "water banker" activities of the Interior secretary suggested above, using aggressive conservation measures throughout the Southwest and devoting the conserved water to the satisfaction of Indian claims could go a long way toward achieving the negotiated resolution of these disputes. Still unresolved at this point, though, is how all of this conservation retrofitting and water banking will be financed.

The nineteenth-century history of the United States is littered with the debris of treaties made between tribes and the U.S. government, in which the tribes relinquished land in return for promises made by a sitting session of Congress, promises that future sessions neglected to appropriate the funds to honor. More recent scholarship[16] has shown that at least through the mid-1970s the situation has changed little with regard to agreements made over water resources. A Congress so saddled with debt that it will have great difficulty in funding major new reclamation projects will also be hard-pressed to consistently come up with the funds to satisfy Indian claims through water banking and retrofitting.

Realizing this, in settling the groundwater dispute between the city of Tucson and the O'Odham reservations, Tucson-area Congressman Morris Udall wrote into the groundwater settlement act a provision establishing a one-time appropriation for the creation of a cooperative fund, the proceeds from which would go to finance the use of CAP water on the San Xavier Reservation. This device has been used in almost every major contemporary settlement since that time.

On a considerably larger scale, such a mechanism could also be used to finance the activities of the proposed American Indian Water Rights Commission, the water-banking activities of the Interior secretary, and at least some of the conservation retrofitting of on- and off-farm reclamation facilities in the West. The trust fund would be established not by a one-time appropriation but by a time-limited surcharge on the sale of water and power from federal facilities in the reclamation states.

The total income accruing to the Bureau of Reclamation from such sales in 1982 was in excess of $20 million;[17] in 1986 it was $731.7 million;[18] and in 1987 it was $799.6 million.[19] This dramatic rise in income in recent years appears attributable to the renegotiation of water-delivery contracts (up almost $10 million from 1986 to 1987 alone), a $4 million increase in water sales to municipalities in the same one-year period, and a huge increase (up over $50 million from 1986 to 1987) in power sales. Thus for the foreseeable future water and power sales from Bureau of Reclamation facilities will average well in excess of $800 million per year. A five-percent surcharge imposed on such sales for a period of ten years would generate an American Indian Water Resources Trust Fund of $400 million, which during the period of its establishment—assuming a ten percent annual yield—would also accumulate another $20 million in interest. At the end of the ten-year period, the politically unpopular surcharge would be dropped; and the commission, the Interior secretary's water banking, and conservation-oriented retrofitting would be funded out of the trust fund's $42 million annual yield.

Although such a suggestion will assuredly provoke a hostile reaction from some political leaders and citizens in the states where it would be implemented, many of those same states are already expending significant public resources in complex and expensive litigation against the tribes and the federal government over reserved water rights; the majority of such cases now inching their way through state and federal courtrooms throughout the West will probably extend well into the next century. Furthermore, these states stand to lose significant quantities of water should the tribes prevail. In nearly all of these cases, it is not a matter of whether the states will lose water to the Indians, but of how much. Finally, these same states for most of this century have been enjoying the benefits of turning to highly profitable use the water that all along was in some measure the Indians'.

EPILOGUE

One of Webster's definitions of *epilogue* is "a short concluding section at the end of a literary work, often discussing the future of its characters."[20] Although this policy study may not be highly literary, it certainly has its share of characters: Indians, soldiers, judges, lawyers, bureaucrats, presidents, and politicians of every stripe. The cast also includes every water user in the West whose rights are affected by Indian claims. And in a sense the entire second half of this study is an attempt to deal with their future, since the way we manage our water resources—including the settlement of disputes over how we manage those resources—will be an important determinant of what lies ahead for the western United States.

In their revealing cross-cultural study of water-resource management in agricultural enclaves, Maass and Anderson[21] point out that efficient, effective settlement of disputes is an integral element of successful irrigated agriculture everywhere they had occasion to study it. Individual prosperity in these situations is contingent on cooperative relations with one's neighboring water users. This may hold true for culturally and economically homogeneous social units, but it certainly does not describe the larger picture of water use currently in the western United States. States are suing each other and the federal government; various interest groups are suing each other, the states, and the federal government; and the Indians appear to be suing everybody. We are transmitting to the next generation a legacy in which the costs of building and maintaining our massive facilities for water management seem rivaled by the costs of fighting over how the waters will be divided.

But the public has grown weary of financing another colossus in the desert every year, and water-management bureaucrats are beginning to pay more attention to increasing the efficiency of systems than to the planning, funding, and building of new ones.[22] Perhaps the same attention will someday be devoted to the way we manage disputes over the management of water. If this does happen it will probably be mostly for the same reason: efficiency. The current interest in nonlitigated settlement of disputes, reflected in some of the literature cited in this study, is to a certain extent predicated on the belief that "delegalizing" American dispute settlement will lead to similar or better outcomes at lower costs. However, arguments of efficiency are most convincing when the debate is between parties with similar economic perspectives. Most Indians don't care much about efficient dispute settlement; they care a lot about water. The farmers in Maass and Anderson's study must cooperate in order to survive economically; protracted squabbling decreases efficiency and ultimately threatens survival.

Conversely, many American Indian tribes feel that at this juncture conflict (water-rights litigation) and not cooperation is the key to their survival as cultural and national entities. The survival instinct in the arid West is not drawing Indian and non-Indian peoples together; it is driving them apart. Until the Euro-American culture can convincingly demonstrate the ability of cooperative effort to ensure the survival of all peoples in the West, the Indians will have no reason to make peace.

The often-heard lamentation over the absence of a free lunch is certainly nowhere more applicable than to the dilemma over American Indian water rights. The debt to the tribes incurred and ignored by our fathers must be paid, either by us or by our children. That payment may be in the form of lost water, as the doctrine of federal reserved rights inevitably makes preemptive inroads into state water law, and in the form of support for the battalions of water lawyers who so far appear to be the only definitive winners in this process.

That debt payment is now also taking the form of expensive new reclamation projects designed primarily to serve non-Indian interests but which concomitantly replace some of the reserved waters the federal government failed to set aside for Indian tribes earlier in this century. To the extent Congress remains willing to purchase ever more costly water projects wrapped in Indian blankets, this policy may continue to gain popularity. But if the powerful congressional leaders responsible for enacting the contemporary settlements were to leave Congress, or if we as a nation fail to resolve our governmental indebtedness and problems with balance of trade, continued reclamation-project bailouts of local disputes over Indian water rights may not turn out to be a long-term solution to the problem. If Congress does not continue to fund these authorized projects, the Indians will go straight back to court.

However, the payment of this moral and legal indebtedness to the tribes might take the form of a temporary use-based surcharge on western water and power consumption (which would itself induce some conservation), the proceeds going both to pay an old debt and to protect our progeny from having to suffer the consequences of its continued "ignore-ance." We are passing enough social and environmental problems along to our children as it is; we should not have to bequeath them the dilemma over American Indian water rights as well. We have been playing this particular glass bead game in courtrooms and lopsided bargaining situations throughout the West since the turn of the century. Perhaps it is time for the game to end.

For over eight decades now American society has had the moral satisfaction of knowing the Supreme Court in *Winters* v. *U.S.* did the right thing in protecting Indian water rights in theory; but we have not taken the fiscal responsibility for acknowledging those rights in fact. With the current onslaught of litigation over reserved water rights, the debt has come due. And in one coin or another, it must be paid.

NOTES

CHAPTER 1. REFLECTIONS IN A GLASS BEAD

1. H. and B. Van Der Zee, *A Sweet and Alien Land—The Story of Dutch New York* (New York: Viking Press, 1978), p. 2.
2. O. Rink, *Holland on the Hudson* (Ithaca, N.Y.: Cornell University Press, 1986), p. 87.
3. Ibid.
4. Manhattan Company, *Manna-Hatin: The Story of New York* (New York: I. J. Friedman, 1929), p. 19.
5. The Spanish, of course, were already busily undertaking similar activities in Central and South America.
6. Herman Hesse, *Magister Ludi (The Glass Bead Game)* (New York: Holt, Rinehart, and Winston, 1969).
7. For a detailed examination of the role played both by elitism and the "iron triangle" phenomenon, see generally M. Reisner, *Cadillac Desert* (New York: Viking, 1986); P. Fradkin, *A River No More—The Colorado River and the West* (New York: Knopf, 1981); and D. McCool, *Command of the Waters* (Berkeley: University of California Press, 1988).
8. For a thoughtful discussion of the influence of anticipated judicial decision making on the negotiated settlement of lawsuits, see Mnookin and Kornhauser, "Bargaining in the Shadow of the Law—The Case of Divorce," 88 *Yale Law Journal* 950 (1979).

CHAPTER 2. THE DEVELOPMENT OF AMERICAN
INDIAN WATER RIGHTS

1. 207 U.S. 564, 28 S.Ct. 207, 52 L.Ed. 340 (1908).
2. J. Folk-Williams, *What Indian Water Means to the West: A Sourcebook* (Santa Fe, N.Mex.: Western Network, 1982), pp. 30–31.
3. Ibid., pp. 3–12.
4. Schmidt, "Meeting in Capitol Today Will Focus on Tribal Water Claims," *New York Times*, Dec. 8, 1982, p. 9, col. 1.
5. See nn. 33–35 and accompanying text.
6. Schmidt, "Meeting in Capitol."
7. Haggling over who was responsible for the original European discovery of the Americas seems destined to continue. A fall 1982 session of the U.N. General Assembly became deadlocked over a proposed resolution commemorating the discovery, owing to a dispute among the Irish, Nordic, Italian, and Hispanic delegations; several African delegates refused to support the measure in any form, viewing it as an obnoxious tribute to the history of colonial exploitation. "The U.N. Holds a 'Historic' Debate," *Newsweek*, Dec. 13, 1982, p. 49.

8. A. Kehoe, *North American Indians—A Comprehensive Account* (Englewood Cliffs, N.J.: Prentice-Hall, 1981), pp. 4–5.

9. D. Snow, *The Archeology of North America* (1976), pp. 20–23.

10. Forbis, "The Paleoamericans," in *North America*, ed. S. Gorenstein (New York: St. Martin's Press, 1975), pp. 17–35.

11. Snow, *Archeology of North America*, p. 29.

12. Masse, "Prehistoric Irrigation in the Salt River Valley, Arizona," 214 *Science* 408 (1981).

13. Ibid., pp. 413–14.

14. J. Jennings, *Pre-History of North America* (New York: McGraw-Hill, 1968), pp. 258–59.

15. Ibid., p. 264.

16. E. Spicer, *Cycles of Conquest* (Tucson: University of Arizona Press, 1962), p. 119.

17. Jennings, *Pre-History of North America*, p. 258.

18. Ibid., pp. 264–81.

19. P. Fradkin, *A River No More—The Colorado River and the West* (New York: Knopf, 1981), pp. 18–21.

20. Betancourt and Van Devender, "Holocene Vegetation in Chaco Canyon, New Mexico," 214 *Science* 656 (1981).

21. Jennings, *Pre-History of North America*, pp. 264–81.

22. Snow, *Archeology of North America*, p. 7. A recent authoritative summary of Indian population estimates at the beginning of continuous European colonization cites a range from "850,000 up to more than a million." E. Spicer, *The American Indians* (Cambridge, Mass.: Belknap/Harvard University Press, 1980), p. 2.

23. E. Spicer, *A Short History of the Indians of the United States* (New York: Van Nostrand, 1960), p. 11.

24. Ibid.

25. V. Holmes, *A History of the Americas* (1950), p. 311.

26. Spicer, *Short History of the Indians*, p. 28.

27. Ibid., pp. 16, 22.

28. S. Tyler, *A History of Indian Policy* (Washington, D.C.: Government Printing Office, 1973), p. 29.

29. F. Prucha, *Indian Policy in the Formative Years* (Cambridge, Mass.: Harvard University Press, 1962), pp. 32–33.

30. W. Washburn, *Red Man's Land—White Man's Law* (1971), p. 52.

31. Ibid., p. 54.

32. Tyler, *History of Indian Policy*, pp. 34–35, 313.

33. U.S., *Constitution*, Art. 6, cl. 2.

34. U.S., *Constitution*, Art. 2, sec. 2, cl. 2.

35. U.S., *Constitution*, Art. 1, sec. 8, cl. 3.

36. M. Young, *Redskins, Ruffleshirts, and Rednecks* (1961), p. 5.

37. Georgia Cession, April 26, 1802, in 1 American State Papers, Public Lands 125 (1832).

38. Ibid.; reprinted in Tyler, *History of Indian Policy*, p. 56.

39. Spicer, *Short History of the Indians*, pp. 54–56.

40. Tyler, *History of Indian Policy*, p. 48.

41. P. Gates, *The Farmer's Age* (New York: Holt, Rinehart, & Wilson, 1960), pp. 52–53.

42. Young, *Redskins*, p. 5.

43. Prucha, *Indian Policy*, pp. 238-44.

44. Ibid.

45. Burke, "The Cherokee Cases: A Study in Law, Politics, and Morality," 21 *Stanford Law Review* 500, 505-7 (1969).

46. Young, *Redskins*, pp. 13-14.

47. D. Getches, D. Rosenfelt, and C. Wilkinson, *Federal Indian Law* (St. Paul, Minn.: West Publishing Co., 1979), p. 158.

48. *Johnson and Graham's Leasee v. William McIntosh*, 21 U.S. (8 Wheat.) 543, 5 L.Ed. 681 (1823).

49. Ibid., p. 587.

50. 30 U.S. (5 Pet.) 1, 8 L. Ed. 25 (1831).

51. Ibid., p. 17.

52. Burke, "Cherokee Cases," p. 519.

53. The Supreme Court disclaimed jurisdiction by rejecting the Cherokees' assertion of their status as a "foreign state" under Article 3, sec. 2 of the Constitution. But the following year, Justice Marshall would find that the Court did have jurisdiction under the same article in *Worcester v. Georgia* (31 U.S. [6 Pet.] 515, 8 L.Ed. 483 [1832]), once he had defined the Indian reservation as a federal protectorate. Burke, "Cherokee Cases," pp. 519-24.

54. Ibid.

55. *Worcester v. Georgia* (1832).

56. See map in Tyler, *History of Indian Policy*, p. 60; also Spicer, *Short History of the Indians*, pp. 66-82. For a more charitable account of the Jacksonian determination to acquire southeastern Indian lands, see Prucha, "Andrew Jackson's Indian Policy: A Reassessment," 56 *American History* 527 (1969).

57. Washburn, *Red Man's Land*, pp. 70-74.

58. Tyler, *History of Indian Policy*, p. 74.

59. Spicer, *Short History of the Indians*, pp. 66-97.

60. Such as the Bear Springs Treaty of 1864; Spicer, *Short History of the Indians*, p. 94.

61. Spicer, *Cycles of Conquest*, p. 249. The fate of the Navajo and the Apache during the early reservation period is thoroughly described, pp. 210-61.

62. Act of Mar. 3, 1871, 16 Stat. 566 (1871).

63. For a case study of the postwar politics of natural resources and the national policies which resulted, see Ellison, "The Mineral Lands Question in California, 1848-1866," in *The Public Lands—Studies in the History of the Public Domain*, ed. V. Carstensen (1963), p. 71; also P. Gates, *The History of Public Land Law Development* (Washington, D.C.: Zenger Publishing Co., 1968), pp. 387-462.

64. As in the first post-Civil War mining laws, Act of July 26, 1866, 14 Stat. 251, *as amended*, 16 Stat. 217 (1870); and the Desert Land Act of 1877, 19 Stat. 377 (1877) *as amended* (codified at 43 USCS 321 [1976]).

65. For an articulation of this view, see Shrago, "Emerging Indian Water Rights: An Analysis of Recent Judicial and Legislative Developments," 26 *Rocky Mountain Mineral Law Institute* 1105, 1106 (1980).

66. 24 Stat. 388 (1887).

67. The federal government had briefly experimented with allotment as a compromise for dislodging the "civilized tribes" of the South from most of their traditional lands in the 1820s and 30s. However, in some of these agreements the allotted lands went only to tribal leaders who signed the treaties, giving the appearance that the allotments were in fact bribes. See, generally, Young, *Redskins*.

68. Tyler, *History of Indian Policy,* pp. 95–124.

69. W. Canby, *American Indian Law in a Nutshell* (St. Paul, Minn.: West Publishing Co., 1981), p. 21. Mr. Canby is a judge on the U.S. Court of Appeals for the 9th Circuit.

70. A detailed account of events resulting in the *Winters* decision is in Hundley, "The Winters Decision and Indian Water Rights: A Mystery Reexamined," 13 *Western Historical Quarterly* 17 (1982).

71. 25 Stat. 113 (1889).

72. Unfortunately, during his second term President Roosevelt also tried to incorporate parts of several western Indian reservations (about 2.5 million acres) into the national forest reserves without tribal consent. His action was subsequently invalidated as exceeding executive discretion, and the lands were returned. Tyler, *History of Indian Policy,* p. 105.

73. R. Clark, ed., *Waters and Water Rights,* 1 (Indianapolis: A. Smith & Co., 1967 and 1978), Sec. 50 et seq.

74. Ibid.

75. Hundley, "The Winters Decision," p. 24.

76. *U.S.* v. *Mose Anderson et al:* Memorandum Order (9th Cir. 1906).

77. *Winters et al* v. *U.S.,* 143 F. 743, 749 (9th Cir. 1906).

78. Ibid., p. 747.

79. *Storey* v. *Wolverton,* 78 P. 590 (Mont. 1904).

80. 207 U.S. 564, 28 S.Ct. 207, 52 L.Ed. 340 (1908).

81. See Hundley, "The Winters Decision," for a discussion of this important point.

82. A more detailed summary of the findings in *Winters* and their implications is in P. Maxfield, M. Dietrich, and F. Trelease, *Natural Resources Law on American Indian Lands* (1977), pp. 207–38.

83. 31 U.S. (6 Pet.) at 582 (M'Lean, J., concurring).

84. 198 U.S. 371, 25 S.Ct. 662, 49 L.Ed. 1089 (1905). A discussion of the present-day implications of the broad reserved-rights doctrine first spelled out in *Winans* is in Pelcyger, "The Winters Doctrine and the Greening of the Reservations," 4 *Journal of Contemporary Law* 19 (1977).

85. Clark, *Waters and Water Rights,* 2, sec. 110.1.

86. Act of June 17, 1902, 32 Stat. 388, 43 USCS 372 et seq. (1976).

87. Clark, *Waters and Water Rights,* 2, sec. 110.2.

88. Folk-Williams, *What Indian Water Means,* pp. 36–39. Some reservation reclamation projects were built during this early period, but their management by the federal government gave rise to questions about who was actually deriving the greatest benefits: the tribes or their non-Indian neighbors who leased the water at federally set bargain rates. See *Review of Conditions of the Indians of the United States: Hearings Before the Committee on Indian Affairs,* 71st Cong., 2d sess., 1930, U.S. Senate, S. Res. 78 and 308. This is the "Preston-Engle Report," cited in Tyler, *History of Indian Policy,* p. 114, n. 16; and in Spicer, *Short History of the Indians.*

89. Act of June 17, 1902, sec. 8, 32 Stat. 390.

90. For a more detailed summary of the historic conflicts in the Interior Department over Indian versus non-Indian access to water resources, see Folk-Williams, *What Indian Water Means,* pp. 7–8.

91. *Skeem* v. *U.S.,* 273 F. 93 (9th Cir. 1921).

92. The basin states had good reason to be nervous. In January 1922 the Supreme Court had based its holding in a water-rights dispute between

Colorado and Wyoming (259 U.S. 419) on strict prior-appropriation doctrine. See Meyers, "The Colorado River," 19 *Stanford Law Review* 1 (1966), p. 11, n. 62.

93. Arizona, California, Colorado, Nevada, New Mexico, Utah, and Wyoming.

94. N. Hundley, *Water and the West* (Berkeley: University of California Press, 1975), p. 80.

95. Subsequent complications with even this general agreement arose when it was discovered that the estimated average annual flow used in apportioning the Colorado River was erroneously high. See Weatherford and Jacoby, "Impact of Energy Development on the Law of the Colorado River," 15 *Natural Resources Journal* 171, 183, Table 1 (1975).

96. It relented in 1944. D. McCool, "Indian Water Rights, the Central Arizona Project, and Water Policy in the Lower Colorado River Basin," 2 *Journal of Energy Law and Policy* 107 (1981); Meyers, "The Colorado River," p. 12.

97. The Colorado River Compact, 70 Cong. Rec. 324 (1928); ratified as the Boulder Canyon Project Act, 43 USCS 617(1) (1976).

98. A case which closely paralleled *Winters* in the 9th Circuit, Conrad Investment Co. v. U.S., 161 F. 829 (1908), interpreted the same 1888 agreement as applied to other tribes. It set aside a fixed amount of water but left the decree open to expansion as Indian needs increased.

99. Colorado River Compact, p. 325.

100. Hundley, *Water and the West*, pp. 211–12.

101. L. Merriam, ed., *The Problem of Indian Administration* (Baltimore: Johns Hopkins Press, 1928), more commonly remembered as "The Merriam Report."

102. 48 Stat. 984, 25 USCS 461 et seq. (1976).

103. This effectively impeded the developing checkerboard pattern of private non-Indian land ownership within reservation borders. Canby, *American Indian Law*, pp. 22–23.

104. Tyler, *History of Indian Policy*, p. 129.

105. Canby, *American Indian Law*.

106. 104 F.2d 234 (9th Cir. 1939).

107. 305 U.S. 527, 59 S.Ct. 344, 83 L.Ed. 330 (1939).

108. Ibid., p. 533.

109. Statement of U.S. Senator Arthur Watkins (R., Utah), Chair, Senate Subcommittee on Indian Affairs, 1952; reprinted in Getches et al., *Federal Indian Law*, p. 90.

110. 43 USCS 666 (1976).

111. Unlike a private dispute over water quantity or quality between two parties, a *general stream adjudication* under a state prior-appropriation system is a consolidated action mandated by statute, in which all appropriators in a given watershed are called upon to come forth in an administrative or judicial proceeding with proof of their date of appropriation and subsequent use of a specific quantity of water for a specified beneficial use or uses. The intent of such a consolidated action is to avoid the endless private litigation of rights on a stream among various users. Clark, *Water and Water Rights*, 1.

112. See 1 *Environmental Law Reporter* 50031 for more detail on these cases.

113. Exec. Order No. 10426 (1953).

114. 43 USCS 1301–1305 (1976).

115. Ibid., 1331 et seq.

116. H. Con. Res. 108, 83d Cong., 1st sess., 67 Stat. B-132 (1953).

117. For a discussion of the intent, content, and impact of this policy, see

Wilkinson and Biggs, "The Evolution of the Termination Policy," 5 *American Indian Law Review* 139 (1977).

118. Ibid., pp. 151-54.

119. Pub. L. 83-280, 67 Stat. 588 (1953) (codified as amended in scattered sections of 18, 25, and 28 USCS) (1976).

120. 236 F.2d 321 (9th Cir. 1956).

121. *Cert. denied* 352 U.S. 988 (1957).

122. E.g., McCool, "Indian Water Rights"; Price and Weatherford, "Indian Water Rights in Theory and Practice: Navajo Experience in the Colorado River Basin," 40; *Law and Contemporary Problems* 97 (1976).

123. The colorful history of the Arizona-California water wars, in and out of court, is reviewed in Hundley, *Water and the West*, and Meyers, "The Colorado River," p. 37, n. 162.

124. 373 U.S. 546, 83 S.Ct. 1468, 10 L.Ed. 2d 542 (1963).

125. See Shrago, "Emerging Indian Water Rights," 1114, n. 36.

126. This distributive criterion had been suggested in the findings of the Special Master, whose report formed the basis of (and in some areas, the points of departure for) the Supreme Court's decision. Rifkind, *Report of the Special Master, Arizona v. California* (1960), pp. 54, 265. Referenced in full in Arizona v. California, 373 U.S. 546 (1963).

127. 82 Stat. 77, 25 USCS 1301 et seq. (1976).

128. E.g., Menominee Restoration Act, Pub. L. 93-197, 87 Stat. 770, 25 USCS 903 (1976).

129. The Upper Colorado River Basin Compact, ratified as Act of April 6, 1949, 63 Stat. 31.

130. Fradkin, *"A River No More,"* p. 167.

131. Price and Weatherford, "Indian Water Rights in Theory and Practice," p. 97.

132. Navajo Tribal Council, Resolution No. CD 86-57, cited in Price and Weatherford, p. 122, n. 99.

133. Act of June 13, 1962, Pub. L. 87-483, 76 Stat. 96, *as amended*, 43 USCS 615 et seq. (1976).

134. Statement of Charles Corke, in *Hearings on H.R. 17619 Before a Subcomm. of the Senate Comm. on Appropriations*, 91st Cong., 2d sess. 2021 (1970).

135. *Navajo Indian Irrigation—Water Entitlement of Navajo Tribe*, memorandum from David E. Lindgren, deputy solicitor, to John C. Whittaker, undersecretary of the Interior, Dec. 6, 1974; cited in Price and Weatherford, p. 98.

136. *State of New Mexico ex rel. State Engineer v. U.S.*, Civ. No. 75-184 (D.N.M., filed Mar. 13, 1975).

137. Folk-Williams, *What Indian Water Means*, p. 72.

138. Fradkin, *A River No More*, p. 173.

139. C. Wilkinson, *American Indians, Time, and the Law* (New Haven, Conn.: Yale University Press, 1987), p. 24.

140. See, generally, P. Gates, *History of Public Land Law Development*. This evolutionary perspective on the history of public-lands policy is also set forth in Clawson, "The Federal Land Policy and Management Act of 1976 in a Broad Historical Perspective," 21 *Arizona Law Review* 585, 587-91 (1979).

141. Tyler, *History of Indian Policy*.

142. New Deal legislation seeking to restrict the flow of commodities into the marketplace and the landmark Supreme Court decisions it triggered are

discussed in G. Robinson, E. Gellhorn, and E. Bruff, *The Administrative Process* (St. Paul, Minn.: West Publishing Co., 1986), pp. 54–60.

143. For a brief discussion of two early twentieth-century federal trial-court decisions in which the *Winters* doctrine was not favorably viewed—*U.S.* v. *Wrightman*, 230 Fed. 277 (D. Ariz. 1916), and *U.S.* v. *Walker River Irrigation Dist.,* 14 F. Supp. (D. Nev. 1936)—see D. McCool, *Command of the Waters* (Berkeley: University of California Press, 1987), p. 118.

144. From 1955 to 1979, western congressmen submitted over fifty bills for the termination or diminution of Indian reserved water rights. See Morreale, "Federal-State Conflicts Over Western Waters—A Decade of Attempted 'Clarifying Legislation,' " 20 *Rutgers Law Review* 423 (1966). See also Note, "Indian Reserved Water Rights: The Winters of our Discontent," 88 *Yale Law Journal* 1689, 1702–4 (1979).

CHAPTER 3. LEGAL ISSUES AND DISPUTE-MANAGING METHODS IN CONTEMPORARY WATER-RIGHTS CONFLICTS

1. See generally C. Wilkinson, *American Indians, Time, and the Law* (New Haven, Conn.: Yale University Press, 1987).

2. 43 USC 666.

3. See Clyde, "Indian Water Rights," in *Waters and Water Rights*, 2, ed. R. Clark (Indianapolis: A. Smith & Co., 1967 and 1978), pp. 373–99.

4. 424 U.S. 800 (1976).

5. For a much more detailed discussion of the generally antagonistic relationship between many of the western states and neighboring Indian reservations and of the extreme tribal mistrust of state adjudication, see Pelcyger, "Indian Water Rights: Some Emerging Frontiers," 21 *Rocky Mountain Mineral Law Institute* 473 (1976). Specific comments on the negative impact of an elected state judiciary on Indian interests are in Corker, "A Real Live Problem or Two for the Waning Energies of Frank J. Trelease," 54 *Denver Law Journal* 499, 500 (1976).

6. The language of jurisdictional waiver in several of these congressional acts and state constitutions is cited in Hostyk, "Who Controls the Water? The Emerging Balance Among Federal, State, and Indian Jurisdictional Claims and Its Impact on Energy Development in the Upper Colorado and Missouri River Basins," 18 *Tulsa Law Journal* 63, n. 300 (1982).

7. 601 F.2d 1116 (10th Cir. 1979), *cert. denied* 444 U.S. 995 (1979).

8. 668 F.2d 723, 729 (9th Cir. 1982).

9. Ibid., p. 1093.

10. Ibid., p. 1100.

11. *Arizona* v. *San Carlos Apaches*, 463 U.S. 545 (1983).

12. *In re General Adjudication of All Rights to Use Water in the Big Horn River System*, 753 P.2d 76 (Wyo. 1988).

13. 426 U.S. 128 (1976).

14. *Shoshone Tribe* v. *Wyoming*, 753 P.2d 76 (Wyo. S.Ct.), *cert. denied* 57 USLW 3860 (U.S. July 3, 1989).

15. *Wyoming* v. *U.S.*, 109 S.Ct. 2994 (1989), affirmed by an equally divided court.

16. Telephone interview with Robert Pelcyger, Fredericks and Pelcyger,

Boulder, Colorado, Feb. 28, 1990; telephone interview with Charles Wilkinson, professor of law, University of Colorado at Boulder, Feb. 28, 1990. Mr. Pelcyger represented the tribes in oral argument before the Wyoming Supreme Court in the Big Horn River case; Professor Wilkinson is a noted scholar of American Indian law and appeared on appeal of the Big Horn River decision before the U.S. Supreme Court.

17. 463 U.S. 545 (1983).

18. *United States* v. *Adair,* 723 F.2d 1394 (1983), *cert. denied* 467 U.S. 1252 (1984).

19. *Kittitas Irrigation District* v. *Sunnyside Valley Irrigation District,* 763 F.2d 1032 (9th Cir.), *cert. denied* 474 U.S. 1032 (1985).

20. *Joint Board of Control of Flathead, Mission, and Jocko Irrigation Districts* v. *Confederated Salish and Kootenai Tribes of Flathead Reservation,* 832 F.2d 1127, *cert. denied* 56 USLW 3789 (1988).

21. Observers have pointed out, however, that the Supreme Court agreed to hear an appeal in the Big Horn River decision only on quantification of the Indian right and not on the state assertion of jurisdiction over groundwater. Pelcyger, Wilkinson, interviews, Feb. 28, 1990. Professor Wilkinson in particular feels that the split vote on the High Court and the narrow scope of the issues it did hear on appeal rob the decision of much precedential value, although it does bespeak very little judicial support for the Indian position.

22. The Indians lost in Supreme Court adjudication in *Colorado River Water Conservation District* v. *U.S.,* 424 U.S. 800 (1976); *Arizona* v. *California* (II), 460 U.S. 605 (1983); *Montana* v. *U.S.,* 450 U.S. 544 (1981); *Pyramid Lake Paiute Tribe* v. *Truckee-Carson Irrigation District,* 463 U.S. 110 (1983); *Arizona* v. *San Carlos Apache Tribe,* 463 U.S. 545 (1983); and *Shoshone Tribe* v. *Wyoming,* 753 P.2d 76, *cert. denied* 57 USLW 3860 (U.S. 7/3/89). The sole tribal victory was a 1979 unsigned supplemental decree to the original 1963 *Arizona* v. *California* decision, in which the Court unanimously held that the tribes should not be restricted to agricultural and domestic uses of reserved waters, even though those uses were the measure of the right. 439 U.S. 419, 422 (1979).

23. 104 F.2d 234 (9th Cir. 1939).

24. In the Supreme Court of the United States, October Term, 1981, Report of Elbert P. Tuttle, Special Master, Feb. 22, 1982, p. 100.

25. Burness et al., "The 'New' Arizona v. California: Practicable Irrigable Acreage and Economic Feasibility," 22 *Natural Resources Journal* 517 (1982).

26. *Arizona* v. *California,* 103 S.Ct. 3201 (1983).

27. For an analysis of the allowability of reserved waters for nonagricultural uses, see P. Maxfield, M. Dietrich, and F. Trelease, *Natural Resources Law on American Indian Lands* (Boulder, Colo.: Rocky Mountain Mineral Law Foundation, 1977), p. 229.

28. *Gila River Pima-Maricopa Indian Community* v. *U.S.,* 9 Cl.Ct. 660 (1986).

29. *State of New Mexico* v. *Aamodt,* 537 F.2d 1102 (10th Cir. 1976), *cert. denied* 429 U.S. 1121 (1977).

30. See Merrill, "Aboriginal Water Rights," 20 *Natural Resources Journal* 45 (1980).

31. For an overview of the quantification debate among tribal leaders, advocates, and other interested parties, see American Indian Lawyer Training Program, *Indian Water Policy in a Changing Environment* (Oakland, Calif., 1982).

32. *Pyramid Lake Paiutes* v. *Truckee-Carson Irrigation District et al.,* 463 U.S. 110 (1983).

33. Shrago, "Emerging Indian Water Rights: An Analysis of Recent Judicial and Legislative Developments," 26 *Rocky Mountain Mineral Law Institute* 1105, 1106 (1980).

34. *U.S. v. New Mexico,* 238 U.S. 696 (1978). In a highly restrictive reserved water-rights decision from the federal standpoint, Justice Rehnquist wrote for a 5–4 majority that if the U.S. Forest Service wished to reserve waters in the Gila National Forest using as an appropriation date the 1899 act that created it, water could be reserved only for the purposes stated in the 1899 legislation—not for the fulfillment of subsequent Forest Service responsibilities in the Gila. The majority then proceeded to construe the purposes of the enabling act quite narrowly.

35. 439 U.S. 419 (1979).

36. Ibid., p. 422.

37. See Maxfield et al., *National Resources Law,* pp. 218–33. However, in the Shoshone dispute decided by the Wyoming Supreme Court and upheld by the U.S. Supreme Court (*Shoshone Tribe* v. *Wyoming,* 1989, and *Wyoming* v. *U.S.,* 1989) the measurement of the tribe's reserved right was restricted solely to agricultural and domestic/municipal uses. If this trend continues, the negative impact on tribal economic development could be substantial.

38. 647 F.2d 42 (9th Cir. 1981), *cert. denied* 102 S.Ct. 657 (1981).

39. 460 F. Supp. 1320 (E.D. Wash. 1978).

40. 647 F.2d at 48.

41. Storey, "Leasing Indian Water Off the Reservation: A Use Consistent With the Reservation's Purpose," 78 *California Law Review* 179 (1989). See also Lichtenfele, "Indian Reserved Water Rights: An Argument for the Right to Export and Sell," 24 *Land and Water Review* 131 (1989).

42. See Shrago, "Emerging Indian Water Rights."

43. Getches, "Management and Marketing of Indian Water: From Conflict to Pragmatism," 58 *University of Colorado Law Review* 518 (1988).

44. 273 F. 93 (9th Cir. 1921).

45. *U.S. v. Powers,* 305 U.S. 527 (1939).

46. *U.S. ex rel. Ray v. Hibner,* 27 F.2d 909 (D. Idaho 1928). A summary of issues related to the conveyancing of Indian water rights is in Palma, "Considerations and Conclusions Concerning the Transferability of Indian Water Rights," 20 *Natural Resources Journal* 91 (1981).

47. Ibid.

48. For a thoroughly documented description of the tension between the Bureau of Indian Affairs and the Bureau of Reclamation over the planning, construction, operation, and maintenance of Indian reclamation projects, see D. McCool, *Command of the Waters* (Berkeley: University of California Press, 1987), pp. 161–92.

49. *Washington* v. *U.S., cert. denied* 50 USLW 3448 (1981).

50. 647 F.2d 52 (1981).

51. 450 U.S. 544 (1981).

52. Ibid.

53. There was not even any allusion to traditional canons of treaty construction in the majority opinion. See Note, "Riverbed Ownership Law Metamorphosed Into a Determinant of Tribal Regulatory Authority—*Montana* v. *U.S.*," 1982 *Wisconsin Law Review* 264 (1982). A stirring indictment of the current Supreme Court's general drift away from protection of the resource rights of Indians throughout the 1980s is Clinton's "State Power over Indian Reserva-

tions: A Critical Comment on the Burger Court Doctrine," 26 *South Dakota Law Review* 434 (1981).

However, it is not possible to characterize the Court as uniformly hostile to the concept of Indian sovereignty. In *Merrion* v. *Jicarilla Apache Tribe*, 102 S.Ct. 894 (1982), Justice Marshall wrote a majority opinion upholding the right of the tribe to impose a severance on oil and gas resources extracted from reservation lands as an "inherent power necessary to tribal self-government and territorial management" (102 S.Ct. at 903). At the same time, in the 1980s the Court's water-rights decisions have been more consistently anti-Indian than in any other realm of resource management.

54. 450 U.S. at 557 et seq.

55. See J. Folk-Williams, *What Indian Water Means to the West* (Santa Fe, N. Mex.: Western Network, 1982), pp. 35, 74–79.

56. Maxfield et al., "Natural Resources Law," pp. 76–80.

57. 33 USC 1251 et seq.

58. 42 USC 6901.

59. 42 USC 300f.

60. *Washington* v. *EPA*, 752 F.2d 1465 (9th Cir. 1985).

61. *Inventory of Hazardous Waste Generators and Sites on Selected Indian Reservations*, report prepared under contract to the EPA by the Council of Energy Resource Tribes (CERT/TR-85-1025, Project No. 061-1025) (July, 1985) (available from the Indian Affairs Coordinator, EPA, Region 9, San Francisco).

62. See Folk-Williams, *What Indian Water Means to the West*, pp. 37–38.

63. *White Mountain Apache Tribe* v. *William French Smith and James Watt*, 51 USLW 3932 (1983).

64. See, for instance, Young, "Interagency Conflicts of Interest: The Peril to Indian Water Rights," 1972 *Law and the Social Order* 313; Veeder, "Confiscation of Indian Water Rights in the Upper Missouri Basin," 21 *South Dakota Law Review* 282, 292 (1976); Price and Weatherford, "Indian Rights in Theory and Practice: Navajo Experience in the Colorado River Basin," 40 *Law and Contemporary Problems* 97, 114–15 (1976); Chambers and Price, "Regulating Sovereignty: Secretarial Discretion and the Leasing of Indian Lands," 26 *Stanford Law Review* 1061 (1974); and McCool, *Command of the Waters*.

65. Folk-Williams, *What Indian Water Means*.

66. Likewise, many of the district and appellate court cases are now being consolidated for appeal on procedural issues such as forum jurisdiction, so many of these cases are now undergoing name changes, removal, and remand.

67. National Water Commission, *Water Policies for the Future* (Washington, D.C.: Government Printing Office, 1973).

68. Ibid., p. 475.

69. Ibid., p. 479.

70. Ibid., p. 477.

71. Ibid., pp. 477–78.

72. Ibid., pp. 481–83.

73. Such as Senator Edward Kennedy's Central Arizona Indian Water Rights Settlement Act of 1977, S. 905, 95th Congress, 1st sess. (1977).

74. From 1955 to 1979, western congressional representatives and senators submitted over fifty bills for the termination or diminution of Indian reserved water rights. See Note, "Indian Reserved Water Rights: The Winters of our Discontent," 88 *Yale Law Journal* 1689, 1702–1704 (1979); and Morreale, "Federal-

State Conflicts Over Western Waters—A Decade of Attempted 'Clarifying Legislation,' " 20 *Rutgers Law Review* 423 (1966).

75. Some observers are skeptical of congressional ability even in this more limited role, unless these acts are drafted with great care. See Dumars and Ingram, "Congressional Quantification of Indian Water Rights: A Definitive Solution or a Mirage?" 20 *Natural Resources Journal* 45 (1980).

76. "Watt Seeks Negotiated Settlement for Indian Water Claims Suits; Will Create Negotiating Teams and Advisory Groups to Guide Settlement" (U.S. Department of the Interior News Release, July 14, 1982).

77. Folk-Williams, "Negotiation Becomes More Important in Settling Indian Water Rights Disputes in the West," *Resolve* (Summer, 1982), p. 1 (the Conservation Foundation's quarterly newsletter of environmental-dispute resolution).

78. Wilkinson, "Perspectives on Water and Energy in the American West and in Indian Country," 26 *South Dakota Law Review* 393 (1981).

79. Schmidt, "Meeting in Capitol Today Will Focus on Tribal Water Claims," *New York Times,* Dec. 8, 1982, p. 9, col. 1.

80. One example is the proposed Indian Water Rights Act, drafted in 1981 by the Western Regional Council, an association of financial and industrial corporations engaged in western development (for its text, see Folk-Williams, *What Indian Water Means,* pp. 139–43); another is the Western Conference of the Council of State Governments' proposed Water Rights Coordination Act (idem, p. 16). Both would extinguish unexercised Indian rights and subject all Indian water rights exclusively to state jurisdiction. These features have appeared in previous stillborn legislation, such as H.R. 9951, 95th Cong., 1st sess. (1977). See also Shrago, "Emerging Indian Water Rights," p. 1145.

81. *Arizona* v. *San Carlos Apache Tribe* (1983).

82. *Arizona* v. *California* (II) (1983).

83. *Montana* v. *U.S.* (1981).

CHAPTER 4. THE PERIL AND PROMISE
OF NEGOTIATION: A CLOSER LOOK

1. Daniel McCool describes this historic tension thoroughly in *Command of the Waters* (Berkeley: University of California Press, 1988).

2. A narrative history of the Kent Decree and subsequent developments may be found in U.S. Senate, Select Committee on Indian Affairs, S. Rep. No. 100–495, to accompany S. 2153, 100th Cong., 2d sess. (1988).

3. For a well-documented history of the Mission Indians affair, see U.S. Senate, Select Committee on Indian Affairs, S. Rep. 100–47, to accompany S.795, 100th cong., 1st sess. (1987).

4. For background on the Globe Equity Decree, see J. Folk-Williams, *What Indian Water Means to the West* (Santa Fe, N. Mex.: Western Network, 1982), p. 37.

5. Ibid.

6. A brief historical summary of the Pyramid Lake Paiute situation accompanies the 1983 U.S. Supreme Court decision, *Pyramid Lake Paiute Tribe of Indians* v. *TCID et al.,* 463 U.S. 110 (1983).

7. Ibid.

8. 48 Stat. 984, 25 USC 461 et seq. (1976).

9. Ibid.

10. 373 U.S. 546 (1963).

11. Price and Weatherford, "Indian Water Rights in Theory and Practice: Navajo Experience in the Colorado River Basin," 40 *Law and Contemporary Problems* 97 (1976). The tribe first agreed to the trade-off in 1957; authorizing legislation was passed in 1962 (ibid.).

12. "Navajo Indian Irrigation—Water Entitlement of the Navajo Tribe," memorandum from David E. Lindgren, deputy solicitor, to John C. Whittaker, undersecretary of the Interior, Dec. 6, 1974; cited in Price and Weatherford, "Indian Water Rights."

13. J. Jacobsen, *A Promise Made: The Navajo Indian Irrigation Project and Water Politics in the American West*, University of Colorado and National Center for Atmospheric Research, Cooperative Thesis No. 119 (1989).

14. Ute Deferral Agreement of 1965. For a discussion of this original agreement, see Fetzer, "The Ute Indian Water Compact," 2 *Journal of Energy Law and Policy* 181, 191 (1982).

15. Thorsen, "Resolving Conflicts Through Intergovernmental Agreements: The Pros and Cons of Negotiated Settlements," in *Sourcebook on Indian Water Settlements* (Oakland, Calif.: American Indian Resources Institute, 1989), p. L–10.

16. UTAH CODE ANN. Sec. 73-21-2 (1980). A point-by-point review of the compact's features is in Fetzer, "The Ute Indian Water Compact."

17. Memorandum from William H. Veeder to Martin Seneca, Seneca & Associates, re the Ute Indian Water Compact, Mar. 21, 1980.

18. Thorsen, "Resolving Conflicts."

19. Pub. L. No. 90-537, Sec. 303, 43 USC 1523. This project is also discussed in Price and Weatherford, "Indian Water Rights," p. 114; and Getches and Meyers, "The River of Controversy: Persistent Issues," in *New Courses for the Colorado River,* ed. G. Weatherford and F. Brown (Albuquerque: University of New Mexico Press, 1986), pp. 51, 64.

20. Kneese and Bonem, "Hypothetical Shocks to Water Allocation Institutions in the Colorado Basin," in Weatherford and Brown, *New Courses for the Colorado River,* p. 97.

21. Price and Weatherford, "Indian Water Rights," pp. 108–31.

22. Kneese and Bonem, "Hypothetical Shocks," p. 97.

23. Interview with Leona Kakar, chairwoman, Ak Chin Indian Community, Ak Chin Farms, Arizona, Nov. 22, 1983.

24. Ak Chin Community Water Rights Settlement Act, Pub. L. 95–328, 92 Stat. 409 (1978).

25. A history of the original Ak Chin Settlement Act is in U.S. House of Representatives, Committee on Interior and Insular Affairs, Rep. No. 98-1026, 98th Cong., 2d sess., p. 6 (1984).

26. Pub. L. No. 98-530, 98 Stat. 2698 (1984).

27. Colorado River Basin Project Act, 82 stat. 885 (1968).

28. For a crisp, authoritative summary of the CAP, see Hundley, "The West against Itself: The Colorado River—An Institutional History," in Weatherford and Brown, *New Courses for the Colorado River,* pp. 9, 35.

29. *U.S.* v. *Cappaert,* 375 F. Supp. 456 (D. Nev. 1974), 508 F.2d 313 (9th Cir. 1974). The Supreme Court affirmed two years later. 426 U.S. 128 (1976).

30. Southern Arizona Water Rights Settlement Act of 1982, Pub. L. No. 97–293, Title III, 96 Stat. 1274 (1982).

31. Ibid., Sec. 304, 96 Stat. 1277.

32. Ibid., Sec. 313, 96 Stat. 1284.

33. Ibid., 96 Stat. 1284.

34. Reclamation Reform Act of 1982, Pub. L. No. 97-293 (S. 1409).

35. U.S. Senate, Select Committee on Indian Affairs, S. Rep. No. 97-375, 97th Cong., 2d sess., p. 33 (1982).

36. Ibid. (There remains to this day some disagreement over the true costs of implementing this act, partly because of its involved reliance on completion of the Central Arizona Project.)

37. E.g., U.S. v. Superior Court, 697 P.2d 658 (Ariz. 1985).

38. See Swan, "The Salt River Pima-Maricopa Indian Community Water Rights Settlement Act of 1988," in *Symposium Proceedings on Indian Water Rights and Water Resources Management*, ed. W. Lord and M. Wallace (Bethesda, Md.: American Water Resources Association, 1989), pp. 87, 90–91.

39. Salt River Pima-Maricopa Indian Community Water Rights Settlement Act of 1988, Pub. L. No. 100–512.

40. Pub. L. No. 100–512, Sec. 10, 102 Stat. 2557.

41. Ibid., 102 Stat. 2558.

42. Ibid., Sec. 8, 102 Stat. 2555.

43. 102 Stat. 2555.

44. For a discussion of these provisions, see Swan, "The Salt River Act of 1988," p. 92.

45. See Hundley, "The West Against Itself," pp. 9–50.

46. Ibid., p. 30.

47. 82 Stat 885 (1968).

48. Hundley, "The West Against Itself," p. 36.

49. Ibid., p. 37.

50. Colorado Ute Indian Water Rights Settlement Act of 1988, Pub. L. No. 100–585, 102 Stat. 2973 (1988).

51. Simon, "Indian Water Claims Negotiations: Conflicting Federal Roles," in *Symposium Proceedings*, ed. Lord and Wallace, pp. 1, 3, Table. 1.

52. *Congressional Record*, October 3, 1988, H9345.

53. Comments of Congressman George Miller of California, *Congressional Record*, October 3, 1988, H9347.

54. 102 Stat. 2975.

55. For background on both the litigation of the Mission Indian bands and the 1988 settlement legislation, see U.S. Senate, Select Committee on Indian Affairs, S. Rept. 100–47, 100th Cong., 1st sess. (1987), pp. 1–5.

56. Ibid., pp. 5–6.

57. San Luis Rey Indian Water Rights Settlement Act, Pub. L. No. 100–675, 102 Stat. 4000 (1988).

58. Ibid., Sec. 105, 102 Stat. 4002.

59. Ibid., Sec. 106(c), 102 Stat. 4003 (1988).

60. By the summer of 1989, the Interior Department and a total of fourteen tribes were actively involved in comprehensive settlement negotiations, in addition to the pending agreements discussed here. Telephone interview with Joseph L. Miller, special assistant for Indian Affairs, Office of the Commissioner, Bureau of Reclamation, U.S. Department of the Interior, Washington, D.C., March 8, 1990.

61. Pyramid Lake Paiutes v. TCID (1983).

62. U.S. Senate, Committee on Energy and Natural Resources and Select Committee on Indian Affairs, S. 1554, 101st Cong., 1st sess. (1989).

63. Ibid., Sec. 301(e).

64. Ibid., Sec. 501.

65. U.S. Senate, Committee on Energy and Natural Resources and Select Committee on Indian Affairs, S. 536, 101st Cong., 1st sess. (1989), Sec. 3(8).

66. Ibid., Sec. 4.

67. Ibid., p. 15; Ute Indian Water Compact, Article 3.

68. *Arizona v. San Carlos Apaches*, 463 U.S. 545 (1983). Indian victories against the state of Montana on the jurisdiction issue, 668 F.2d 723 (9th Cir. 1982), were reversed on consolidated appeal with the San Carlos Apache case before the Supreme Court.

69. The Fort Peck–Montana Compact, Article 3 (1985).

70. A summary of this pact is in Thorsen, "Resolving Conflicts," pp. c–52.

71. Ibid.

72. For a summary of agreement terms, see Blain, "Florida Seminole Indian Dispute Settlement Including Water Rights Compact and Manual," in *Symposium Proceedings*, ed. Lord and Wallace, p. 145.

73. Seminole Indian Land Claims Settlement Act of 1987, Pub. L. No. 100–228, 101 Stat. 1556 (1987).

74. See McCool, *Command of the Waters*, for a well-documented discussion of federal government ambivalence over how ardently to litigate tribal reserved water rights.

75. See P. Fradkin, *A River No More—The Colorado River and the West* (New York: Knopf, 1981), pp. 176–77.

76. McCool, *Command of the Waters*, pp. 140–42.

77. Simon, "Indian Water Claims Negotiations." Benjamin Simon serves in the Interior Department's Office of Program Analysis.

78. As of March 1990, however, MWD and some other signatories to the agreement resulting in the Mission Indians settlement act were refusing to abide by its terms, alleging that they had never explicitly agreed to some of its terms and conditions. They are apparently fearful that while a set quantity of water is guaranteed to the Indians, it is as yet unclear whether that much water would actually be saved by lining the All American Canal and that they might be forced to make up the difference. As of this writing, it is unclear whether a private negotiated solution to this problem will be found or if instead the agreement is doomed. Interview with Joseph L. Miller, Mar. 8, 1990.

79. The Navajos' purported five-million-acre-foot claim to the upper Colorado River, if/when that case is litigated, may well result in the negotiated settlement of provable claims in the two-million-acre-foot range, which would be five times greater than the Fort Peck allotment. See Kneese and Bonem, "Hypothetical Shocks," p. 97; and Price and Weatherford, "Indian Water Rights," pp. 108–31 and accompanying text.

80. At the same time, these marketing limitations may come to be seen by future historians as the least fair aspect of late twentieth-century settlements and therefore the most vulnerable to subsequent legal attack, as perspectives on substantive Indian justice continue to evolve. The notion that the tribes should in perpetuity be regarded as lesser governmental entities than neighboring municipalities and conservancy districts is one that, legally, is not likely to stand the test of time. For an insightful and thoroughly documented short treatise on the evolution of Indian legal status over the past three hundred years, with an

emphasis on the gradual reclamation of tribal sovereignty, see C. Wilkinson, *American Indians, Time, and the Law* (New Haven, Conn.: Yale University Press, 1987).

81. Pub. L. No. 101–121, 103 Stat. 715 (1989).

CHAPTER 5. GROUNDWATER RIGHTS, PLANNING, AND BARGAINING IN SOUTH-CENTRAL ARIZONA

1. J. McGregor, *Southwestern Archeology* (1965), pp. 10–12.
2. Ibid., p. 15.
3. Masse, "Prehistoric Irrigation in the Salt River Valley, Arizona," 214 *Science* 408 (1981).
4. A. Kehoe, *North American Indians—A Comprehensive Account* (1981), p. 107.
5. "Papago" was the term early Spaniards used for the indigenous population of southern Arizona; it was derived from the word the natives used for a desert plant that featured prominently in their diet. When the tribe adopted a new constitution in 1986, it also officially changed the tribal name to the traditional term of self-reference from its own language—"O'Odham."

"Tohono O'Odham" properly refers to tribal members residing on the main reservation, whose headquarters are at the town of Sells, about sixty miles southwest of Tucson. However, other O'Odham refer to themselves according to the district where they reside. That distinction is used in this chapter; "San Xavier O'Odham" refers to the tribal members on the satellite San Xavier Reservation who lost their groundwater to Tucson and neighboring mines and farms; "Tohono O'Odham" is now the official name for the tribe as a whole—the legal entity that entered into the groundwater rights agreement resulting in a 1982 congressional act. This distinction is important, since dissension between the Tohono and San Xavier O'Odham has caused serious implementation problems for their settlement legislation. Telephone interview with Austin Nunez, chairman, San Xavier District, Tohono O'Odham Nation, San Xavier del Bac, Arizona, Apr. 5, 1990. (See accompanying text.)
6. E. Spicer, *Cycles of Conquest* (Tucson: University of Arizona Press, 1962), p. 134.
7. Ibid., p. 126.
8. Ibid., p. 136.
9. Ibid., p. 137.
10. Ibid., p. 138.
11. P. Fradkin, *A River No More—The Colorado River and the West* (New York: Knopf, 1982), p. 78.
12. Ibid., p. 79. See also J. Hastings and R. Turner, *The Changing Mile* (1965).
13. C. Sonnichsen, *Tucson—The Life and Times of an American City* (Norman: University of Oklahoma Press, 1982), p. 9.
14. Ibid., p. 210.
15. Ibid., pp. 102–4.
16. Ibid., pp. 110–12.
17. As reported in the *Tucson Weekly Citizen*, May 29, 1885.
18. Arizona Office of Economic Planning and Development, *Arizona Indian Community Profiles*, as reprinted in R. Foreman, *Indian Water Rights—A Public Policy and Administrative Mess* (1981), p. 149.
19. Spicer, *Cycles of Conquest*, p. 140.

20. See *Arizona Indian Community Profiles,* in Foreman, *Indian Water Rights.*

21. Information reprinted in American Indian Lawyer Training Program, *Self-Determination and the Role of Tribal Courts* (Oakland, Calif.: American Indian Resources Institute, 1982), p. D-27.

22. Ibid., D-30.

23. Sonnichsen, *Tucson,* p. 196.

24. D. Mann, *The Politics of Water in Arizona* (1963), p. 46.

25. Sonnichsen, *Tucson,* p. 196.

26. Ibid., p. 280.

27. The most authoritative historical data on the status of the groundwater in the geographic area of these case studies may be found in Anderson, "Electrical Analog Analysis of Groundwater Depletion in Central Arizona," U.S. Geological Survey, Department of the Interior, Water Supply Paper No. 1860 (1968).

28. Ibid.

29. Anderson, "Electrical Analog Analysis of the Hydrologic System, Tucson Basin, Southeastern Arizona," U.S. Geological Survey, Department of the Interior, Water Supply Paper No. 1939-C (1972), pp. C-12, 13.

30. Davidson, "Geohydrology and Water Resources of the Tucson Basin, Arizona," U.S. Geological Survey, Department of the Interior, Water Supply Paper No. 1939-E (1973), p. E-74.

31. Ibid.

32. Mann, *Politics of Water.*

33. *Maricopa County Municipal Water Conservation District* v. *Southwestern Cotton Co. et al.,* 39 Ariz. 65, 4 P. 369 (1926).

34. Mann, *Politics of Water,* pp. 49-64.

35. Ibid., p. 65.

36. *Arizona* v. *Anway,* 87 Ariz. 206, 349 P.2d 774 (1960).

37. *Farmers Investment Co.* v. *Bettwy,* 113 Ariz. 520, 558 P.2d 14 (1976).

38. Colorado River Basin Project Act, Pub. L. No. 90-537, 82 Stat. 885, 43 USCS 1501 et seq. (1980).

39. Regarding the Arizona legislature's history of excruciating inaction on the question of groundwater regulation, see D. Mann, *Politics of Water,* pp. 43-66.

40. Interview with Hilda Manuel, legislative aide, Papago Tribal Council, Sells, Arizona, Nov. 21, 1983.

41. Ibid.

42. *Jarvis* v. *State Land Dept.,* 104 Ariz. 527, 456 P.2d 385 (1969) (*Jarvis* I); 106 Ariz. 506, 479 P.2d 169 (1970) (*Jarvis* II); 113 Ariz. 230, 550 P.2d 227 (1976) (*Jarvis* III). The findings of the *Jarvis* litigation are summarized in FICO v. Bettwy (1976).

43. U.S. General Accounting Office, *Reserved Water Rights for Federal and Indian Reservations: A Growing Problem in Need of Resolution* (Washington, D.C.: Government Printing Office, 1978), pp. 33-34.

44. *U.S. and Papago Indian Tribe* v. *City of Tucson et al.,* No. CIV. 75-39 TUC (JAW) (1975).

45. Telephone interview with Daniel O'Neil, district assistant, District Office of U.S. Congressman Morris Udall, Tucson, Arizona, Feb. 9, 1984. Although on Congressman Udall's Tucson staff at the time of the interview, in 1978 Mr. O'Neil was an employee of the Tucson City Attorney's Office, representing city interests in the O'Odham groundwater-dispute bargaining

process. As of the date of this interview, he was also chairman of the Water Resources Coordinating Committee.

46. U.S. G.A.O., *Reserved Water Rights.*

47. Interview with William Strickland, general counsel, Papago Indian Tribe, Tucson, Arizona, Nov. 25, 1983.

48. 426 U.S. 128 (1976).

49. In *Cappaert,* the Court ruled (1) that if groundwater withdrawals by neighbors of a federal reservation (in this case, Devil's Hole National Monument) were having the effect of defeating the purpose for which the reservation was created; and (2) if a "hydrologic connection" could be demonstrated between groundwater being withdrawn and surface waters needed to fulfill a reservation's purpose; then (3) such withdrawals could be enjoined under the reserved-rights doctrine. Although Indian reservations were not the subject of this case, few observers doubted that the *Cappaert* ruling would apply to them as well.

50. Telephone interview with Norbert Ludwig, Tucson City Attorney's Office, Tucson, Arizona, Feb. 16, 1984.

51. Several of the parties I interviewed during the course of this research revealed a kind of Sisyphean fatalism in their attitudes toward water-rights litigation—regarding it as an interminable, burdensome process resorted to less out of choice than from an absence of effective institutional alternatives. It is an interesting perspective, conveyed as it was by a group of western water lawyers whose livelihood depends on how well they can roll the rock up the hill.

52. Ludwig, interview, Feb. 16, 1984.

53. Ibid.

54. Authorization cited in Corps of Engineers (Los Angeles District), U.S. Department of the Army, *Tucson Urban Study, Draft Regional Water Supply Appendix* (Dec. 1981), at 1-1. Unpublished preliminary draft, subject to revision.

55. The official membership of the Water Resources Coordinating Committee varied, but at one time or another included representatives of U.S. Senators Goldwater and DeConcini, the Army Corps of Engineers (chair of the meetings), several irrigation districts and private agribusiness firms, the Bureau of Indian Affairs, the Papago Indian Tribe and individual Papago allottees, four mining companies, Tucson-area public utilities, Davis-Monthan Air Force Base, the University of Arizona, and the Arizona Department of Water Resources. Tucson Active Management Area, Arizona Department of Water Resources, *A Water Issues Primer for the Tucson Active Management Area* (June, 1982), p. 45.

Principal Corps staff involved in chairing WRCC proceedings were Michael Thuss, H. W. "Will" Worthington, and Joseph Dixon. Telephone interview with Will Worthington, former chief, Urban Studies Section, Army Corps of Engineers, Phoenix Regional Office; currently chief, Dams Planning Branch, Bureau of Reclamation, Arizona Projects Office; Phoenix, Arizona, Nov. 23, 1983.

56. The principal function of Corps staff in the early stages of these negotiations was to get the disputants speaking the same language in terms of the hydrologic data base. Once there was a threshold level of agreement on how much water was being withdrawn, by whom, what the rate of recharge was, and how serious the overdraft problem was, Congressional staff assumed a more central role in getting the principal parties to consider and ultimately to accept a negotiated settlement. The process had to be undertaken twice since President

Reagan vetoed the first Papago settlement act because of a lack of local financial contribution to the settlement.

57. The Corps borrowed the area identification and base map in Figure 4 from an earlier publication of the University of Arizona, which in turn relied on USGS hydrologic province definitions. Matlock and Davis, *Groundwater in the Santa Cruz Valley, Arizona*, Agricultural Experiment Station, University of Arizona, Tucson, Technical Bulletin No. 194, p. 3. This definition of the upper Santa Cruz basin conforms substantially to that described in Anderson ("Electrical Analog Analysis of the Hydrologic System") and Davidson ("Geohydrology and Water Resources") insofar as the western, northern, and eastern boundaries of the basin are concerned; but unlike these USGS papers, the Tucson Urban Study encompasses the upper basin as far south as the Mexican border.

58. Corps of Engineers (Los Angeles District), U.S. Department of the Army, *Past and Present Groundwater Usage, Eastern Pima County, Arizona* (April, 1981); hereafter cited as *Tucson Urban Study* or *Urban Study Summary*. Although the document was later to undergo some revision (it was criticized for underestimating the severity of the overdraft situation), negotiators relied on the figures in this 1981 draft in achieving a settlement of the groundwater litigation.

59. Ibid., p. 17.

60. N. Hundley, *Water and the West* (Berkeley: University of California Press, 1975), pp. 211–12.

61. Ibid., citation to Hoover quote, see ibid., n. 96.

62. Ibid., pp. 211–12.

63. Colorado River Compact, Art. 7; H. Doc 605, 67th Cong., 4th sess. (1923), pp. 8–12.

64. *Arizona v. California*, 373 U.S. 546, 601 (1963).

65. 43 USCS 1524 (1980).

66. Telephone interview with Larry Lindser, chief of planning, Arizona Department of Water Resources, Phoenix, Arizona, Feb. 16, 1984.

67. 41 Fed. Reg. 45883 (Oct. 18, 1976).

68. 45 Fed. Reg. 52938 (Aug. 8, 1980); 45 Fed. Reg. 54452 (Aug. 15, 1980).

69. Lindser, interview, Feb. 16, 1984.

70. 45 Fed. Reg. 81265 (Dec. 10, 1980).

71. *Tucson Urban Study*, Draft of Regional Water Supply Appendix (1981), pp. 1–6.

72. *Urban Study Summary*, p. 92. Arizona's recommended CAP allocations to the upper and lower Santa Cruz and Avra-Altar basins, as considered by Secretary James Watt in 1981, totalled 191,348 acre-feet for the year 2005. See *Water Issues Primer*, p. 19.

73. Ibid., p. 17.

74. The University of Arizona's Water Resources Center clearly demonstrated this point—that the CAP would not be the ultimate technological fix disputants were seeking—in research published as early as 1978. Water Resources Center, University of Arizona, "Groundwater Projections for 11 Basins," *Arizona Water Resources News Bulletin*, No. 3 (1978), p. 2.

75. Lindser, interview, Feb. 16, 1984.

76. Mann, *Politics of Water*.

77. Ibid., pp. 61–63.

78. The Central Arizona Project was twenty-five percent completed as of April 1, 1982. At that time, it was estimated that total project costs, assuming a

scheduled completion date of 1989, would come to $3.6 billion in 1982 dollars. *Water Issues Primer,* p. 15.

79. S.B. 1001, Ariz. 34th Legis., 4th Special Sess. (1980); Ariz. Rev. Stat. Ann. Sec. 45-441 et seq.

80. Arizona Governor Bruce Babbitt's "personal dedication and negotiating skill" in chairing the "hundreds of hours of meetings" necessary to produce the statute have been credited for much of the bill's success. Johnson, "The 1980 Arizona Groundwater Management Act and Trends in Western States Groundwater Administration and Management: A Minerals Industry Perspective," 26 *Rocky Mountain Mineral Law Institute* 1031, 1061 (1980).

81. Ludwig, interview, Feb. 16, 1984.

82. H.R. 7640, 96th Cong., 2nd sess. (1980). See *Tucson Urban Study,* Draft of Regional Water Supply Appendix (Dec. 1981), pp. 1-6. Unpublished preliminary draft, subject to revision.

83. H.R. 4363, 97th Cong., 1st sess. (1981); ibid., pp. 1-8.

84. Ibid.

85. Telephone interview with Deborah Sliz, counsel to the Subcommittee on Energy and the Environment of the House Committee on Interior and Insular Affairs, U.S. Congress, Washington, D.C., Feb. 10, 1984.

86. Ibid.

87. Ibid.; and Strickland, interview, Nov. 25, 1983.

88. Letter from Morris Udall, chairman, House Committee on Interior and Insular Affairs, to President Ronald Reagan, June 4, 1982, p. 4 (copy of letter available from Cong. Udall's office).

89. Office of the Press Secretary, the White House (Presidential Announcement of the Veto of H.R. 5118), June 1, 1982.

90. Ibid.

91. Udall to Reagan, p. 5.

92. House Committee on Interior and Insular Affairs, U.S. Congress, *News Release:* "Udall Applauds Papago Negotiating Schedule," July 14, 1982.

93. Ibid.

94. Telephone interview with William P. Horn, deputy undersecretary of the Interior, Washington, D.C., Feb. 24, 1984.

95. Ibid.

96. Telephone interview with Wesley Steiner, director, Arizona Dept. of Water Resources, Phoenix, Arizona, Feb. 15, 1984.

97. Ibid.

98. This provision may have been included for at least two reasons. First, several of Arizona's nineteen Indian tribes might someday bring groundwater-adjudication actions against the state; tacit acknowledgment of the applicability of the *Winters* doctrine to groundwater in the Papago bill would strengthen their legal arguments. Second, Mr. Steiner told me that the state executives and congressional delegations of several western states were seriously concerned about the precedential impact of the Papago settlement; the *Winters*-doctrine disclaimer was something they wanted in return for their agreement not to oppose the bill. Since Arizona needed the legislation, the DWR director insisted on the disclaimer provision. Ibid.; also Sliz, interview, Feb. 10, 1984.

99. Strickland, interview, Nov. 25, 1983.

100. Some observers (including selected respondents in this research who preferred not to go on the record) believe Congressman Udall attached the

Papago bill to the 960-acre-limitation act because of suspicions that the ad-minstration would otherwise try to alter the federal funding commitment in the bill during last-minute floor debate—threatening another veto if opposed. However, Deputy Undersecretary Horn felt that the Papago bill was tucked under the wing of the acreage-limitation amendment to protect it from enemies in the Senate who disliked the "generosity" and precedential implications of the Papago measure but would swallow them in order to get acreage-limitation reform. Horn, interview, Feb. 24, 1984. It is possible, of course, that both reasons are accurate. However, the Senate had passed an almost identical Papago bill by unanimous consent earlier in the same session of Congress, so if Mr. Horn is correct, the upper chamber had undergone a substantial change of heart in the intervening period.

101. Pub. L. 97-293, 97th Cong., 2nd sess. (1982).

102. Pub. L. No. 97-293, Title 3, Sec. 303.

103. Ibid., Sec. 313.

104. Ibid., Secs. 303(a)(3) and 306(a)(3).

105. Ibid., Secs. 304 and 305.

106. Ibid., Sec. 306.

107. Ibid., Sec. 307.

108. Ibid., Sec. 309.

109. Horn, interview, Feb. 24, 1984.

110. Strickland, interview, Nov. 25, 1983.

111. H.R. REP. No. 855, 97th Cong., 2d sess., at 49 (1982).

112. U.S. Department of the Interior, Southern Arizona Water Rights Settlement Act of 1982, Contract between the United States and the Papago Tribe of Arizona to Provide Water and to Settle Claims to Water, Oct. 11, 1983.

113. Interview with Leona Kakar, chairwoman, Ak Chin Indian community, Ak Chin Farms, Arizona, Nov. 22, 1983.

114. Sheridan, "The Desert Blooms—At A Price," 23 (3) *Environment* 9, n. 27 (1981).

115. Kakar, interview, Nov. 22, 1983.

116. Pub. L. No. 95-328, The Ak Chin Indian Community Water Rights Settlement Act, 95th Cong., 2d sess. (1978).

117. Ibid., Sec. 2(c).

118. Ibid., Sec. 4.

119. Office of the Secretary, U.S. Department of the Interior, Ak Chin Indian Community Water Rights Settlement Act, Contract Between the United States and the Ak Chin Indian Community to Provide Water and to Settle Claims to Water, May 20, 1980.

120. Ak Chin Act, Pub. L. No. 95-328, sec. 2(c).

121. Horn, interview, Feb. 24, 1984.

122. Perry, "Delayed Project Has Tribes Leery on Watt Water 'Settle-ments,'" *Arizona Republic,* January 2, 1983, p. 1–A.

123. Ibid.

124. Ibid.

125. Ibid.

126. Office of the Secretary, U.S. Department of the Interior, Agreement in Principle for Revised Ak Chin Water Settlement, Sept. 23, 1983.

127. Letter to the author from Wesley Steiner, Mar. 27, 1984.

128. Horn, interview, Feb. 24, 1984.

129. Steiner, letter, March 27, 1984.

130. Ibid.

131. Ak Chin Community, Water Rights, Pub. L. No. 98-530, 98 Stat. 2698 (1984).

132. 98 Stat. 2699.

133. 98 Stat. 2700.

134. Telephone interview with Leona Kakar, executive director, Ak Chin community, Ak Chin Farms, Arizona, Apr. 5, 1990.

135. Ibid.

136. 98 Stat. 2701.

137. Ibid.

138. Ibid.

139. Telephone interview with Austin Nunez, chairman, San Xavier District, Tohono O'Odham Nation, San Xavier del Bac, Arizona, April 5, 1990.

140. Pub. L. No. 97-293, Sec. 307(a)(1), 96 Stat. 1281 (1982).

141. Ibid., 96 Stat. 1276.

142. Nunez, interview, Apr. 5, 1990.

143. Pub. L. No. 97-293, Sec. 307(a)(1), 96 Stat. 1280.

144. Ibid.

145. Nunez, interview, Apr. 5, 1990.

146. Ibid.

147. Telephone interview with Joseph L. Miller, special assistant for Indian Affairs, Office of the Commissioner, Bureau of Reclamation, U.S. Department of the Interior, Washington, D.C., March 8, 1990.

148. Nunez, interview, Apr. 5, 1990.

149. Ibid.

150. Strickland, interview, Nov. 25, 1983.

151. Horn, interview, Feb. 24, 1984.

152. Pub. L. No. 97-293, Sec. 313(f).

153. Nunez, interview, Apr. 5, 1990.

154. Telephone interview with James Magner, currently executive director, National Water Alliance; formerly legislative aide to U.S. Senator Dennis DeConcini (D., Ariz.), Washington, D.C., Feb. 28, 1984.

155. *Tucson Urban Study,* p. 92, Table 32.

156. *Water Issues Primer,* p. 7.

157. Telephone interview with Jody Emel, assistant director, Tucson Active Management Area, Arizona Department of Water Resources, Tucson, Arizona, Feb. 7, 1984.

158. In all candor, this may not be completely true. In the closing pages of the *Tucson Urban Study* Appendix are suggestions for the construction of three storm-runoff impoundment projects in the upper Santa Cruz basin, which the Corps believes would enhance the basin's groundwater recharge capability. *Tucson Urban Study,* sec. 5, p. 2. Unpublished preliminary draft, subject to revision.

159. This unified, basin-wide perspective is precisely what the state's groundwater-regulation reform act finally imposed, with the creation of the Tucson Active Management Area. There is now a single planning jurisdiction with implementation authority—the TAMA office of the state DWR. Still, the O'Odham are only indirectly subject to its administration, through the translating device of U.S. Interior Dept. directives.

160. Sliz, interview, Feb. 10, 1984.

CHAPTER 6. CONCLUSION: IMPROVING THE PROSPECTS
FOR NEGOTIATED SETTLEMENTS

1. Bloom, "Law of the River: A Critique of an Extraordinary Legal System," in *New Courses for the Colorado River,* ed. G. Weatherford and F. Brown (Albuquerque: University of New Mexico Press, 1986), pp. 139–54.

2. E.g., the fourteen tribes now seriously discussing settlement terms with the Department of the Interior. Telephone interview with Joseph L. Miller, special assistant for Indian Affairs, Office of the Commissioner, Bureau of Reclamation, U.S. Dept. of Interior, Washington, D.C., Mar. 8, 1990.

3. For a discussion of the role of racism in American Indian water-rights disputes—and it is more often than not a significant one—see D. McCool, *Command of the Waters* (Berkeley: University of California Press, 1987), pp. 157–58.

4. 424 U.S. 1 (1976).

5. 108 S.Ct. 2597 (1988).

6. Tucson Active Management Area, Arizona Department of Water Resources, *A Water Issues Primer for the Tucson Active Management Area* (June, 1982), p. 45.

7. Meyers and Posner, "Toward an Improved Market for Water Resources," National Water Commission, Legal Study No. 4 (1971).

8. Z. Willey, *Economic Development and Environmental Quality in California's Water System* (Institute for Governmental Studies: University of Calif., Berkeley, 1985).

9. San Luis Rey Indian Water Rights Settlement Act, Pub. L. No. 100-675, 102 Stat. 4000 (1988).

10. However, it was beginning to appear in spring 1990 that the MWD was balking at even this compromise since the act specifies a quantity of water (14,000 acre-feet annually) to be given to the Indians, whether or not that much is actually saved by lining the canal. Miller, interview, Mar. 8, 1990.

11. U.S. Department of the Interior, U.S. Department of Agriculture, and U.S. Environmental Protection Agency, *Irrigation Use and Management: An Interagency Task Force Report* (Washington, D.C.: Government Printing Office, 1979).

12. Ibid., p. 28.

13. Ibid., p. 86, Table 14.

14. Ibid., p. 73.

15. Back and Taylor, "Navajo Water Rights: Pulling the Plug on the Colorado River?" 20 *Natural Resources Journal* 71, 74, n.12 (1980).

16. Price and Weatherford, "Indian Water Rights in Theory and Practice: Navajo Experience in the Colorado Basin," 40 *Law and Contemporary Problems* 97 (1976).

17. Bureau of Reclamation, U.S. Dept. of Interior, *1982 Summary Statistics,* vol. 1, *Land, Water, and Related Data* (Washington, D.C.: Government Printing Office, 1982), p. 27, Table 1.

18. Bureau of Reclamation, U.S. Dept. of Interior, *1986 Summary Statistics,* vol. 1, *Land, Water, and Related Data* (Washington, D.C.: Government Printing Office, 1986), p. 25, Table 1.

19. Bureau of Reclamation, U.S. Dept. of Interior, *1987 Summary Statistics,* vol. 1, *Land, Water, and Related Data* (Washington, D.C.: Government Printing Office, 1987), p. 25, Table 1.

20. *Webster's II New Riverside Dictionary* (Boston: Houghton Mifflin, 1984), p. 438.

21. A. Maass and R. Anderson, . . . *And the Desert Shall Rejoice: Conflict, Growth, and Justice in Arid Environments* (Cambridge, Mass.: MIT Press, 1978).

22. See, for instance, Office of Water Program Operations, U.S. Environmental Protection Agency, *The Alternative Is Conservation* (Washington, D.C.: Government Printing Office, 1980).

INDEX